ANNALS OF THE
IRISH HARPERS

ARDRIGH

EDWARD BUNTING
From a daguerreotype in the possession of Dr Louis MacRory

ANNALS OF THE IRISH HARPERS

CHARLOTTE MILLIGAN FOX

Edited by
SARA C LANIER

ARDRIGH BOOKS
KILWAUGHTER
MMXIII

First published in 1911 by John Murray, Alblemarle Street, London.

This edition 2013 Ardrigh Books,
P.O. Box 78, Larne, N.I. BT40 9AU.
www.ardrighbooks.com

Introduction and editorial material
© Sara C. Lanier

A CIP catalogue for this book is available from
the British Library.
ISBN 978-1-909721-01-2

Printed and bound at GPS, Alexander Road, Belfast.

AUTHOR DEDICATION

TO THE
RIGHT HON. THE EARL OF SHAFTESBURY, K.C.V.O.,
PRESIDENT OF THE IRISH FOLK-SONG SOCIETY

CONTENTS

LIST OF ILLUSTRATIONS

INTRODUCTION

INTRODUCTION

THE *ANNALS OF THE IRISH HARPERS* IS A COLLECTION OF ESSAYS, LETTERS AND memoirs edited from the personal manuscripts of the Belfast musician Edward Bunting (1773-1843). This compelling work includes the story of Bunting's historic encounter with the Irish harpers at the Assembly Rooms in Belfast in July 1792, an encounter which started Bunting's life-long career in recovering and preserving the music of the traditional Irish wire-strung harp. His three published collections of Irish harp music saved this most important element of the Irish musical tradition from sinking into historical obscurity. At the time of its original publication in 1911, *Annals of the Irish Harpers* succeeded once again in retrieving the Irish harp and its role in the history of Irish traditional music from cultural amnesia and it has been a major influence upon the modern development of traditional Irish music.

The Irish composer Sean Ó Riada (†1973) has been called the Father of modern Irish music by many, including the Irish mystic and 1980's pop diva Sinead O' Connor. Without Milligan Fox's rediscovery of the Bunting manuscripts, Ó Riada's 1960s folk ensemble Ceoltóirí Chualann (whose members later formed The Chieftains), would have had a much more limited archive of music to draw upon for their conscious recreation of Irish traditional music. In 1998 an historical harp recital was given at the World Music Centre at the University of Limerick organised by the composer and musician Micheál Ó Súilleabháin, an ex-pupil of Ó Riada. The Scottish harper Alison Kinnaird MBE and the Irish American harper Ann Heymann performed traditional Scottish and Irish airs upon both gut and wire-string harps and then talked to the students both about harp technique and history. Ann Heymann's musician partner Charlie Heymann memorably stated that "if it wasn't for Bunting none of us would be here." And if it wasn't for Charlotte Milligan Fox's *Annals* Bunting's musical manuscripts would still be mouldering in an attic, his publications relegated to an academic footnote.

Charlotte Olivia Milligan was born at Gortmore Cottages, north of Omagh, County Tyrone, on St Patrick's Day in 1864, the eldest of ten children. Charlotte's mother, Charlotte Elizabeth Milligan (nee Burns), was herself an accomplished musician who instilled a love of music in her children, four of whom would later attend European Conservatoires. She had received her musical education from an older cousin who had managed a small dame school in Dungiven. The pupils had been instructed in what was even then an old-fashioned manner with the liberal use of globes and an insistence upon a familiarity with heraldry and Irish mythology. A proper French accent was also required from the pupils, their teacher having acquired hers, in turn, from a French refugee who regaled her charges with stories about the baskets of human heads she had seen carried away from the guillotine during the French Revolution of 1789. Notably, Charlotte's mother's musical education had included a familiarity with the Irish harp, for her school had employed harpers from the old Drogheda School to instruct the pupils in the proper repertoire and technique.[1] Following her marriage to Seaton Milligan their children were raised as staunch Irish Unionists and the first Irish folk songs her daughter Charlotte Olivia learned at the knee of their much loved nurse, who was an ardent Orange woman, included 'The Boyne Water' and 'Derry's Walls'.

Charlotte's father Seaton Forrest Milligan was a trade representative for the Belfast-based general merchants Hawkins, Robinson and Ferguson. He was passionate about the importance of a good education and so he ensured that all of his children attended the best of the local schools. Seaton Milligan was an extremely successful salesman, and through his diligence his business expanded rapidly throughout the 1860's and 70's. In 1875 he was offered a promotion to head office and his entire family moved

---

1. For the Drogheda Harp School, see chapter VI, p. 54 of the present edition of *Annals*. Also, Hurrell, Nancy. 'A Drogheda harp: instrument and icon,' *History Ireland*, vol.XXI, no.I, (Jan/Feb 2013), pp. 34-37.

to Belfast. This enabled him easy access to the many vibrant learned societies of late nineteenth-century Belfast, and Milligan was able to use his increased leisure time to pursue his interest in antiquarianism. He was elected as a Fellow of the Royal Society of Antiquaries of Ireland in 1888 and served as regional Vice-President in Ulster from 1895-99. Milligan was also a founder member of the scholarly committee established by the Belfast solicitor and antiquarian F. J. Bigger in order to launch the second series of the *Ulster Journal of Archaeology* in 1895. By the late 1890s the Milligan family had moved into a house on the Antrim Road just along from F. J. Bigger's own home 'Ardrigh', and the family frequently entertained writers and musicians from Bigger's Irish Revival circle.

Charlotte Milligan chose music as her vocation from an early age. Her mother gave her every encouragement and even while the family was living in Tyrone had ensured that Charlotte attended concerts held by visiting musicians playing in Belfast, even though this entailed an arduous and lengthy train journey. She was given so much musical input early on that at just eleven years of age she confided to a friend that she knew so much about music that she could not possibly learn any more and that her musical education was now complete. Despite this her education continued and after she left school she spent two years studying classical music and piano at the musical Conservatoire in Frankfurt, spending a further year at the Royal College of Music in London. She completed her formal musical education with a spell at the Conservatoire in Milan.

While in London she met her future husband, the young solicitor, Charles Elliot Fox. They were married on the 17th March in 1892, Charlotte's thirty-first birthday. The wedding took place in Belfast at her family's home on the Royal Terrace off the Lisburn road. Her younger sister Alice described the event in her diary noting that Charlotte wore a deep green velvet wedding dress. The couple settled in London and their only child, Seaton Henry Elliot Fox, was born the following year in Hampstead, in 1893.

Charlotte Milligan Fox published her first musical arrangements of Irish traditional airs in 1898. This was the year the Folk Song Society (FSS) was formed in London by Kate Lee, Lucy Broadwood, Fuller Maitland and a number of other antiquarians, folklorists and musicians, many of whom had strong Irish connections. The FSS was founded under the auspice of the Irish Literary Society (ILS), and its first meetings were held at the rooms of the ILS in Adelphi Terrace in Piccadilly, London. The declared work of the FSS was the collection of folk music with 'no geographical limit set.' Milligan Fox was an early member of the Society and the collection of folk music was to become such a compelling pursuit for her 'that she spared nothing for it – time, money, health and life itself.'[2] Her first published prose work would be an article for the opening issue of Standish O'Grady's *All Ireland Review* which described how FSS was working to make Irish music accessible to London audiences.[3]

Kate Lee, described by A.P. Graves as the 'moving spirit' of the FSS, undertook the pivotal role of Honorary Secretary from its inception. When in 1902 Lee developed cancer, four years after the founding of the FSS, her illness ensured that the Society's affairs entered a temporary hiatus. By 1903 the Society had ceased to hold regular meetings. This state of affairs lasted until Kate Lee's untimely death in 1904. Frustrated by the inevitable lapse in the Society's activities, Milligan Fox and A.P. Graves organised a meeting amongst their fellow Irish members in order to propose founding an entirely separate society devoted specifically to Irish folk music and so it came to pass that 'Mrs Milligan Fox, though a Unionist in politics, led a Home Rule secession for Irish Folk Song.'[4] Their eventual secession from the parent FSS was entirely amiable

---

2. Graves, A.P. 'Mrs C. Milligan Fox,' *Journal of the Irish Folk Song Society*, vol.xvi, (Dublin, 1918), p. xi.

3. [C.M.F.] 'Irish Music in London,' *All Ireland Review*, vol.i, no.i, (6th January 1900), p. 5. A further anonymous article on 'Irish music in London,' on p. 2 of issue no.5, 3rd Feburary 1900, is almost certainly by Milligan Fox, see p. 315 of this work.

4. Graves, A.P. op.cit. p. xi. For Charlotte's politics, see also Morris, Catherine. *Alice Milligan and the Irish Cultural Revival*, Four Courts, (Dublin, 2012), p. 53.

and they were soon to be followed in developing national bodies by the Welsh, and under the leadership of Mrs Kennedy-Fraser, the Scots contingent of the Society.[5] Milligan Fox was appointed Honorary Secretary of the newly formed Irish Folk Song Society, a position she would hold for the remaining twelve years of her life. Early membership included the Irish musicians Charles Wood and Charles Villiers Stanford, the musicologist Henry Grattan Flood and the Irish antiquarian and song collector P.W. Joyce.

The Irish Folk Song Society (IFSS) held its inaugural concert at Londonderry House in Park Lane, London, England, on the 20th May 1904. The proceedings were opened by IFSS President the Earl of Shaftesbury, a thirty-five year old peer related to the Earls of Donegal through his mother's family.[6] The evening's programme of events included a talk on Irish folk song by A.P. Graves illustrated by two songs arranged by Charles Wood, a performance of four airs by Kathleen Purcell 'on the Gothic harp' and a presentation upon the Irish Pipes by Lord Castletown and Irish harp (cruit) by May Coleman. The 'Connaught Caoine', or 'Lament of Connaught', was performed by Miss Coleman in an arrangement by Charlotte Milligan Fox and the concert ended with a talk on "Ulster Folk Song" illustrated by songs performed by Miss Kirkwood and Lord Shaftesbury.

Milligan Fox co-edited the *Journal of the Irish Folk Song Society* (*JIFSS*) in collaboration with Herbert Hughes. Hughes was originally from Belfast and had been a musical protégé of F.J. Bigger. In 1903 Hughes had been the musical conductor at the commemoration

---

[5.] The parent society did not become moribund with Kate Lee's death. The Folk Song Society was resurrected through the work of Lucy Broadwood and Cecil Sharp. In 1932 it amalgamated with the English Folk Dance Society to form the English Folk Dance and Song Society (EFDSS) which continues to florish to this day.

[6.] Shaftesbury's maternal grandfather Lord Belfast was patron for the publication of Edward Bunting's last volume of Irish music in 1840 and presented the book to its dedicatee, Queen Victoria.

festival for the 1792 Harpers' Assembly, held in Belfast at the Linen Hall Library. The first volume of the *JIFSS* was issued in April 1904 and the later series included contributions from P.W. Joyce and Cecil Sharp. The following year, a journal publication committee was formed. Its membership was made up of John Todhunter, a friend of the Irish poet W.B. Yeats, the musical comedy composer Claude Aveling and Michael Moloney. However, Milligan Fox continued in her role as principal editorial advisor for the *JIFSS* until her death in 1916 and the journal continued to bear the imprint of her strong personality.

At some point during this period Milligan Fox paid a visit to Morley's, a music shop at Battersea in south London, in order to purchase a harp for the daughter of a friend. Once inside the door she obeyed a pressing inner prompting to ask whether "any wandering harpers ever come in here to buy strings?" The assistant could not actually recall any actual wandering harpers, however her query put him in mind of a recent customer who had said that it was only right that he should have a harp in his home "for it was my grandfather who preserved the music of the ancient Irish harpers." The man was a certain Dr McRory of Battersea who had inherited from his grandfather, Edward Bunting, a number of unpublished notebooks and manuscripts. Milligan Fox had first come across the story of Edward Bunting in *Historical Notices of Old Belfast* (1896) by her father's friend R.M Young and recognised the importance of this musical discovery. Bunting's manuscripts are, arguably, one of the most historically significant collections of Irish music ever assembled. They were principally compiled between 1792 and 1809, at a time when the last notable body of itinerant Irish harpers were still living. In addition to the preservation of the harpers repertoires, Bunting's extensive notes offered invaluable information regarding the wire-strung harp technique as practiced at this period by those harpers he met and questioned.

Bunting's first exposure to this music began with the Belfast

Harper's Assembly in July 1792. The Harper's Assembly had been organised by a committee of prominent Belfast citizens in order to attempt to preserve the fast disappearing music and poetry of Ancient Ireland.[7] Bunting's own role in the preservation of the music came about almost by chance. He had been a young assistant organist at St Anne's church, Belfast, in the early 1790's. When the chief organist of St. Anne's, William Ware, was unable to fulfil his engagement to transcribe the music played by the harpers, his assistant Bunting had been sent in his stead as transcriber. Bunting formed relationships with many of the performers and under the patronage of several members of the original Harper's Assembly Organising Committee he continued to visit the harpers and to transcribe their repertoire.

Bunting published selections of the music he had collected transcribed for pianoforte in three separate volumes over the course of his life (1796, 1809 & 1840). The Bunting collection would enter the culture of 19th century Ireland through the songs of his rival, the poet Thomas Moore. Moore employed many of Bunting's airs in his *Irish Melodies* (1808-34) and it was these *Melodies* that became part of the canonical repertoire for amateur singers and pianists performing in Irish drawing rooms and parlours throughout the nineteenth century. The publications never fulfilled Bunting's hopes that his own settings of the airs would award him with both popular and financial success. By the time that Milligan Fox was born in 1863 the traditional music painstakingly rescued by Edward Bunting at such great personal cost would have been most widely recognised merely as the airs to which Moore's *The Minstrel Boy*, *The Last Rose of Summer* and *Let Erin Remember* had been set. However, the historical context of

---

7. For a detailed account of the Belfast Harper's Assembly and of the events surrounding it, see Lanier, S.C. 'It is new-strung and shan't be heard,' *British Journal of Ethnomusicology*, vol.VIII, (1999), pp. 1-26. Despite Milligan Fox's general use of the term 'Belfast Harp Festival,' the term the 'Belfast Assembly of Harpers' or 'Belfast Harper's Assembly' is the contemporary usage for the event during 1792 in the published newspaper reports and, most significantly, in Charles Fanning's own published letter of thanks.

the musical collections transcribed by Edward Bunting had by this time fallen into obscurity. Milligan Fox's *The Annals of the Irish Harpers* rescued the memory of the Irish harp tradition he had encountered, and revived cultural interest in the Irish harp and its music.

The earliest fruits of Milligan Fox's rediscovery of the Bunting manuscripts were first published in volume IV of the *JIFSS* in 1906. This was Edward Bunting's *Prospectus of a General Collection of the Ancient Music of Ireland comprising Notices of the Tunes, and of the more eminent Harpers of later times, with some account of the various efforts towards a Revival of the Irish Harp.* The *Prospectus* was presented alongside previously unpublished pictures of Edward Bunting's children, Sarah and Anthony Bunting. Over the following years, Charlotte Milligan Fox worked assiduously at editing the Bunting manuscripts into an accessible popular publication. Her younger sister, the poet and dramatist Alice Milligan, helped her with the Irish she encountered in the manuscripts. Alice had studied Irish under the Irish scholar and Gaelic League luminary P.J. O'Shea who wrote in Irish under the pen name of 'Conán Maol.'[8] O'Shea had been born above Kenmare and taught his pupils the Munster Irish of his distinctive Kerry dialect. The modern Irish language movement was then in its infancy and issues of dialect and spelling were still an arena for heated debate.[9] Alice Milligan's translations of Irish for her sister's *Annals of the Irish Harpers* therefore cannot be readily compared with regularised modern Irish.

Charlotte Milligan Fox's *Songs of the Irish Harpers* was published in 1910. It included her arrangements for five of the unpublished songs she

---

8. O'Shea, (Pádraig O'Séaghdha), was born at Gort Breac between Kenmare and Killarney. He wrote a number of works in Irish, including a fantasy-satire novel *Eogan Paor*, and a short life of Shane O'Neill for children, *Seághan an Díomais*. His published short stories made a significant contribution in modernising the short story form in Irish.

9. On the rare occasions where the contemporary Irish usage employed in *Annals* may possibly create confusion over names I have inserted modern Irish usage in square brackets within the text, with the help of Dr Stiofán Ó Direáin.

had discovered in the Bunting Manuscripts. Several of these songs were performed at the 1910 Grand Bardic Concert held at Londonderry House the in Park Lane, London, England on the 24th June and hosted by the Marchioness of Londonderry. Charlotte Milligan Fox introduced them as 'Songs of the Irish Harpers and Ancient Bardic Airs arranged for the harp and produced after a long silence.' During the course of the concert she made a personal appeal for the revival of the harp in Ireland. There was also an exhibition of harps which included a traditional Welsh harp with a triple-row of strings, a small single-row traditional Welsh harp, a contemporary small English Morley Celtic lever harp painted green, an early 19th century Egan Irish lever harp and a large ornately carved 18th century French pedal harp.

The final edited version of the Bunting material, now known as *The Annals of the Irish Harpers*, was at the publishers John Murray by early 1911. With the manuscript finally out of her hands Charlotte Milligan Fox undertook a whirlwind tour of North America in order to increase awareness of Irish traditional music. In February 1911, she successfully established a New York branch of the Irish Folk Song Society at a meeting held at the National Arts Club in New York.[10] A month later, the day before her forty-seventh birthday on 16th March, short plays by both Charlotte Milligan Fox and her sister Alice Milligan, were performed in Washington D.C. at the National Theatre in Pennsylvania Avenue. Charlotte Milligan Fox had written the romantic one-act play entitled *The Bardic Recital*. It was the dramatised story of Murtagh, a wandering Irish bard and an itinerant Irish harper, Fial. It recounted the ancient days and faded glories of Kincora during the 11th century in the kingdom of the most famed High King of Ireland, Brian Bóruma. At the end of that month Charlotte Milligan Fox gave a lecture illustrated by Irish songs in New York entitled 'Songs by the Fireside.' In the following month of April she travelled on to Boston to examine the Irish musical manuscripts held in

---

10. Milligan Fox, C. 'The Irish Folk Song Society,' *Journal of the Irish Folk Song Society*, vol.IX, (Dublin, 1911), pp. 7-14.

the special collections of Harvard University. To her disappointment she found nothing that she had not already met with in Ireland. However, whilst she was in Boston she also visited the Public Library there. This visit was to prove more fruitful. It held in its collections 'five green volumes of MS. music' containing Dr William Elliot Hudson's musical collection of over a thousand Irish folk songs 'taken down from the peasantry' during the early part of the 19th century. Charlotte Milligan Fox edited and published material from this collection in subsequent volumes of the *JIFSS*. [11]

The Annals of the Irish Harpers finally appeared in print in late 1911. The following spring Milligan Fox started on another of the field trips which she had undertaken in recent years with her sisters in order to collect songs.[12] She travelled to County Waterford equipped with 'a fine Edison phonograph and a plentiful supply of blank cylinders.'[13] With considerable local help she successfully collected yet more folk songs in English and Gaelic as well as some instrumental pieces.

However, during the following year of 1913, Milligan Fox's health began to fail. As a result only one annual volume of the *JIFSS* appeared for the years 1913-15. Her mother, Charlotte Elizabeth Milligan, died on 13th January 1916 after a long debilitating illness. Alice Milligan, who had been engaged in nursing their mother through her last years now felt free to travel to London to visit her older sister Charlotte, who was now gravely ill. Alice Milligan arrived in London in time to attend the Irish Folk Song Society's 1916 St Patrick's Day Concert at the Albert Hall on March 18th. Milligan Fox was by that date in the final throws of her

---

11. Milligan Fox, C. 'Concerning the William Elliot Hudson Collection of Irish folk songs,' *Journal of the Irish Folk Song Society*, vol.x, (Dublin, 1911), p. 5.

12. See Morris, Catherine. op cit, p. 45.

13. Milligan Fox, C. 'Folk song collecting in County Waterford,' *Journal of the Irish Folk Song Society*, vol.xii, (Dublin, 1912), p.11. Her sisters Edith Wheeler and Alice Milligan accompanied Milligan Fox.

illness but insisted on attending the event. Alice Milligan later wrote that her sister's 'attendance at the concert was visibly an effort.'[14]

Charlotte Milligan Fox's death took place a week later on the afternoon of Saturday 25th March 1916 at the age of 52. The day after her death, the designs for a gold medal sponsored by the Irish Folk Song Society for the best original Irish composition at the annual competitions held by the Feis Ceoil committee, arrived for her personal approval.[15] It bore 'the names of Mrs Milligan Fox and the Earl of Shaftesbury as Founder and President of our Society.'[16]

Alice Milligan took charge of escorting her sister's body home to Ireland for burial in the family plot at Drumragh Churchyard, Omagh, County Tyrone. However, by the time arrangements were in hand for the journey to Ireland travel throughout England had been brought to a standstill by a late snow storm of such intensity that trains caught in transit became snowbound for a number of days. After this untimely delay Charlotte Milligan Fox was finally laid to rest in the family plot where her mother had been buried a mere three months before. Seaton Forrest Milligan, already broken by grief at the recent loss of his wife, survived the death of his eldest child by less than two weeks. He died on 6th April 1916, his subsequent burial providing the families third funeral of the year. Within two weeks of Milligan Fox's death the Easter Rebellion in Dublin and its aftermath of executions ensured the marginalisation of those aspects of the Irish Cultural Revival that had successfully restrained the passions of political factionalism. Her early death spared Charlotte Milligan Fox from witnessing the eclipse of the complex Irish culture with which she had grown up, as Ireland again descended into political violence, revolution and civil war.

---

[14] Milligan, Alice. 'Mrs C. Milligan Fox,' *Journal of the Irish Folk Song Society*, vol.xvi, (Dublin, 1919), p. x.

[15] Correspondence regarding the medal is held in the Feis Ceoil Archive at the National Library of Ireland MS. 40/240/3.

[16] *Alfred Perceval Graves to Francis Joseph Bigger*, 16th January 1917, letter, MS. GR.1, the F.J. Bigger Archive, Central Library, Belfast.

In the settlement of Milligan Fox's estate the unpublished Bunting manuscripts in her possession at the time of her death would eventually be gifted to the Queen's College of the University of Ireland, now Queen's University Belfast. Her father Seaton Forrest Milligan had been named as executor of her affairs and in the two weeks he survived his daughter there was some discussion regarding the eventual repository for the manuscripts. An approach was made by the committee of the Linen Hall Library. In a letter to Francis Joseph Bigger, Alice Milligan had already expressed concern at the manuscripts being "donated to a private institution to be entirely reserved for privileged subscribers."[17] With her father's death, it fell to Alice Milligan to make the final decisions in the matter. She offered the material to Queen's College, Belfast and with their acceptance of her conditions she undertook the work necessary for the manuscripts to be packed and conveyed to the college. She personally spent June and July of 1916 in London arranging the books and papers, and settling her sister's other affairs. Milligan Fox's younger sister Edith Wheeler finally lodged the manuscripts at Queens College early in 1917.

The bequest entailed forty-five items. It contained Edward Bunting's musical personal notebooks and manuscripts from every period of his life, his letters, the journal and song collections of Bunting's musical associate Patrick Lynch and a manuscript copy of the memoirs of the 18th century harper Arthur O'Neill. In 1917 Dr McCrory's cousin, Lady Deane, also placed a number of Edward Bunting's other papers at Queen's University. Through Milligan Fox's gift the Bunting manuscripts and papers are available for study in the special collections department of the library at Queen's University in Belfast. In 2000 Collette Moloney's exhaustive full length study of the manuscripts, *The Irish Music Manuscripts of Edward Bunting (1773-1843), An Introduction and Catalogue,* was published by the Irish Traditional Music Archive, Taisce Cheol Dúchais Éireann. Any future researcher of Milligan Fox's bequest must begin with this work.

---

17. *A.L Milligan to F.J. Bigger,* undated, letter no. 20, envelope MS. MI.5. The F.J. Bigger Archive, Central Library, Belfast.

Charlotte Milligan Fox never held music or knowledge or service back from others. She was so passionate in her pursuit of lost songs that her scholarship could occasionally become rather chaotic. Arthur O'Neill's *Memoirs* are alternatively referred to in *Annals* as 'O'Neill's *Life*' and as 'O'Neill's *Autobiography*' in different places. However, during Milligan Fox's lifetime this aspect of her work was generally forgiven because she was 'so delightfully disarming that she made friends of the severest critics'. Her vivid personality imbues her narrative style with her infectious enthusiasm. Accordingly, *Annals of the Irish Harpers* is far from being simply the dry academic preservation of a musical tradition. It also carries the reader into a compelling journey through the vanished world of eighteenth-century Irish harpers.

ANNALS OF
THE IRISH HARPERS

Yours always
C. Milligan Fox

PREFACE

IN PREPARING FOR PUBLICATION THE *ANNALS OF THE IRISH HARPERS*, MY constant aim has been to do justice to the memory of Edward Bunting, who rescued from oblivion the last authentic records of ancient Irish Minstrelsy. The honour of this achievement belongs rightly to him and is shared, moreover, by the town of Belfast. Here he listened to the strains of the last minstrels; here, cheered and encouraged by an enthusiastic band of fellow workers, he lived and laboured from childhood till middle age. It is a somewhat remarkable fact that the capital of the Ulster Plantation Colony should have been the scene of such efforts to preserve the relics of the civilisation of native Gaeldom.

Edward Bunting's collections of Irish music were first brought to my notice by one who is now amongst the most venerable of Belfast citizens, the Right Hon. Robert Young, P.C. I had then just recently completed my musical studies on the Continent, and had come home to settle in Ireland. It was news to me that this commercial centre had anything to boast of in connection with music.

When in course of time I became Hon. Secretary of the Irish Folk-Song Society (founded 1904), Mr Young contributed to our journal an article on Bunting and his work, which awakened great interest. Meantime through the medium of the Feis Ceoil and the Gaelic Revival in Ireland renewed attention was directed to the harp. Belfast was not behindhand, the instrument again became popular on concert platforms, and indeed occasionally a picturesque band of harps graced the orchestra of the Ulster Hall.

In consequence a friend wrote asking me to select a harp for her daughter, at one of the leading London warehouses. I went there, and, having selected an instrument, was about to leave, when it came into my head to ask, "Do any old wandering harpers ever come in here to buy strings?" The attendant smiled somewhat cynically, and I felt that my question had been a foolish one, for the days of the last minstrels are surely over. "Well, no," he said; "we have no such customers; but, by the way, a gentleman was in here not long ago, who would interest you. He bought a harp, and when giving the order he said, 'It is only right that I should have a harp in my house; for it was my grandfather who preserved the music of the ancient Irish harpers.' "

Eagerly I asked for the name and address of this purchaser, who turned out to be Dr Louis MacRory of Battersea. A brief correspondence resulted in his inviting me to his home to inspect certain papers belonging to his grandfather, who was no other than Edward Bunting. On my arrival at the doctor's house, he met me with the abrupt remark, "Now I hope you are an Irish woman, for I think some one from Ireland should handle my grandfather's papers."

When I said that I came from Belfast, his countenance cleared, for had not Bunting's labours from first to last been connected with it, and he seemed satisfied that he had found a fit and proper person to go over the old manuscripts.

At this time I hoped for nothing more than some gleanings of unpublished airs and some personal memoirs and letters for the *Irish Folk-Song Journal*; but as I went through the mass of documents which Dr MacRory put before me, I saw that a great amount of unpublished material had survived. Here were musical note-books, letters, faded documents, which demanded most careful consideration. I grew more and more absorbed in the study of them, and in the end the doctor decided that I must take the box away with me, and investigate them at leisure. Then he added to my delight by telling me that there were other papers in a box in Dublin, and that he would try to obtain them for me. He explained that Edward Bunting had two daughters, Mary Ann and Sarah. The latter, who married Mr R. MacRory of Belfast, was his own mother. Mary Ann Bunting, who married a Mr James Wright in Dublin, had a daughter Florence. This lady is the wife of an eminent Dublin architect, Thomas Manley Deane, son of Sir Thomas Newenham Deane. Certain of the Bunting manuscripts were in her possession.

On the occasion of my next visit to Ireland, I went armed with an introduction from Dr MacRory and interviewed Mrs Deane, with the satisfactory result that another box of Bunting manuscripts was confided to me.

I may here in passing comment on the fact that Bunting's family has been largely connected with engineering and architecture. His father was a mining engineer, his son Anthony, who died in early manhood, showed great talent as an engineer, and his granddaughter's marriage connected her with a family in which architectural skill has shown itself hereditary. Her husband is now Sir Thomas Deane, having been knighted by King George, on the occasion of the opening of the College of Science, Dublin, of which he was one of the architects.

The investigation of all this mass of papers occupied me pleasantly for many months. In the note-books I found many beautiful airs which Bunting had never published, and which I drew on for the *Irish Folk-Song Journal*. Some I arranged and published as *Songs of the Irish Harpers* with words in English and Irish. However, as I pored over the manuscripts, I felt that there was material here for a book. The manuscript *Life* of Arthur O'Neill, the harper, deserved to be published in full, though Bunting, with the assistance of Samuel Ferguson, had used many anecdotes from it in the preface to his last collection. The journal of Patrick Lynch had never seen the light, and Dr MacDonnell's letters were of great interest. Above all, I felt that a memoir of Bunting was called for, and so embarked upon the task of authorship.

From first to last I have relied much on the help of my sister, Miss Alice Milligan, who has had considerable literary experience and a knowledge of Irish history.

Amongst books of authority on our subject matter, I must acknowledge indebtedness to Eugene O'Curry's *Manners and Customs of the Ancient Irish*, Benn's *History of Belfast*, and *Old Belfast*, by R. M. Young, M.R.I.A. (the latter volume was invaluable as a guide to local history), Dr P. W. Joyce's various works and writings of Dr Hyde and Dr Sigerson, and the *Autobiography of Wolfe Tone*, edited by K. Barry O'Brien. Dr W. H. Grattan Flood's *History of Irish Music*, was always at hand for reference. From it I have quoted an account of Patrick Lynch, a Clare man and author of a Gaelic Grammar, whom he takes to be the same as the Lynch who taught Irish in Belfast and toured Connaught for Bunting. It is only right to state here that this has been questioned. Mr Seumas Casaide, a Dublin Gaelic scholar and Bibliophile, has prepared a short biography of Lynch, the Clare grammarian, and was not aware that he had ever been in Belfast. He assumed that Bunting's Lynch was an entirely different person. On examining and comparing handwriting, his belief was somewhat shaken, as the script of Lynch in the Bunting papers bore a decided resemblance to that of the Clareman. Moreover, Mr Casaide allowed that there were a few years of the life of his Lynch which he could not account for, and which might have been occupied by his residence in Belfast and County Down. On looking through the Irish poetry taken down by Lynch in Connaught, his opinion again changed and he asserted that the words were spelled to represent the Northern pronunciation of Irish, and that no Clareman that ever was born or schooled, could have spelt like that. So there the mystery remains unsolved, and perhaps I have erred in naming Lynch "The Pentaglot Preceptor." There may have been two men, where I, with Dr Grattan Flood's assistance, have given an account of one. In any case he stands forth in these pages a typical preceptor of the gay old times, when schoolmasters were itinerants like the harpers, ere ever a National Board had arisen to cabin and confine them behind the doors of school-houses.

For information on different points I am indebted to Mr Isaac Ward of Belfast (an inveterate reader of old newspapers, and great authority on all connected with the history of the city), Dr the Rt. Hon. Michael Cox, P.C., Sir William Whitla, Mrs Chambers Bunten, Miss Lucy Broadwood, Sir Charles Brett, and above all to Dr Louis MacRory and Sir Thomas and Lady Deane for prompt response to all questionings.

The time is ripe to recall Bunting's labour and claim for him a full meed of fame. The subject of national folk music has been recognised as of much importance by the school boards of England and Wales. In the United States, which I visited recently, a mingling of races, makes possible a comparative study of the folk-song of many nations, and I found interest on the subject keen, and many educational agencies at work in this sphere. In New York that most cosmopolitan of cities, Dr Leipziger, superintendent of the lecturing department of the public schools, is full of interest in the subject, and it is kept prominently before the public.

Where the world's folk music is studied and compared, that of Ireland is assured of due attention, and the Irish population in the United States will have reason to boast of their heritage.

In conclusion let me say that the dedication of this volume to Lord Shaftesbury, is in keeping with its aim and purpose, for his Irish kindred come into the story. It was to a Lady Donegall that Moore dedicated his melodies; and Lord Belfast (Lord Shaftesbury's own grandfather) encouraged and assisted Bunting in his final enterprise, and brought his work before the notice of Queen Victoria and the Prince Consort. The next Lord Belfast was intensely musical, had talent as a composer and supported the Belfast Anacreonotic Society, which had good reason to deplore his early death, and honoured his memory by a requiem concert. His nephew to whom this volume is dedicated, sustains these musical traditions, has done much for the Belfast Philharmonic Society, the Irish Folk Society, and occasionally appears as a vocalist on a concert platform. He has, moreover, held the office of Lord Mayor of Belfast, thus strengthening his connection with the city whose musical history is recorded here.

CHARLOTTE MILLIGAN FOX.

BELFAST, SEPTEMBER 1911.

CHAPTER I

EDWARD BUNTING—AN INTRODUCTORY MEMOIR

THERE IS AN OLD IRISH STREET BALLAD TO AN AIR NOW KNOWN AS THE 'Wearing of the Green', which commences with the rythmical announcement:

Oh, I'll go down unto Belfast to see that seaport gay,

and with this we may fitly begin our record, for before bringing on the stage of description our dramatis personæ, it will be well to realise the scene in which they are to move. This is all the more necessary when the scene is mainly in Belfast of a century ago, for there is no place in Ireland that has changed more than that city which boasts itself the commercial capital of Ireland, and counts its population by hundreds of thousands.

In this Ireland of decaying towns and cities and dwindling population, the growth of Belfast seems indeed a marvel, and, turning back the pages of history, the contrast is heightened, for we find it to have been a place of little importance.

To the head of a deep inlet of the sea, which opens into the North Channel, directly facing the entrance to the Scottish Clyde, the River Lagan flows down from the interior of Ulster. Near that river mouth there was in ancient times a fordable place. This was *Beulfearsaide*, the ford, important as a passage from one known centre of habitation to another. Carrickfergus, a few miles off on the northern shore of the Lough, got its name in legendary times, and was one of the keys of Ireland held by the early Norman invaders. Bangor, on the southern side, at the gate of the sea, was in the seventh century the site of the most famous of Irish ecclesiastical schools, sending out Christian missionaries to France and Switzerland and Northern Italy. With their Gospel books, they carried also the Irish book of Church Song that remains to this day the treasure of a European library.

The invading Norsemen blotted out the glory of Bangor in fire and blood, and ultimately their kinsmen, the Normans, planted their strong castles on the coast of Down. *Beulfearsaide* retained its importance as a place of passage for riders between the towers of Carrick and the Ards of Down. Sometimes it was in the keep of the native Irish. Edmund Spenser in his view of Ireland mentions it among northern places which had been anglicised, but had fallen away to be "one of the most out-bound and abandoned places in the English Pale, and, indeed, not counted of the English Pale at all."

The foundation of its present greatness was, however, laid ultimately in the reign of James I., after the passing over-sea of the great Chieftains of the Gael, when Sir Arthur Chichester took in hand the business of the Plantation of Ulster. You may see his tomb and read his epitaph in the Church of St Nicholas at Carrickfergus. He may take his place in history, as the founder of that Belfast, which nowadays stands for the continuance of English rule and speaks in the name of that Ulster, which would still fain be considered a plantation. The connection with his family is perpetuated in the names of many of the streets Donegall Street, Donegall Square, Donegall Place, Chichester Street, Arthur Street. He had laid firm hand and holding on Donegal after the passing of the brothers of Red Hugh O'Donnell, and the family took title from that territory. Strangely enough certain members of the Donegall family come in at the end of this story of the preserving of the treasures of the Irish bards and harpers, as extending encouragement and help to those engaged in the work. The benign images of a Lady Donegall, who was the best friend of Moore, and of Lord Belfast, who encouraged the last labours of Bunting, are some set off against the grim masterful figure of Chichester, who swept Ulster of her bard-protecting native chieftains.

Here, then, at Belfast was the chief part of that great plantation, and the inhabitants from the outset displayed certain qualities of thrift and independence that mark them to this day. In Oliver Cromwell's time its Presbytery indeed displayed too much independence for the liking of that man of blood and iron, and by his command his secretary, John Milton, thundered at them in language of sternest invective as having "the appearance of a co-interest, and partaking with the Irish rebels," and being no better than "a generation of Highland thieves and redshanks." In this latter phrase he points at the Scotch origin of so many of the Presbyters, and maybe had in mind Spenser's erudite disquisition on the racial ties of the Albans and Scythians, and his conclusion to the effect that "Scotland and Ireland are all one."

In 1690, on the 14th June, Dutch William, landing at Carrickfergus, was met by General Schomberg and accompanied by him to Belfast, where he lodged at the Castle, and stayed from Saturday till the following Thursday. He spent his time in receiving addresses and reviewing his army, preparatory to his march south, to his victory of the Boyne.

This was a great event for Belfast, and quite in keeping with the tradition of Chichester's foundation and the spirit of the city we know to-day. In fact, Belfast would seem to have not yet recovered its equilibrium, and the figure of William of Orange still stands out as of supreme importance, overshadowing the repute and popularity of living sovereign or popular politician. In every Protestant working-man's dwelling you will see his image in crockery, or on the walls in a showy picture. When the 12th of July comes round hundreds of pictures of King William are lifted to the breeze on the great banners of the Orange lodges. There you will see him on his white, prancing horse, pointing his sword towards the smoke of James's guns, and to the stirring notes of 'The Boyne Water', that great victory is recalled.

One might easily imagine that this has been going on ever since William and Schomberg rode southward along the Dublin road; but in the intervening eighteenth century there was a time when Belfast would have deserved Spenser's lament concerning its retrogression from the English Pale, and when Milton might again have taunted its people with their kinship to the Highlanders.

Mention of the July procession brings us to this moment of history, and to the dramatic opening of narrative, which is our immediate concern.

It is 11th July 1792. There are bands, banners, and marching men. Amid popular enthusiasm a procession winds its course along the High Street, going by one bank of the river, which flows seaward between the houses, and returning by another. There is a review in a field on the Falls Road, a convention, and, finally, a banquet. This is, in short, a muster of the Irish Volunteers, who have already made history. The occasion of their assembly is to celebrate the fall of the Bastille, and declare themselves in favour of Catholic Emancipation and the Rights of Man.

Side by side with this political demonstration there was proceeding, what would be called nowadays a feis ceoil or musical festival, a gathering of the Irish harpers, the successors of the ancient bards of the Gaeldom. What a strange contrast is afforded here, between the politicians of the new era, fired with the principles of the French Revoluion, and the musicians mostly aged and blind assembled in the Exchange Rooms, who waited for the sound of the drums and the cheering to pass into the distance, ere they wakened the clear sweet music of their harps. Before we come to describe the festival in which they shared, it will be well to say something briefly and then dismiss the political celebration.

On this occasion of action and oratory, a leading part is taken by a keen-faced young man from Dublin, Wolfe Tone, who is proud to wear the uniform of the Belfast Company. He has left in his vivacious diary a vivid account of the proceedings and of the persons concerned. He held office as secretary of the association formed by the Irish Catholics to further their own emancipation. A Protestant himself, he was exerting all his powers to win the Protestants of Belfast to make a strong pronouncement at the convention in favour of the Catholic claims. He was opposed on this occasion by certain important men, chief of whom was Mr Henry Joy, who advocated caution and gradual reform. A great suspicion and curiosity was excited by the fact that he had driven into the town, with a gentleman from the College in Dublin, whom nobody knew. This was no other than his great friend, Whitley Stokes, a Fellow of Trinity College, a cultivated scholar and distinguished scientist. The Belfast moderates feared that he had been brought to exercise undue influence in the convention, and to allay these suspicions Wolfe Tone diverted his attention to the musical festival, and put him in the hands of the man who was the guiding spirit thereof, that is, Dr James MacDonnell. Tone himself took a look in at the old harpers, but writes of their efforts with impatience and only acknowledges three of the performers to be good.

It remains an undecided question, whether the political situation or the musical festival had brought Whitley Stokes to Belfast, probably the former was the reason, the latter the excuse, till Tone found that the Belfast men resented the presence of this outsider. Then again he was a United Irishman, but not in favour of revolution; and though Tone may have brought him with a view to his assisting in leading the moderates forward, his influence might have tended to hold the extremists back. Anyhow, he was left out of the political councils; and if he expressed his views at all on the burning questions of the day, it was in the course of argument and conversation at the dinners and festivities to which he was invited. Perhaps it was just this personal influence that Tone had counted on, for he himself had felt it, and in his analysis of the characters of his friends, places Stokes as coming nearest to his own views, save in the matter of revolution.

> He is an enthusiast in his nature, [writes Tone,] but what he would highly, that would he holily. In the full force of the phrase I look upon Whitley Stokes as the very best man I have ever known.

Stokes, it may be added, left the United Irish body in this year, when it began to advocate physical force.

Dr James MacDonnell, who must be regarded as the moving spirit in the matter of the harp festival, was without doubt one of the most public spirited men associated with Belfast at any period of its history.

Later in this book will be found an appreciation of his services in the sphere of medical practice and of scientific research. In politics he was liberal, and had spoken in favour of Catholic emancipation, avowing that though a Protestant himself, he had many Catholic kindred. He was never, however, entangled in the United Irish conspiracy, though Wolfe Tone seems to have sought after him, and dubbs him in his diary 'The Hypocrite,' not signifying that he fell short of his professions, but that he was a better Nationalist than he would allow himself to be considered.

Thomas Russell, Tone's intimate friend and associate, was for some time resident in Dr MacDonnell's house, and cooperated with him in collecting geological specimens and fossils, making the nucleus of the present Belfast Museum in College Square (where by the way there is a fine marble bust of the doctor).

Amid all this intimacy with the Belfast Republicans, MacDonnell remained unattached. It was perhaps to provide himself with a separate sphere of action on the occasion of 'The Fall of the Bastille' celebration and convention, that he set about organising the harper's festival along with Henry Joy and Robert Bradshaw. A present day parallel will be found in the Gaelic festivals held all over Ireland in the summer months, to which persons of every political creed are invited, but which serve to stir the deep well springs of national sentiment.

Dr MacDonnell could boast himself a Northern Gael of most illustrious line. He was born at Glenarrif, in County Antrim, where his father Michael, surnamed Roe MacDonnell, had some property, remaining from greater estates. Michael was son of Alexander, son of Coll a Voulin (of the Mill), so named because on his land in the Antrim Glens he used water mills, where humbler folk still ground at the quern. Going beyond Coll a Voulin, to his father, Sir Alexander MacDonnell, we step across the Irish Channel to the Scottish Isles, and into an era that makes blood-stained pages in history. In short, the great-grandfather of our gentle Belfast doctor was that tremendous personage, Sir Alastair MacColkitto MacDonnell, who figured in the rising of Montrose in Scotland and in the wars of Owen Roe in Ireland.

We dare not tarry to describe his great deeds here, nor to speak of his father before him, the Colkitto, from whom he derived his patronymic and with whom he is often confused. English writers, not understanding the Gaelic system of naming, often alluded to Alastair as Colkitto, or even as Mr Kitto or Colonel Kitto. These confusions are likely what led Milton to demand in his sonnet on Tetrachordon, whether that name was,

> *harder Sirs than Gordon*
> *Colkitto, or MacDonnell or Galasp,*
> *Those rugged names to our mouths grow sleek*
> *That would have made Quintillian stare and gasp.*

Michael MacDonnell of the Antrim Glens had somewhat declined from the position of his father and grandfather, yet retained all the Gaelic pride of birth, and counted kindred with the Earl of Antrim, his neighbour at Glenarm. To his house in Glenarrif came a blind youth, then going his first itinerary of Ireland as a harper in some year of the seventeen seventies.

This was Arthur O'Neill, clansman of the noble family that had once reigned in Tyrone. Michael MacDonnell gave hospitable welcome to the blind harper, and made him tarry in the glens to teach his three sons the art of playing on this instrument. What he thought of his pupils will be found in the chronicle of his life-story. Much as they loved music, the young men had other tastes, and had not patience to become expert; but as the years passed by, and when Dr MacDonnell, having graduated at Edinburgh, was settled in Belfast as a doctor and heard the stir of preparation for the Bastille celebrations, his mind went back to the blind harp-player at Glenarrif. He thought of the Highland festivals he had heard of in Scotland, and of the attempts which had been made to imitate them in the Granard harp gatherings. A fund was started, a circular sent out, subscribers found, and then an advertisement was put in the *Belfast Newsletter* summoning the harpers of Ireland to assemble and compete.

Arthur O'Neill, who was still on his wanderings, was laid up in the house of one of his friends after a severe wetting. Being disinclined to play by reason of rheumatic fingers, he had the newspaper read to him, and so came to hear the advertisement.

So came it that master and music-pupil met again. Nine other harpers were there, including those he had competed with again and again at the Granard competitions; but on this occasion, more than transient pleasure, or the excitement of a trial of skill was in view. As the harpers played, a young man, just nineteen years of age blue-eyed with Irish complexion and brown wavy hair was called forward and requested to transcribe the airs, as accurately as possible, and without any attempt to modernise or modify any peculiarities of the strains. The music was to be studied and recorded from the point of view of the antiquary eager to preserve a heritage of melody that had been handed down from one generation to another for centuries.

Whilst Dr MacDonnell, organiser of the festival, issued these commands, they were faithfully obeyed by the young musician and scribe, who bore the name of Edward Bunting.

CHAPTER II

EDWARD BUNTING—AN INTRODUCTORY MEMOIR (continued)

E DWARD BUNTING, ACCORDING TO THE ACCOUNT GIVEN BY HIMSELF, FIRST drew breath in the city of Armagh about 1773, his brother Anthony, who is frequently mentioned in this record, having been born in 1765. There was a third brother, John, about whom little is known, and all three grew up to be organists and cultured musicians.

The father was a mining engineer, who came from Shottle in Derbyshire, to assist at the opening of coal mines at Coal Island, Co. Tyrone. Dr Grattan Flood has pointed out that several families of the name of Bunting had been settled in the neighbourhood of Lough Neagh since the seventeenth century around Ballinderry.

He would like to have us believe, that Bunting had on his father's side a connection of some generations with Ireland; but the family records do not bear this out. It is quite likely, however, that Engineer Bunting may have heard of the opening of these Tyrone mines through kinsfolk already planted in Ireland. On the mother's side Bunting traced his descent to a pure Gaelic source, as she was a descendant of one Patrick Gruana [Grauma] O'Quinn, who had fallen in the great Irish rising of 1642. In his notes and writings he refers to having in boyhood heard the country-folk of County Armagh crying over the dead. We may almost certainly assume that he had mixed with his mother's Irish kindred and heard the Caoine in the house of mourning.

His taste for the native music he was accustomed to ascribe to his Irish descent, but in Armagh he was most fortunately situated for its cultivation.

The Primatial Cathedral of Ireland has been, from the time of its foundation to our own day, a training place for musicians. Here the three Bunting boys were trained by Barnes, then organist there; and Anthony, the eldest, qualified to become an organist, and secured a position in Drogheda.

It has been suggested that little Edward must have gone to Belfast in response to an advertisement which appeared in the *Belfast Newsletter,*

11th September 1781, as follows:

> Wanted an Apprentice from the age of nine to twelve by William Ware
> Organist of St Anne's Church Belfast. A fee is required. No one need
> apply who cannot be well recommended and who has not a taste for the
> Musical profession.

The advertisement may indeed have caught the attention of the friends and
guardians of the boy, and they may have got into communication with Mr
Ware, but his going to Belfast was deferred till his eleventh year.

Our authority is an article which appeared in the *Dublin University
Magazine*, written by an intimate friend, and whilst his brother and wife
were living in Dublin in 1847. The writer says:

> At a very early age he had the misfortune to lose his father, who left
> him unprovided for; and at the age of nine, having already shown a
> decided predilection for music, he was removed to Drogheda, where his
> eldest brother Anthony, an estimable gentleman and citizen of Dublin
> who yet survives him, was then located as a music teacher and organist.
> Here he remained for two years during which he received musical
> instruction from his brother and made such progress in his art, that
> his fame spread to Belfast, whither at the age of eleven, he proceeded at
> the invitation of Mr Weir (Ware) the organist of the Church there, to
> take his place at the instrument while that gentleman made a visit to
> London. It was very soon discovered at Belfast that the boy substitute
> was a better Organist than his employer and Mr Weir was glad to
> secure his services as assistant by articles for a limited number of years.
> While thus engaged he had in addition to his duties as assistant or
> sub-organist to the Church, to act also as deputy teacher to Mr Weir's
> pupils on the pianoforte throughout the neighbouring country, and the
> zeal of the young master to fulfil his duties were often productive of
> the most ludicrous results, for his young lady pupils who were often
> many years older than himself were accustomed to take his reproofs
> with anything but an angelic temper, and we have heard him tell how

a Miss Stewart of Welmot in the County of Down, was so astonished at his audacity that she indignantly turned round upon him and well boxed his ears.

To this account it may be added that the organ was a comparative novelty in Belfast, and that in the Parish Church of St Anne's, where Ware was organist, was, as yet, the only one.

From a *Newsletter's* advertisement we learn Ware's terms of tuition to have been:

> For harpsichord, a guinea entrance, and half-a-guinea the twelve lessons; guitar, half-a-guinea entrance, half-a-guinea the twelve lessons.

It was part of the duty of the music teacher to tune the instrument, and Mr Ware's tuning-key is still preserved in Belfast. Bunting became efficient, not only at tuning, but actually at repairing and constructing pianos. The mechanical skill, inherited from the engineering father, showed itself in the two musical sons, and there is a reference, in one of Bunting's letters to a daughter, to his brother Anthony and himself working at making the instruments. In the correspondence with Mr John McCracken in 1802 (see p. 224), it would seem that Bunting dealt in pianos for the firm of Broadwood, as there is a reference to his collecting money, and paying them a business visit. Anthony Bunting, both in Drogheda and Dublin, acted as agent for Messrs Broadwood through a long term of years.

The same Dublin University writer states, that on arriving at Belfast, the boy went to live with the family of Mr John McCracken, a prosperous merchant and shipowner, resident in Donegal Street, near to the Parish Church. Mr McCracken's wife had been a Miss Joy, and we hear of four sons and two daughters, of these John McCracken, junior, and Mary are most intimately associated with the life of Bunting. The other brothers were William and Frank and Henry Joy. The second sister was called Margaret. Bunting's note-books give evidence of the fact that they were musical and lovers of folk-song, for we find airs jotted down as "Mr John McCracken's tune," "William McCracken's tune," and a manuscript psalm tune book bears the inscription, "Mary McCracken, her book, Donegal Street, Belfast." In addition to psalm tunes, it contains a copy of the beautiful Irish air, 'Cean dubh Dilis'. The brothers and Mary were deeply involved in the political plots of the day; but it will be seen that Bunting differed from the views of his friends on political matters, though in a time of danger and sorrow he was found to be trustworthy and courageous when others failed who had made louder professions.

We must assume that his general education was in some way attended to whilst he resided with the McCrackens, for he showed himself a highly-cultivated man, with critical literary tastes, yet our Dublin University writer tells us that he ran in danger of the usual fate of an over-flattered genius, "After a few years spent in this manner," he writes, "he became a professor on his own account and his abilities as a performer had become developed, his company was courted by the higher class of the Belfast Citizens, as well as by the gentry of its neighbourhood and in short the boy prodigy became an idol among them. But need we say that this was a most perilous position for a young man subject to no control, imperfectly educated, with social spirit and high animal spirits, obtaining with ease sufficient means to supply his wants and without any higher objects of ambition to gratify them than that which he had already compassed. Or should we wonder that courted, caressed, flattered and humoured as he was, he should have paid the usual penalty for such pampering, that his temper should have become pettish and his habits wayward and idle. Such indeed is too commonly the fate of young musicians precociously gifted with extraordinary powers and who falling into premature habits of incurable dissipation, have seldom realised in after life the promise their early talents had given. It was happily not so with Bunting. Wayward and pettish he remained through life, and for a long period at least, occasionally idle and we fear dissipated, for hard drinking was the habit of the Belfastians in those days; but while still young, not more than nineteen, an event occurred which gave his ardent and excitable temperament a worthy object of ambition on which to employ it and which necessarily required a cultivation of his powers to enable him to effect it. The event we allude to was the assemblage in Belfast in 1792 of the harpers from all parts of Ireland, the aged and feeble Minstrels, who had given pleasure in a state society now rapidly undergoing a radical change."

So far we have quoted from one who enjoyed his intimacy at the end of life, and what he tells us is corroborated by the diary of Wolfe Tone, which throws so much light on the social as well as the political life of Belfast at that era. From his pen we get a glimpse of Bunting in the year previous to the Harp Festival, and though only a youth of eighteen we meet him at a club with men of the world, and arguing politics at a men's dinner-party. In October 1791 Tone came up to Belfast on a special political mission, and stayed with his friend, Thomas Russell, meeting all the leading men of the town and neighbourhood. Their political doings do not concern us, but there was much entertaining, and after each night's proceedings Tone notes late hours, much political argument and wine. Here is his description of his Sunday (23rd *October,* 1791).

Dinner at A. Stewart's with a parcel of Squires of County Down. Foxhunting, hare hunting, buck hunting and farming. No bugs in the northern potatoes; not even known by name, &c. A farm at a smart rent always better cultivated than are at a low rent; *Probable enough.* Went at nine to the Washington club. Argument between Bunting and Boyd of Ballycastle. Boyd pleasant. (*N.B.* perhaps Bunting was the opposite). Persuaded myself and P.P. (*i.e.* Russell) that we were hungry. Went to the Donegal Arms and supped on lobsters. Drunk. Very ill natured to P.P. *Mem. To do so no more.*

On 25th October he records a dinner at Mr McTier's, and "a furious battle on the Catholic question which lasted two hours."

Bruce an intolerant high priest declared . . . . that thirty-nine out of forty Protestants would be found, whenever the question came forward to be adverse to the liberation of the Roman Catholic . . . . It may be he was right, but God is above all. Sad nonsense about scavengers becoming members of Parliament, and great asperity against the new fangled doctrine of the Rights of Man. Broke up rather ill-displeased towards each other. More and more convinced of the absurdity of arguing over wine.

In this after-dinner debate he notes, "almost all the company agreed with Dr Bruce except Russell, M°Tier, Getty and myself. Against us Bruce, Cunningham, Grey, Holmes, Bunting and H. Joy."

It will be noticed that no member of the M°Cracken family with whom the boy Bunting resided was present at this dinner, and strange to say we do not meet the name of any one of the brothers in connection with these festive events. Nor are they mentioned as taking any lead in political discussions, either in private or at the Convention of 1793. Later on, when the day of danger and action arrives, they are found in the front.

Enough has been said to give an idea of the society and the influences by which Bunting was surrounded, when, as Petrie writes, the assembly of the harpers roused his enthusiasm and gave him an uplifting aim in life.

In a circular printed before the issue of his third volume in 1840 he refers to this event and possibly in the opening sentences, to the ambitions awakened by converse between Whitely Stokes and Dr MacDonnell which he was privileged to hear. The letters of the latter towards the end of the book exhibit him as urging Bunting on to tremendous efforts, almost too great for his enfeebled age, and we can gather thence what must have been his attitude of mentor to the talented but somewhat spoiled youth. We now quote from the circular:

The hope of being enabled, by reviving the National Music, to place himself in the same rank with those worthy Irishmen whose labours have from time to time sustained the reputation of the country for a native literature, had the Editor admits, no inconsiderable share in determining him on making the study and preservation of our Irish melodies the main business of his long life, and he is free to confess, the same hope still animates him in giving these, the last of his labours, to the public. But what at first incited him to this pursuit and what has chiefly kept alive the ardour with which for nearly fifty years, he has prosecuted it, was and is, a strong, innate love for these delightful strains for their own sake, a love for them, which neither the experience of the best music of other countries, nor the control of a vitiated public taste, nor the influence of declining years, has ever been able to alter or diminish.

The occasion which first confirmed the Editor in this partiality for the airs of his native country, was the great meeting of the Harpers of Belfast in the year 1792. Before this time there had been several similar meetings at Granard in the County of Longford, which had excited a surprising degree of interest in Irish music through that part of the country. The meeting in Belfast was however better attended than any that had yet taken place and its effects were more permanent, for it kindled an enthusiasm throughout the North, which still burns bright in some honest hearts. All the best of the old class of harpers—a race of men then nearly extinct and now gone for ever, Denis Hempson, Arthur O'Neill, Charles Fanning and seven others, the least able of whom has not left his like behind, were present. Hempson, who realised the antique picture drawn by Cambrensis and Galelei for he played with long crooked nails and in his performance the tinkling of the small wires under the deep tones of the bass was peculiarly thrilling, took the attention of the Editor with a degree of interest which he can never forget.

He was the only one who played the very old the aboriginal music of the country, and this he did in a style of such finished excellence as persuaded the Editor that the praises of the old Irish harp in Cambrensis, Fuller and others, instead of being as the detractors of the country are fond of asserting, ill-considered and indiscriminate, were in reality no more than a just tribute to that admirable instrument and its then professors.

But more than anything else, the conversation of Arthur O'Neill, who though not so absolute a Harper as Hempson, was more of a man of the world and had travelled in his calling over all parts of Ireland, won and delighted him. All that the genius of later poets and romance writers has feigned of the wandering minstrel was realised in this man. There was no house of note in the North of Ireland as far as Meath on the one hand and Sligo on the other in which he was not well known and eagerly sought after.

Carolan had been his immediate predecessor, and those who have taken any interest in the life of the elder minstrel will readily recognise the names of Charles O'Conor of Belnagare, Toby Peyton of Lisduff, James Grivin of Streamstown, Mrs Crofton of Longford, Con O'Donnell of Larkfield, Squire Jones of Moneyglass; not to detain the reader with a longer enumeration all of whom are to be found in the list of O'Neill's friends and entertainers. He had also when a youth been through the South where his principal patron was the famous Murtagh O'Sullivan at Bearhaven, a man who led quite the life of an old Irish chieftain, and whose memory is still vividly preserved in the lays and traditions of the County Cork. O'Neill was of the great Tyrone family and prided himself on his descent, and on supporting to some extent the character of a gentleman Harper. Although blind from his youth he possessed a singular capacity for the observation of men and manners. He had been the intimate friend of Acland Kane who played before the Pretender, the Pope and the King of Spain. He himself had played on Brian Borou's harp strung for the occasion, through the streets of Limerick, in the year 1760; in a word he was a man whose conversation was enough to enamour anyone of Irish music, much more, one so enthusiastic in everything Irish as the Editor.

By reference to Arthur O'Neill's *Autobiography*, it will be seen that Dr MacDonnell entertained all the harpers to a banquet, and detained O'Neill himself for some days as guest. During this time we may be sure Edward Bunting was still in attendance noting down the airs. In some instances the words of songs may have been taken down, and we find amongst the manuscripts the Irish words of 'The Green Woods of Truagh', with this inscription "for Mr W. Stokes." We have, however, no record of an attempt to preserve Gaelic song words at this meeting, though that had been in view, and the Harper O'Neill had attempted to bring with him a native Gaelic speaker, providing the man with suitable clothes for the occasion; but the poor scholar so fancied his improved appearance, that he went of to show himself to his friends and never turned up in Belfast.

The collecting of Gaelic lyrics was anyhow deferred to a later date, and attention concentrated on the harp melodies.

For four years after the harper's festival, Bunting devoted himself to the work of collecting airs, and in the circular already quoted refers to his labours at this period.

Animated by the countenance and assistance of several townsmen of congenial taste and habits, of whom his excellent friend, Dr James MacDonnell is now, alas, the only survivor, and assisted to a great extent by O'Neill and the other Harpers present on this memorable occasion, the Editor immediately after the termination of the meeting, commenced forming his first collection. For this purpose he travelled into Derry and Tyrone, visiting Hempson, after his return to Magilligan in the former county, and spending a good part of the summer about Ballinascreen and other mountain districts in the latter, where he obtained a great number of admirable airs from the country people. His principle acquisitions, however, were made in the Province of Connaught, whither he was invited by the celebrated Richard Kirwan of Creggs, the philosopher and founder of the Royal Irish Academy, who was himself an ardent admirer of the native Music, and who was of such influence in that part of the country, as procured the Editor a ready opportunity of obtaining tunes from both high and low. Having succeeded beyond his expectations, he returned to Belfast, and in the year 1796 produced his first Volume, containing sixty-six native Irish Airs never before published.

The Society for Promoting Useful Knowledge assisted the publication by subscribing a sum of money, which was, however, regarded as a loan, and returned.

Thomas Russell, the intimate friend of Tone, a south of Ireland man, who had come to Belfast with his regiment, had, on retiring from the army, taken the position of first librarian to this society. His intimacy with Dr MacDonnell has been already mentioned, and his work in the connection with starting the library was a labour of love. It was at that time placed in rooms in Anne Street, and here he was accustomed to have Irish lessons from a tutor (also a southern) called Patrick Lynch,[1] who had been imported to Belfast to teach Gaelic as a sound basis for literary research. Russell doubtless considered a knowledge of it as a necessary equipment for a librarian, who might have to collect and care for Gaelic manuscripts.

He had not been present at the Harp Festival, and passed through several changes of fortune in the interval between 1791 and the appearance of Bunting's collection in 1796. To recapitulate these briefly. Through indiscreet generosity to an undeserving friend he had got into debt, and was obliged to part with his commission, obtaining through the influence of the Knox family, a magistracy in Dungannon. This position he resigned from conscientious motives, being unable to concur with his brother magistrates in their method of deciding actions between Protestants and Catholics. Returning to Belfast, he was the guest of Dr. MacDonnell, who obtained for him, January 1794, the post of librarian with a small salary. It was during this period that he was enabled to show an active interest in Bunting's projected work; and in 1796 he was writing from a Dublin prison, for in the autumn of that year, the Government, awakening to impending danger, made a swoop on the Belfast centre of conspiracy, suppressed their newspaper, *The Northern Star*, and took its editor, Samuel Neilson, into captivity along with Henry and William McCracken, Russell, and many northern men, and among other

---

[1.] Later on collector of the words and music in Connaught.

Dubliners, Mr Thomas Emmet.

Russell's letters from prison were addressed to a Belfast friend, John Templeton, and contain many anxious enquiries about the library about matters of scientific research, and in 1797 he writes:

> I am told that the Irish Music is finished. I have no doubt that it will have great success and raise the reputation of the collectors of the Institution which brought it forward.

In 1800, writing still from prison in Fort George, Scotland, he writes:

> I enclose a tune for my friend Bunting which I beg you to give him; it is one I do not recollect him to have had.

In 1802, when he was at length liberated and about to seek a refuge in France, he finally wrote:

> Farewell, my dear friend. Give my kindest and warmest regards to Miss Mary McCracken and all the good family. Remember me affectionately to Bunting. I have a copy of his music with me, and will do all I can to introduce it to notice. You will best know to whom I would be remembered. Assure them of my best regards.

This may have been an indirect message from those who remained of his political friends, or to the lady for whom he had cherished an attachment.

We have passed over a pathetic scene connected with the political events of that time, in which Edward Bunting figured.

In 1795, Wolfe Tone with his family, came as a political fugitive to Belfast in order to embark there for America. Thence he was destined to pass to France, to launch three forces of invasion against England and finally to die in a condemned cell.

Passing through Belfast, he was entertained and cheered by former friends who rallied around him. Many delightful excursions were planned, the last of which was on the 11th June, to Ram's Island on Lough Neagh. On the return of the picnic party to Belfast there was a final gathering, for it was now the eve of departure. Russell, Neilson, and the McCrackens were present, and Bunting, whose collection was now well on the way to completion, was asked to play.

He chose an appropriate air known as 'The Parting of Friends'. It is recorded that the wife of Tone, though unused to the melting mood, was overcome with the pathos of the music, and, bursting into tears, left the room.

Had they had power to see into the future, the music chosen was singularly appropriate, for tragedy loomed darkly over the future; for two there, the scaffold waited, for a third, death in a condemned cell.

What was the air played by Bunting is questionable. That published with the title of 'The Parting of Friends', though sweet and pathetic, lacks the poignant grief of another with the same name, which lies buried in one of the musical note-books. It is also given the title of 'An Cuman', or 'The Bond', and there are Irish words for it; [2] but among the manuscript poems there is only one quatrain bearing the title of 'The Parting of Friends' or the 'Scattering of the Company'. It would peculiarly apply to the case of Tone, who had been courted in Belfast, then taken note of as a conspirator, and, finally, was separating from these conspirators with danger and death in prospect. The air has all the character of a Gaelic lamentation, and here is literal English for the Gaelic words.

> *I have been for some time in this town, I have been greatly caressed,*
> *That did not last long till notice was taken of me,*
> *No two things on earth I account to be more grievous*
> *Than the death of friends and the separating of companions.*

---

2. Published by Bailey Ferguson of Glasgow in *Songs of the Irish Harpers*, arranged by C. Milligan Fox.

CHAPTER III

EDWARD BUNTING—AN INTRODUCTORY MEMOIR (continued)

I N ORDER TO ESTIMATE THE IMPORTANCE OF BUNTING'S FIRST COLLECTION, WE must recollect that nothing approaching such a work had previously existed. In his own circular, summing up his life work and soliciting support for his last publication, he dwells on this.

> Before this time there had been but three attempts of this nature. One by Burke Thumoth in 1720, another by Neill of Christ Churchyard soon after, and a third by Carolan's son, patronised by Dean Delaney about 1747. In all these the arrangement was calculated rather for the flute or violin than for a keyed instrument, so that the tunes were to a great extent deprived of their peculiar character, and as they were deficient in arrangement, so were they meagre in extent. On the whole, the Editor may safely say that his publication, above alluded to, was the first and only collection of genuine Irish harp music given to the world up to the year 1796.

The book stands, therefore, as the earliest standard authority on this department of study.

View it with regard to its after effect in popularising and saving Irish music, it must be classed as an epoch-making book. Not that its circulation was very extensive, for indeed it brought little profit to the young man who gave it to the world.

A Dublin pirate-publisher speedily brought out a cheap edition, underselling Bunting's half-guinea volume, thus depriving him of a great part of his possible sale; but the object of the compiler and of his enthusiastic supporters in Belfast was accomplished indirectly through the medium of others, who followed in Bunting's track and gleaned the reward of his labours. In short, he gave the material and inspiration to Moore for his Irish melodies, which are known and sung in every country of the civilised world.

Moore's first volume of melodies did not appear for eleven years after Bunting's collection, but we have evidence from himself that the book had fallen into his hands very shortly after its publication. One quotation will illustrate this, and the anecdote embodied in it has interest from the fact that it relates to the young Irish patriot, whose tragic fate is alluded to in the exquisitely pathetic songs, 'Oh, breathe not his Name', and 'She is far from the Land'.

Thomas Moore was a student at Trinity College, Dublin, at a time when Ireland was seething with the spirit of insurrection. Even inside the sedate walls of the college conspirators were meeting and whispering. What the authorities considered a dangerous spirit was evident in the speeches at the debating societies. Finally, there was a visitation and investigation into this matter resulting in the expulsion of certain students. Moore, who was called before the visiting inquisitors, behaved with great firmness and courage, and refused to answer questions calculated to injure his friends. Chief of these was Robert Emmet, the younger brother of Dr Thomas Emmet, one of the leading men of the United Irish party, who was confined in prison along with Thomas Russell. Concerning his memories of his student days Moore has written:

> Edward Hudson, an amateur flute-player and a United Irishman, first made known to me Bunting's First Volume, which I brought to my home in Angier Street. [Also,] Robert Emmet, during those college days, used frequently to sit by me at the pianoforte while I played over the airs from Bunting's Irish Collection, and I remember one day, when we were thus employed, his starting up as if from a reverie while I played 'The Fox's Sleep' exclaiming passionately, "Oh, that I were at the head of twenty thousand men marching to that air."

The air so much admired by Emmet is that to which Moore afterwards composed his song, 'Let Erin Remember the Days of Old'. We may here incidentally remark that the northern insurgents, marching in the summer of 1798 from the neighbourhood of Belfast to their defeat at Antrim, tried to cheer their spirits with music; and, though led by Henry Joy McCracken, a member of the family with whom Bunting had his home, they did not sing an old Irish air, but in imitation of the French revolutionists tried to chant 'The Marseillaise' (whether in French or English we are not told). However, the song lagged to the slowness of a psalm tune, and dwindled away. Then Jamie Hope, a weaver, who was McCracken's chief lieutenant, started what he calls a brisk Irish air, now known as 'The Lass of Richmond Hill'.

Musical matters had evidently been somewhat neglected amongst the active conspirators, though the Belfast United Irishmen, stimulated by the harp festival of 1792, had adopted as their badge an Irish harp with this motto: *It is new strung and shall be heard*. In this connection, it is also interesting to recollect that Wolfe Tone, when in France, whiled away the time, when an army of invasion was being got ready, by jotting down Irish airs for the band of his regiment to play, in case he ever got so far as to have a regiment with a band.

To return to the subject of Moore, we have many references in his diary and letters to his dependence on Bunting. He sometimes notes that he has spent a morning trying over tunes; and after a visit to Ireland writes back to Dublin in urgent haste for his volume of the ancient music which he had inadvertently left behind. Petrie, in the *Dublin University Magazine* article already quoted, gives a very fair appreciation of the book, estimating its influence on other composers.

Of the excellence of the melodies in this first collection of Bunting's, it is hardly possible to speak in terms too high, there is hardly an air in it undistinguished for beauty and character; and as a whole it is confessedly superior in this particular to either of the more splendid volumes which he afterwards produced. It has now been long out of print, and, too, generally forgotten; but the majority of its airs have been made familiar to the world by the genius of Moore, to whom it served as a treasury of melody, as may be gathered from the fact that of the sixteen beautiful airs in the first number of the Irish melodies, no less than eleven were derived from this source. And yet he did not exhaust its wealth. Lover, who came to it for gems of melody after him, found there the exquisite air, 'Mary, do you fancy me?' which he worthily made known as 'The Angel's Whisper' and the air, 'I'll follow you over the Mountains'. And there still remain in this store-house of song unnoticed airs of a vocal character of equal beauty to any that either Moore or Lover has extracted from it too intensely Irish, perhaps, in their structure for fashionable ears and taste, but not the less touching to Irish feelings, and for which only a poet of the highest powers and musical sensibility could furnish appropriate words. Such, for example, is the very first air in the collection, 'If to a Foreign Clime I go', which Bunting placed in that prominent position from his intense admiration of it, and which we know he considered as the most ancient and characteristically Irish tune in this collection.

It is very true that the material for Irish musical composition was not exhausted, by even such lavish borrowers as Moore and Lover. The published volumes contain many airs which are rarely heard. Moreover, on searching through the manuscripts placed in her keeping by Bunting's descendants, the present writer has found many airs of a very distinctive character which have never yet been published. Some of these have appeared in the journal of the Irish Folk-Song Society, as facsimiles from Bunting's note-book, and have since then been arranged as songs and published under the title of *Songs of the Irish Harpers*.

When we consider the immense circulation attained by Moore's melodies, in spite of their association with Sir John Stevenson's settings, we cannot help regretting that Bunting and Moore had not met and arranged to collaborate. Petrie is our authority for a supposition that Moore had made advances to this end, but had been repelled.

We have often heard it asserted, we will not, however, vouch for the truth of the statement, as we never heard it corroborated by Bunting himself, that some time after the publication of his first collection, Mr Moore offered to supply him with words for the finer vocal airs in his possession, and that Bunting declined or neglected to avail himself of such assistance. But be that as it may, it is certain that he deeply regretted when it was too late, that he had not secured the aid of the great lyrist, though it may be doubted that two instruments so differing in character would have run together long in smooth harmony.

A spirit of reverence for old tradition, a desire to preserve religiously the ancient music of Ireland as he received it from the harpers, restrained and guided Bunting, who worked as an antiquary as well as a musician. Moore would have been impatient of such restraints, and never scrupled to make the melody mould and mollify itself at his pleasure. We need scarcely regret that the collaboration never took place, as it would have been impossible without compromise on one side or the other. It is, however, pleasing to note that towards the ends of their lives the poet and musician paid homage to one another, and that the bitterness due to comparative failure, the result of Moore's rivalry, did not blind Bunting to the merits of the lyrics, and he praised them in a way which gratified Moore's heart.

We quote from Moore's diary an expression of his feeling on reading Bunting's praise. It contains a candid avowal of the use he had made of the ancient music, and, in addition, a most interesting account of the share he had in connection with the settings.

> *July* 15th, 1840. Received from Cramers & Co. a copy of Bunting's newly-published collection of Irish Airs, which they have often written to me about, as likely, they thought, to furnish materials for a continuation of the Melodies. Tried them over with some anxiety, as, had they contained a sufficient number of beautiful airs to make another volume, I should have felt myself bound to do the best I could with them, though still tremblingly apprehensive lest a failure should be the result.
>
> Was rather relieved I confess on finding with the exception of a few airs, which I have already made use of, the whole volume *is a mere*

mess of trash.

Considering the thorn I have been in poor Bunting's side by supplanting him in the one great object of his life (the connection of his name with the fame of Irish Music) the temper in which he now speaks of my success (for some years since he was rather termagant on the subject) is not a little creditable to his good nature and good sense. Speaking of the use I made of the first volume of airs published by him he says: "They were soon adapted as vehicles for the most beautiful popular songs that perhaps have ever been composed by any lyric poet." He complains strongly, however, of the alterations made in the original airs, and laments that "the work of the Poet was accounted of so paramount an interest that the proper order of song writing was in many instances inverted, and instead of the words being adapted to the tunes, the tune was too often adapted to the words: a solecism which could never have happened had the reputation of the writer not been so great as at once to carry the tunes he designed to make use of, altogether out of their old sphere among the simple tradition-loving people of the Country with whom in truth many of the new melodies to this day are hardly suspected to be themselves.

He lays the blame [Moore continues] of all these alterations upon Stevenson, but poor Sir John was entirely innocent of them; as the whole task of selecting the airs and in some instances shaping them thus, in particular passages, to the general sentiment, which the melody appeared to me to express was undertaken solely by myself. Had I not ventured on these very admissible liberties many of the songs now most known and popular would have been still sleeping with all their authentic dross about them in Mr Bunting's first Volume.

The same charge is brought by him respecting those airs, which I took from the Second Volume of his collection. "The beauty of Mr Moore's words," he says, "in a great degree atones for the violence done by the musical arranger to many of the airs, which he has adopted."

These entries in Moore's journal are of profound interest, not only as a plain avowal of indebtedness to Bunting, but as casting a light on the fact, that he was himself accustomed to give a hand in the matter of musical composition. However, we cannot believe for a minute that the Stevenson arrangements so elaborated and florid can have any resemblance to the accompaniments, which Moore played or improvised when he melted hearts and drew tears from the eyes of his hearers in the most fashionable circles of London Society.

This is borne out by a description left us by Willis, who, in 1834, heard him sing at an after-dinner reception at Lady Blessington's.

My letter is getting long and I have no time to describe his singing. It is well-known, however, that its effect is only equalled by the beauty of his own words and for one, I could have taken him into my heart with delight. He makes no attempt at music. It is a kind of admirable recitative in which every shade of thought is syllabled and dwelt upon, and the sentiment of the song goes through your blood, warming you to the very eyelids and starting your tears if you have a soul or sense in you. I have heard of a woman's fainting at a song of Moore's, and if the burden answered by chance, to a secret in the bosom of the listener, I should think from its effect on so old a stager as myself, that the heart would break with it. We all sat round the piano and after one or two songs of Lady Blessington's choice, he rambled over the keys awhile and sang, 'When first I met thee' with a pathos that beggars description. When the last word had faltered out, he rose, took Lady Blessington's hand, said "Good-night," and was gone before a word was uttered. For a full minute after he had closed the door no one spoke. I could have wished myself to have dropped silently asleep where I sat, with the tears in my eyes and the softness upon my heart.

From this description, borne out by others that have come down to us, we feel sure that Moore never marred the beauty of the airs by the ornate quasi-Italian preludes and movements of Stevenson, but that he improvised as he went along, a chord here, a chord there, to emphasise a word and assist interpretation, leaving the clear stream of melody to flow on undisturbed.

In his journal of December 1826, we find an account of Moore's collaboration with so famous a composer as Bishop.

> Bishop, having failed at giving my idea of the song for the War-dance, I played him a few bars when in town as my notion of the sort of subject it ought to be. He took down from the notes I played and when his new setting came, I found he had exactly preserved them. The rest of the composition not being at all what I liked I again suggested a totally different harmony as well as melody, and he very good humouredly adapted it almost note for note; so that the composition now, though under his name, is nearly as much mine as anything I ever wrote.

In the same manner, without doubt, the poet handled and altered the measure and melodies, of the old airs in Bunting, improving them according to his own opinion, in any case, getting rid of their archaic characteristics, which had been so faithfully preserved, and thus smoothing the way for their world-wide popularity.

Bunting was of opinion that the harpers had accurately transmitted the melodies from one generation to another, but that in the mouths of singers, unacquainted with the county tradition, they had greatly altered. The achievements of Moore must have tended to confirm him in this view, and, indeed, with our own experience of folk-song collecting to judge from, we have to conclude that if Moore erred in this matter he was not the first. A great many songs are to be found which are simply variants of some one melody modified by alterations in the measure and style, according to the fancy of the poet who set words to them.

It is pleasing, however, to find, that Bunting, who was generally credited with having an embittered temper, should have made the graceful acknowledgment of Moore's genius which the poet thus quoted side by side with the condemnation for altering the airs. Moore, in spite of the adulation which had been heaped on him since boyhood, was eager for universal appreciation and was evidently exceedingly gratified by Bunting's pronouncement that he had written "the most beautiful popular songs that had ever been composed by any lyric poet." He responded with an outspoken acknowledgment of his indebtedness to Bunting's patient research, which appeared in his preface to the fourth volume of his collected works published in 1841 as follows:

> There can be no doubt that to the zeal and industry of Mr Bunting, his country is indebted for the preservation of her own National Airs. During the prevalence of the penal code the music of Ireland was made to share in the fate of its people. Both were alike shut out from the pale of civilized life; and seldom anywhere but in the huts of a proscribed race could the sweet voice of the songs of other days be heard.

It may here be noted by reference to the *Life* of the Blind Harper, Arthur O'Neill, that this description of the minstrels sheltering in huts is inaccurate. The harp was, as O'Neill himself calls it, a passport, which won entrance not only to the homes of the remaining old families of Irish race, but many of the newly-planted lords of land became enthusiastic patrons of music, and we find amongst O'Neill's entertainers Boyd of Ballycastle, and the ancester of Colonel Saunderson of Orange fame, whilst harp-loving Protestant parsons are mentioned as well as Catholic priests but to come back to Moore, he writes after describing the Belfast Harp Festival:

> It was in the year 1796 that this gentleman published his first volume; and the national spirit and hope then wakened in Ireland could not but insure a most cordial reception for such a work, flattering as it was to the fond dreams of Erin's early days, and containing in itself indeed remarkable testimony to the truth of her claims to an early date of civilisation. It was in the year 1797, that, through the medium of Mr Bunting's book, I was first made acquainted with the beauties of our native music. A young friend of our family, Edward Hudson,[1] the nephew of an eminent dentist of that name, who played with much taste

---

[1.] See vol.x. *Irish Folk-Song Society's Journal* for essay on the Hudson family.

and feeling on the flute, and, unluckily for himself, was but too deeply warmed with the patriotic ardour then kindling around him, was the first who made known to me this rich mine of our country's melodies a mine, from the working of which my humble labours as a poet, have since then derived their sole lustre and value.

In poetic phrase, addressing the harp of his country, he had before this written in one of his best known songs:

> *If the pulse of the patriot, soldier, or lover*
> *Has throbbed to our lay 'tis thy glory alone;*
> *I was but the wind passing heedlessly over*
> *And all the wild sweetness I waked was thine own.*

Moore's acknowledgment to Bunting came only two years before the death of the latter, but it must have given him content at the end of his days to think, that the work of this rival, whose success had overshadowed all his efforts was declared by its author to owe its inspiration to the harp music, which he had rescued from oblivion.

CHAPTER IV

EDWARD BUNTING—AN INTRODUCTORY MEMOIR (continued)

THE PERIOD BETWEEN THE PUBLICATION OF BUNTING'S FIRST AND SECOND volumes was occupied in Ireland by stormy happenings. In 1798 and in 1803 occurred unsuccessful revolutions, in which his intimate friends were implicated. In the earlier rising the efforts of the northern insurgents were considerably hampered by the arrest of the leaders they had chosen, and by the failure of others to fill the gap of danger. In this crisis it was Henry Joy McCracken who took the lead in Belfast, and brought a little army to attack the town of Antrim. His attempt ended in defeat and arrest. He was brought to Carrickfergus prison, thence to Belfast, where he was tried and executed. It is not in our domain to refer to these tragic events, except in as far as they form the background of the life of the musician, who lived and worked on, in the midst of conspiracy and tumult. In the early years of the nineteenth century we find Miss Mary McCracken actively and ardently interested in his work, and she remained a constant friend and adviser till the end of his life. She was then a young woman about his own age, of very remarkable character. No more striking and noble personality has appeared in the annals of Ireland's later history. Her virtues and talents are to be counted as all the more remarkable in that she entered no sphere of life where they would have competed for public recognition. She is not known as an author, yet is deserving of the fame due to a historian. When Dr Madden came to write the *History of the United Irishmen*, he found that her faithful heart had treasured the memories of all that had happened. The story of the north in those "dark and evil days" was related to him mainly by Miss McCracken, who knew all who had fought and suffered, and who had been as a protecting angel to the widows and orphans of those who had fallen.

When her brother was tried for his life, and no defence seemed possible, overcoming her natural timidity and repressing her emotions, she rose in the Court, to the astonishment of all, and pleaded his cause, not as a woman crying for mercy, but in the calmly-reasoned speech of a lawyer, pointing out all possible weak places in the case for the prosecution. When sentence was pronounced, she walked leaning on his arm to the foot of the scaffold, to comfort him and sustain his courage, and only at his earnest plea did she consent to leave before the last dread offices of execution were performed. Even at that late moment she had attempted to save him, and it is generally believed that she had bribed the executioner. She had used powerful influence to have the body delivered up to the family at the earliest possible moment, and on receiving it they sent for Dr MacDonnell to attempt every known method of resuscitation. He sent in his stead his brother Alexander, a qualified surgeon, but all his efforts failed. In a brief time a small funeral cortege bore the body towards St George's Churchyard in High Street. No other of the relatives had sufficiently recovered from grief to accompany it, and indeed the brothers were threatened with arrest. Mary walked along sustained by a kindly neighbour, till her brother John, seeing that she was determined to be present at the burial, hastened after the little procession and drew her arm through his. Her indomitable courage sustained her till the sods rattled down on the coffin, then she gave way to natural grief.

Recently her brother's remains have been reverently removed from that resting place, and laid in her own grave in Old Clifton Cemetery, so that after a hundred years we can at length say, "In death they are not divided."[1]

In the dark years that followed, the strains of the old Irish songs, softly played by Edward Bunting in the stricken home in Donegal Street, must have often touched and soothed her sorrowing heart.

In 1802 we find Dr MacDonnell and McCracken's family eagerly at work in an effort towards saving, not only the music, but the ancient language of the Gael. Bunting's first volume had consisted simply of harp melodies; now a more ambitious scheme presented itself. Every air should find its match in a Gaelic song. These would be examples of the efforts

---

[1.] This re-interment was effected through the exertions of Mr F. J. Bigger, M.R.I. A., and a simple slab with Irish and English inscriptions marks the spot.

of the Belfast writers to put the songs into English verse. These efforts were on the whole not very satisfactory to Bunting, who has dashed down a terse criticism on each, such as a teacher might write on his scholars' exercises. "Good" "Bad," "Middling," "Take this," and finally in sarcastic vein, "Take this if there's nothing worse."

A schoolmistress, Miss Balfour, was the most diligent and on the whole the most successful of these writers, though Bunting shows impatience at her over-refinement of the naïve peasant songs. We shall come back presently to the matter of these English song words, and must first speak of the Irish originals and the manner of their collection and the possible reason for the fact that they were never published. It has already been mentioned that Thomas Russell, who was by this time liberated from prison, but exiled and resident in France, had been at one time librarian of the Belfast Library, and had studied Irish with one Patrick Lynch, a native-speaking Gaelic scholar.

Early in the summer of 1802 the said Patrick Lynch was despatched on a song collecting mission to Connaught. He departed in May travelling *via* Drogheda, where he saw Bunting's brother Anthony, and then went on through the middle of Meath and Cavan to Sligo and Connemara. Edward Bunting had gone off on a business trip to London, and Lynch kept in correspondence with John and Mary M\u1d9cCracken, suffering, however, many adversities till Bunting joined him at Westport in the middle of July.

The Gaelic song collection was the fruit of this journey. The full account of Lynch's experiences will be found in this volume on a later page and makes interesting reading as recorded in his diary and in the letters he wrote appealing for funds to his friends in Belfast.

For some of the songs that he brought back with him, Bunting had already collected the airs in his visit to Kirwan in 1794, but he had never taken down the words, and Lynch brought the words of these and of many others. Here we may select one for quotation, which must have appealed with poignant force to the heart of sorrowful Mary. It is called 'Donachu Ban', and the speaker is a sister who has seen her brother die on the gallows. In the first verse she laments the walks at night, the conspiracy and the informer's envy which had wrought his ruin. Then she grieves that she had not him in her care, as a young child borne in her arms, and that she would not have carried him to the place of danger.

The song proceeds:

> *I gave a leap to the banks of the Lough*
> > *And the second leap to the middle of the bridge,*
> *The third leap to the foot of the gallows*
> > *Where I found my brother stretched.*
>
> *Mother! Mother rise up on your feet*
> > *Your darling son is coming home*
> *Not from his wedding, nor from the feast*
> > *But in his coffin of deal firmly bound.*

But the tragic drama of the United Irish insurrection was not yet completed. Wolfe Tone had died in prison, after bringing a French invading force to Ireland's shores. Others, notably his friend Russell, were known to be in Paris, and the menacing star of Napoleon Bonaparte's fortune was in the ascendant.

The ballad singers were voicing the hopes of the people in songs like that which told:

> *Boney's on the shore*
> > *I can hear his cannon roar.*

According to the popular tradition in Belfast, Mary M'Cracken is supposed to have been engaged to Russell, and the romance of her love and sorrow is told as a parallel to that of Emmet and Sarah Curran.

We shall see presently that tradition has erred, for Russell cherished another attachment. He was, however, her friend, and had sent when leaving prison a message of affectionate regard to her and to Edward Bunting. Her admiration for him was intense, and she seems to have regarded him with distant awe according to the following description supplied by her to the historian, Dr Madden:

> A model of manly beauty, he was one of those favoured individuals, whom one cannot pass in the street, without being guilty of the rudeness of staring in the face, while passing and turning round to look at the receding figure.
>
> Though more than six feet high, his majestic stature was scarcely observable owing to the exquisite symmetry of his form. Martial in his gait and demeanour, his appearance was not altogether that of a soldier. His dark and steady eye, compressed lip and somewhat haughty bearing were strongly indicative of the camp, but in general the classic contour of his finely-formed head, the expression of almost infantine sweetness which characterised his smile, and the benevolence that beamed in his fine countenance seemed to mark him out as one, who was destined to be the ornament, grace and blessing of private life. His voice was deep-toned and melodious, and though his conversational powers were not of the first order, yet when roused to enthusiasm, he was sometimes more than eloquent. His manners were those of the finished gentleman combined with native grace, which nothing but superiority of intellect can give. There was a reserved and somewhat haughty stateliness in his mien, which to those who did not know him had at first the appearance of pride; but as it gave way before the warmth and benevolence of his disposition it soon became evident that the defect, if it were one, was caused by too sensitive delicacy of a noble soul; and those who knew him loved him the more for his reserve, and thought they saw something attractive in the very repulsiveness of his manner.

A person of such marked distinction would be at any time observed in a crowd, and Russell must have had considerable difficulty in disguising himself when he returned to Ireland in 1803. However, he seems to have been able to do so, and we find him in the middle of July, "on the day of the Maze races," appearing in the heart of County Down in a district where he was exceedingly well known. One of the first persons to meet him was the "Pentaglot Preceptor," as from the title of one of his own books, we may call the learned Patrick Lynch, Bunting's emissary to Connaught. Considerably startled, he was yet inquisitive enough to hang around Russell for some days overhearing much of his conversation and plans. He had hoped to rouse insurrection in the north, and to march to the assistance of his friend Robert Emmet, who would be, he expected, by that time in possession of Dublin. All these hopes were doomed to failure. No force of any account could be persuaded to rally to Russell's aid, and in a few day's time he was a fugitive with a price upon his head, having learned of the premature outbreak of riot and disorder in which Emmet's elaborate plans had ended.

It is now that we can dwell on the contrast between the story of Sarah Curran and Emmet and that of Mary McCracken's devotion to her friend. It is now, too, that the fidelity of Edward Bunting was tested. He had never been involved in the United Irish conspiracy, still cherished moderate and loyal political ideas, yet he was the first man from Belfast to go out to meet the outlaw in his place of refuge among the hills, and to offer active assistance.

But Mary McCracken had gone earlier, taking her sister with her, to the house of a Covenanter, James Witherspoon, of Knockbracken, beyond the Castlereagh Hills. It was she who brought home the message that Russell desired to see Bunting, and James Hope adds in his narrative of these events that he desired to enquire of Bunting about the lady to whom he was attached. This was a Miss Simms, a reigning belle in Belfast Society. She does not seem to have reciprocated Russell's affection, or to have sent any message or offer of help to him in this time of trouble. Probably she had been pleased to make a conquest of him when he was the object of general admiration.

Russell soon removed to a place called Ballysallagh, not far from Bangor, and was in constant communication with Miss McCracken till a means of escape was planned. At last she sent money to provide for his journey, and at Craigavad he embarked in a Bangor sailing boat in care of two men called Campbell. They conveyed him safely to Drogheda, where he lay concealed in the house of a Protestant gentleman. We cannot help thinking that Bunting must have had a hand in arranging for this refuge in Drogheda, where he frequently visited his brother Anthony. From Drogheda Russell removed to Dublin, and after remaining for some time in hiding was arrested, and lodged in Kilmainham on 9th September.

Miss M'Cracken, at the earnest entreaty of her mother and relatives, yielded so far as not to attend the trial of her friend, but she collected money to pay for the defence, and engaged her uncle, Henry Joy, to act as counsel. In a letter of farewell, written two days before his trial, Russell thanked her for all her efforts on his behalf, but his characteristic reserve and punctilious courtesy is shown in that throughout, he refers to the kindness of "you and your sister."

The trial took place on the 20th of October, and resulted in the conviction of Russell, who, after an affecting but dignified speech from the dock, was sentenced and duly executed.

Two persons, whose handscript is abundantly in evidence in our Bunting papers, were present at the Russell trial in different capacities.

The unfortunate Patrick Lynch, who, it will be remembered, had hovered around Russell when he was trying to stimulate insurrection in July, had been arrested in Belfast not long before the trial, kept in prison on the charge of high treason, and only released on promising to appear as a Crown witness against Russell.

He duly appeared, and said in evidence that he knew the accused having given him lessons in Irish in the library in Belfast, and detailed some of the conversation that had taken place relative to the projected insurrection. We refrain from dwelling on this painful scene, as the unfortunate Lynch, who had not the stuff of a hero in him, seemed to realise the meanness of his position. At the end of his evidence he faltered out a few words that might be taken as an appeal to the prisoner for forgiveness. "I had a regard for the man; he was my friend."

In the body of the court, meantime, sat an attentive listener, who busily tried to commit to paper every word that fell from the prisoner's lips. Debarred from being present at the trial, Mary M'Cracken had entrusted to one Hughes, a lawyer's clerk, the task of preserving for futurity Russell's speech before sentence.

This was, we believe, no other than the Tom Hughes, who acted as scribe to blind Arthur O'Neill, the harper, when dictating his *Autobiography*. The speech which he preserved for the perusal of Russell's friends does much to illumine his memory, for in it was no bombastic justification of his conduct, but a solemn appeal to men of wealth and station to pay heed to the condition of the poor.

After the execution and burial Hughes returned, still by the faithful Mary's order, to place a stone in Downpatrick Cathedral Yard with this inscription:

THE GRAVE OF RUSSELL.

CHAPTER V

WE WOULD NOT HAVE DEALT AT SUCH LENGTHS WITH THE CIRCUMSTANCES surrounding the tragedy of Thomas Russell's death, but that the fortunes of Bunting's projected second collection were thereby affected.

We can well believe that Lynch, the unfortunate "Pentaglot Preceptor" was no longer employed by the MᶜCrackens and their ally. He, in fact, withdrew to another sphere of labour in Dublin, and is lost to our view. With his departure difficulties likely arose about his Gaelic manuscripts, although they remained in Bunting's possession, and had been all fairly copied.

But the loss of Lynch was not the only misfortune; an estrangement arose between the MᶜCracken family and Dr MacDonnell.

In the period succeeding Russell's first arrest and imprisonment, MacDonnell had shown himself a steadfast friend, as may be concluded from the letters written to John Templeton, of Belfast, from Russell in Kilmainham. In them the prisoner asks his financial necessities to be made known to the doctor, or to have his state of health explained and advice given. There are constant references to the Library and museum collection, and other subjects of common interest.

Dr MacDonnell, however, had never identified himself with the insurgent cause, and, we suppose, whilst he stood to his friends as long as he could, he considered himself under no moral obligation to suffer or make sacrifices.

When Russell was a fugitive in the north, the authorities became suspicious that Dr MacDonnell had extended aid to him. A visit was paid to him, and he was invited and urged to sign a document denouncing the attempted insurrection, and offering a reward for the apprehension of Russell. He urged that he did not believe that Russell was in Ireland, had no news or knowledge to that effect, and that he saw no need to sign the proclamation. A sister-in-law, who was in the room, added her entreaties with the specious plea, that if he was so confident that Russell was not in Ireland, he should have no hesitation in signing the paper, especially as he was decidedly opposed to the revolutionary designs.

He was thus persuaded to sign, but writing to Dr Madden said:

> I had not done it an hour until I wished of all things it was undone. I need not dwell upon what passed soon after, when Patrick Lynch was apprehended and fixed upon to identify Russell, in which transaction Lynch was entirely blameless in my opinion.
>
> Three friends of mine, John Templeton, his sister and Miss Mary McCracken refused soon after to speak well of me, and a subscription I had been in the habit of paying to Miss Russell was returned to me. These things vexed me more than I can express, but without any explanation upon my part, all these persons returned to my friendship.

In 1807, the first volume of Moore's *Melodies* appeared, and, as already explained, his free and easy method of borrowing from Bunting's collection provoked intense resentment.

The advantage of popularising the airs by turning them into drawing-room songs was seen, and Bunting determined to try and rival Moore. It was now that the Muse was invoked by that obliging preceptress, Miss Balfour, and she sat down to modify the Gaelic songs of love and war and drinking into something more delicate.

We open the manuscript book of English translations at random, and come on a rendering of a little Gaelic lyric that has become famous in the rendering by Douglas Hyde, which opens:

> *Oh were you on the mountain*
> *And saw you my love?*

Here is how Miss Balfour deals with it:

> *Saw you the rock that the hazel embowers?*

Saw you my love as she trimmed the wild flowers?
Or saw you the lustre of Beauty the rarest?
Or saw you the female in Erin the fairest?

and here is the style in which a Mr McNeill[1] treats 'The Coolin':

Have you seen the proud maid with the loose flowing hair
As she tripped through the woods with a negligent air,
Have you seen my cold love with her feet gemmed with dew?
Still dear to my heart though to love never true.

There are, of course, better verses than this, but Wordsworth had not yet convinced the writing world of the artificiality of accepted styles of poetic diction, and the Belfast writers were skilled in the accustomed conventions and endeavoured to remould the Gaelic translations by their standard.

Other specimens might be quoted as the song words include translations by Dr Drennan, by a Mr Boyd, "the celebrated translator of Dante," Mr McNeill, Robert Emmet, Thomas Russell (in a very sentimental eighteenth century style), Gilland (a fairly good song-writer), and Stott, a County Down man, who enjoyed the doubtful distinction of being mentioned in Lord Byron's satire on 'English Bards and Scotch Reviewers' as "grovelling Stott." Poems by Dean Swift and Campbell are copied as adaptable for the music.

Bunting, however, determined to try and arouse Thomas Campbell to a rivalry with Moore, and, with that in view, started for London in March 1809. The result was far from satisfactory. Campbell was a man, who, having secured easy success and early fame, was inclined to rest on his oars. At a later page will be found quotations from letters to Miss McCracken, in which Bunting alludes to his negotiations with Campbell. We find among the manuscripts a document he had drawn up for the guidance of this poet and others who might be induced to supply song-

---

[1.] Author of a famous temperance poem, 'Scotland's Scaith'.

words for the airs.

He gives in all cases the subject matter of the Irish poems and a specimen verse in the metre suited to the music, and he also explains the character of the epithets usual in Irish songs; that there are "frequent allusions to the perfumes of the apple-blossom," that "the cuckoo is frequently introduced into their songs."

His attempt to direct the verse writers on to Gaelic lines is profoundly interesting, and we rejoice for his sake to know that before he passed away he had seen a young poet rise up in Belfast in the person of Samuel Ferguson, who must have realised his ideal of a translator in such lines as these:

> *Oh, had you seen the Coolun*
> *Walking down the Cuckoo's street*
> *With the dew of the meadow shining*
> *On her milk-white twinkling feet,*
> *Oh, my love she is and my Coleen oge*
> *And she dwells in Balnagar*
> *And she bears the palm of beauty bright*
> *From the fairest that in Erin are.*

Ferguson was strangely enough born 1810 in Belfast, shortly after the time when Bunting was sorrowing for want of a poet to translate the Gaelic songs of his collection, and he was destined to collaborate with the musician in his last labours. One would almost be led to believe that the strong desire of his townsfolk had summoned that poet spirit from the vasty deep.

The merits of the 1810 volume have been very justly estimated by Petrie, whose criticism of the 1792 collection we have already quoted. Having given the first criticism we let the other follow. He refers first to the words:

If the well of Campbell's genius ran deep and clear, it was exceedingly difficult to pump anything out of it, and so after a long delay and innumerable fruitless applications, Bunting was ultimately obliged to content himself with two indifferent songs and permission to use two of the poet's ballads written long previous to the agreement, and which however excellent they confessedly were in their way, were entirely out of place in a collection of Irish melodies . . . but notwithstanding the want of merit or so-soishness generally of the words associated with so many of the airs, this volume was not only a beautiful, but a truly valuable one; and though, as a whole, it was not so rich in melodies of the finest character as his first volume, it yet contained very many in no degree inferior equally new to the public, and moreover arranged with such an exquisite grace, skill and judgment, as at once placed its Editor, in the opinion of the musical world, in the foremost rank of British Musicians, and as the most accomplished of those of his own country.

This alas! was the only reward it procured him. Like his former collection its sale barely paid the expenses of its publication, and this chiefly through his friends in the North who had become subscribers to the work to encourage him to undertake it. It was too costly, too repulsively learned with a long historical dissertation on the antiquity of the harp and bagpipes prefixed, to give it a chance of suiting the tastes or purses of the class of society which had bought the earlier work ; and among the higher classes there was then too little of Irish taste to incline them to receive it. So, after a fruitless effort to force a sale for it, while in his own hands, Bunting was at length glad, for a trifling sum, to transfer it altogether into those of his publishers, the Messrs Clementi; and like its predecessor the work is now rarely to be seen.

According to Petrie[2] Bunting had in any case the pleasure of seeing his merit recognised by impartial critics in the musical world of London, and during the period, when the preparations for publication detained him there, he enjoyed much literary and intellectual society.

[2.] In the *Dublin University Magazine* article already frequently quoted.

At the hospitable table of the Messrs Longman he had the pleasure of meeting the men most distinguished in literature, and at the Messrs Broadwood he was made known to the most eminent men of his own profession. At these houses he used to delight his hearers by his performance of the Irish music; and with the Broadwoods in particular, he was on this account as well as others, throughout his long life, an especial favourite; so much so, that on his last visit to London in 1839, they presented him with a grand pianoforte which they allowed himself to choose out of their extensive manufactory.

The interest of the Broadwood family in Irish music, which was aroused by Bunting, has continued to the present day, as is evident from the work of Miss Lucy Broadwood, of the Folk-song Society. Her attitude towards Irish traditional music is one of sympathy and understanding.

At the end of the year 1809 his Belfast admirers celebrated the publication of his book by giving a banquet in his honour. It took place in O'Neill's Hotel, Rosemary Street, on 20th December, with Gilbert McIlveen in the Chair, and William Stevenson as Vice-Chairman. Old Arthur O'Neill, who had now settled as instructor to the Harp Society in Belfast, was present with twelve pupils, all blind, and performed selections of music.

This festive ceremony was turned into a sort of anti-Moore demonstration, as the list of toasts included the names of men famous in the literary world, that of Moore being of set purpose omitted.

We find in Moore's *Life* by Lord John Russell a most interesting correspondence on the subject, for the poet of the melodies was actually very much hurt by the omission, as, of course, Bunting's Belfast supporters meant that he should be.

Mr Corry, a North of Ireland man, tried to gloss over the matter and to soothe Moore's feeling, explaining that the Belfast banquet was not so much a social and literary gathering as a mere demonstration got up to advertise and puff Bunting's volume, in which the banquet promoters were financially interested.

The affair, however, rankled in Moore's mind, for, not content with the adulation of royalty, the aristocracy, and literary world of England, he was eager to be recognised as the uncrowned laureate of Ireland. The refusal of homage from Belfast was a bar to his claim. With this in mind, we can understand the exultation with which he at length read Bunting's acknowledgment of his supremacy, which has already been quoted.

Reference to the Sidebotham letters[3] show us that his devotion to Irish music had not prevented Bunting from spreading in Belfast a taste for classical music. Mr Sidebotham, who resided in Belfast before going to practise law in London, was one of a party of distinguished amateurs who met under Bunting's direction to practise Beethoven's symphonies.

We will deal presently with the annals of the Harp Society, as this department of Bunting's work more especially concerns us, but not less to his credit is the fact that he conducted the first production of Handel's Messiah in Belfast. This took place in Dr Drummond's Church, Rosemary Street, in October 1813, when a whole week was occupied by a musical festival on a large scale. The Oratorio was rendered by the choir of Christ Church Cathedral, Dublin. We shall here add some details from Bunting's private papers as to the expenses. "Mr Cooke and his wife" (the prima donna) Bunting enters as having been paid one hundred guineas; Spray (the tenor) and daughter, forty-five guineas; Mahon Wedner, thirty guineas; Sidebotham, as secretary, regulating everything, received thirty guineas for his trouble; and, after paying for the choir and a band of fifty, the expenses amounted to a total of six hundred and thirty-eight pounds. The concerts took place in the theatre, or, when an organ was required, in Dr Drummond's meeting-house.[4] There is an addendum to the list of expenditure. "Paid

---

3. See pages 289-298.

4. So much attention has been given to Bunting as a song-collector, that his career as an organist has been scarcely sufficiently alluded to. The Belfast churches in which he officiated were St Anne's (as assistant), Dr Drummond's church in Rosemary Street, where the Oratorio part of the Musical Festival was held, and finally St George's, High Street, Belfast. His longest stay was at Rosemary Street, where his position was more independent than at St Anne's. He was able at times to appoint a deputy, and devote himself to his song collecting.

Spray out of my own pocket five guineas, as he said that his rank as first tenor deserved it," by which we see that concert directors had to cope with the same difficulties as at the present day.

CHAPTER VI

EDWARD BUNTING—AN INTRODUCTORY MEMOIR (continued)

IT IS NOW NECESSARY FOR US TO RETRACE OUR STEPS, AND GIVE SOME account of the results of the Belfast Harp Festival, and of Bunting's earliest publication in influencing public taste. We have dealt separately and at length with the subject of Thomas Moore's derivation of so many of his melodies from Bunting's gleanings.

Another literary personage, who had much influence in arousing the enthusiasm of the fashionable world, was Sydney Owenson, author of *The Wild Irish Girl* and other novels, later known to fame as Lady Morgan. Her memoirs and correspondence are of great interest, throwing light on the state of society in town and country.

In Arthur O'Neill's *Life* will be found a reference to "Owenson the Comedian" as an admirable singer of Irish airs. This popular actor, who flourished in the latter part of the eighteenth century, had at one period of his career inaugurated a National Theatre and Music Hall in Dublin, in which his singing formed as powerful an attraction as the drama. His venture was ruined by the Theatre Royal obtaining a monopoly, and he later became deputy-manager of it. His family, consisting of two daughters, were brought up under the opposing influences of an actor-father and a puritanical mother, whose whole pleasure was in the society of the followers of John Wesley. Lady Morgan has left a delightful account of her own christening, saying in conclusion:

> I am sorry not to be able to tell all this as a "credible witness" of the scene narrated, for being but a month old I understood nothing about it; but I have so often heard of it from my father as I sat upon his knee, that my testimony, although hearsay evidence, may be accredited.

The company included Father Arthur O'Leary, a Dominican Friar, famous as a preacher and controversialist, who had broken lances in attacking the penal laws with John Wesley himself. Next to him was the Rev. Mr Langley, a missionary of Lady Huntingdon's College; and amongst others present were Counsellor MacNally, Kane O'Hara, and Captain Jephson, three dramatists Richard Daly, patentee of the Theatre Royal; Signor Giardiani, the composer; Edward Tighe of Woodstock, a dramatic critic, "Counsellor Lysaght," the Irish *improvisatore* in his youth, the eloquent barrister and prime wit in his middle age, who acted as sponsor.

> The Rev. Charles Macklin, nephew to Macklin the actor and dramatic critic, [who, she adds,] was so great a favourite with my father that he chose him to perform the ceremony of inaugurating me into the Church militant. But his preaching, however eloquent, was not equal to his skill in playing the Irish bagpipes, that most ancient and perfect of instruments. 'The Piper that played before Moses' is still an Irish adjuration, and a personage who is at any rate sworn by. . . . A branch of Shillelagh from its own wood near Dublin flourished as a Christmas tree in the centre of the table. . . . My father sang first in Irish and then in English Carolan's famous song of 'O'Rourke's Noble Feast', whilst the chorus was swelled by the company. . . .

Many years after this notable event, Counsellor Lysaght, an eminent barrister, going the Munster Circuit, bivouacked for the night at the house of a friend in Tipperary. He stole into the drawing-room, which was full of company, not to interrupt a song which a young girl was singing to her harp, it was the Irish cronan of 'Emun a Cnuic', 'Ned of the Hill'; the air was scarce finished when he sprang forward and seized the harpist in his arms, exclaiming, "This must be Sidney Owenson it is her father's voice none but an Irish voice could have such a curve in it, and, she is my god-child."

We quote at this length to introduce the reader to a picture of *The Wild Irish Girl* with her harp. Her memoirs throughout afford a complement to O'Neill's evidence of the popularity of music, and the manner of education in Irish country houses. In the eighteenth century young people of quality were not sent to schools, nor was a general governess or tutor "of all work" kept. Tutor specialists went from house to house; one time it was the writing master, next a French *emigré* or a Latin-learned parson, a dancing-mistress succeeded to a person who had dealt with more serious branches of culture, and the wandering minstrel was detained on his journey as a guest in some great house to give sets of harp-lessons to the family and neighbours.

An Irish Government Department has, by the way, inaugurated in late years a somewhat similar system of itinerant instruction.

Sydney Owenson gives a description of her own *debût* as a governess, which contrasts delightfully with the dismal experiences of Charlotte Bronte. Leaving a dance in Dublin attired in muslin and pink silk stockings, with no time to change, she bundled herself up in a great Irish cloak, and went by coach to the country house of a Mrs Fetherston-haugh in Westmeath. The dinner party on her arrival included the lady of the house, her two daughters, two itinerant preceptors, Mr O'Hanlon, a writing and elocution-master, and a dancing-master, Father Murphy, the P. P., and the Rev. Mr Beaufort, Protestant curate.

The parish priest proposed the health of the new governess, and after dinner the butler announced,

> that the piper had come from Castletown to play in Miss Owenson, upon which the girls immediately proposed a dance in the back hall, and when I told them I was a famous jig-dancer they were perfectly enraptured. So we set to, all the servants crowding round the two open doors in the hall.

She concludes this account of her terpsichorean debut into the scholastic profession by describing the last occasion on which she had danced a jig in public during the Viceroyalty of the Duke of Northumberland, when at Dublin Castle she accepted a challenge from Lord George Hill, and defeated him.

Like Thomas Moore, Lady Morgan found, through the music of

Ireland and her fresh and charming mode of rendering it, an enthusiastic reception into aristocratic society. She became the pet of the Marchioness of Abercorn, and was married in the drawing-room of Baronscourt to Charles Morgan, the family physician, who was knighted to give the wild Irish girl the title of Lady.

She exerted herself on behalf of the preservation of the Irish harp, and Egan at Dublin, who started as a harp-maker after the Belfast Festival, owed many orders to her recommendation.

Lady Abercorn, in a letter to her, wrote on receiving one:

> Your harp is arrived, and for the honour of Ireland, I must tell you, is very much admired and quite beautiful. Lady Aberdeen[1] played on it for an hour last night, and thought it very good. . . . Pray tell poor Egan I shall show it off to the best advantage, and I sincerely hope he will have many orders in consequence.

In 1805, Sydney Owenson had bought her own harp out of the earnings resulting from the sale of her first novel.

To her interest we owe the description of Harper Hempson, which finds a place later in this volume. Interested by the reference to him in Bunting's book, she sent Mr Sampson, a Derry gentleman, to interview him in his home at Magilligan, as she found it impossible to journey there herself. She encouraged the various harp festivals and the Harp Society founded in Dublin, and finally, through her exertions, a beautiful bas-relief portrait of Carolan playing on his harp was executed by the famous sculptor Hogan, and erected in St Patrick's Cathedral, Dublin.

Though her musical taste was obviously inherited from her father, much of her enthusiasm was inspired by Bunting's efforts. This account of the part she played in making Irish music and the Irish harp fashionable may find a place here without our being accused of unwarrantable digression.

We shall now deal with the various societies formed to preserve

---

1. Lady Abercorn's married daughter.

and popularise the harp.

A year before Bunting's second volume was published, Dr James MacDonnell and other leading Belfast men, with Bunting as musical organiser, and John McAdam as secretary, founded the Irish Harp Society of Belfast. Perhaps a mistake was made in trying to connect the musical effort with a philanthropic aim namely, to provide occupation for the blind. The first Harp Society, in fact, organised a regular institute for the blind, and the pupils were boarded as well as instructed, with the exception of a few day-pupils resident in Belfast. Old Arthur O'Neill was employed as preceptor, and we owe to his residence in Belfast between the years 1808-1813 the fact that his interesting autobiography has been preserved. It was taken down from his dictation by Tom Hughes, a lawyer's clerk, who figures otherwise among our manuscript collection as "Nibbs," Mr Bunting's private secretary.

Dr W. H. Grattan Flood, in his *History of Irish Music*, briefly but sufficiently summarises the record of the first Belfast Harp Society:

At length, on St Patrick's Day 1808, the Belfast Harp Society was formally inaugurated at Linn's Hotel, the White Cross, No.1 Castle Street. In the list of original subscribers (one hundred and ninety-one) the total annual subscriptions amounted to three hundred pounds, Lord O'Neill being appointed first president, vice Bishop Percy of Dromore, who declined the honour. The first teacher was Arthur O'Neill, and the classes opened with eight day-pupils and a girl, Bridget O'Reilly. Of these two were dismissed in June 1810 for inaptitude to learn, thus leaving seven boarding-pupils, viz. : Patrick O'Neill, Patrick McGrath, Edward McBride, Nathaniel Rainey, Abraham Wilkinson, James McMolaghan and Bridget O'Reilly, in addition to Edward O'Neill, Hugh Dornan and John Wallace as day-scholars. Harps were supplied by Messrs White, McClenaghan and McCabe, of Belfast, at a cost of ten guineas each. From 1809 till 1811 there were Irish classes in connection with the Belfast Harp Society, with James Cody as Professor, the grammar used being that by Rev. William Neilson, D.D. In 1812 the society was in difficulties, and it collapsed in 1813, having expended during the six years of its existence nine hundred and fifty-five pounds. To the credit of the society poor O'Neill was given an annuity of thirty pounds[2] a year, but he did not long enjoy it, as his death occurred at Maydown, Co. Armagh, on October 29th, 1816, aged eighty-eight. His harp is in the Museum of the Belfast Natural History and Philosophical Society.[3]

To this we may add, in relation to Irish being taught to the harp pupils, that Bunting says all harpers previous to O'Neill had used Irish terms in regard to their instrument and music. A Miss O'Reilly, of Scarva, was the last person to be taught the harp through the medium of Irish. Through her and other sources Bunting carefully collected all the Irish technical musical terms, which were duly published in 1840.

The unfortunate Patrick Lynch had assisted Dr Neilson with the Irish grammar. It is quite a literary production, containing a splendid phraseology, and amongst other things the famous 'Lament of Deirdre for the Sons of Uisneach' is given as a reading and recitation exercise.

The work of the first Belfast Harp Society was emulated in Dublin, where John Bernard Trotter, a talented but eccentric man of means, who had been secretary to Charles James Fox, became the guiding spirit.

Patrick Quinn, who had been one of the youngest harpers in Belfast, 1792, was brought from the North as instructor. The society was inaugurated 13th July 1809 with an influential list of subscribers, including Tom Moore and Walter Scott. The last-named, by the way, must have surely realised that he had been premature in poetically chronicling *The Last Minstrel*.

Bernard Trotter gave 200 a year to the Harp Society, and at his residence of Richmond, near Clontarf, he entertained in great style. Quinn, seated in a picturesque arbour, used to delight the numerous

---

2. Dr James MacDonnell was the donor.

3. Transferred to the Municipal Collection, 1810.

guests on festive occasions with the strains of his harp. Trotter also carried out a grand Carolan Commemoration, where Quinn figured along with many distinguished musicians including Sir John Stevenson, of *Melodies* fame. Trotter became bankrupt in 1817 owing to his extravagance, and his Harp Society expired. His own death occurred in Cork, 1818.

In the following year, 1819, just when Bunting, who had for a couple of years been organist of St George's, was about to leave Belfast, a pleasant surprise occurred in the arrival of a gift of one-thousand two-hundred pounds for the purpose of reviving the harp and the ancient music of Ireland. The money was subscribed by a number of Irishmen resident in India, headed by the Marquis of Hastings, formerly prominent in Irish affairs as Lord Moira.

This generous subscription re-started the Harp Society, which was inaugurated 6th April 1819. Classes were started with Edward McBride, and afterwards Valentine Rennie, as teachers. The scheme was carried on for fully twenty years. The teacher Rennie, dying in 1837, was succeeded by James Jackson, who taught harp classes in Cromac Street for one year more, when the society finally expired. References to the last efforts of the Harp Society will be found in Dr MacDonnell's letters, where we find him boasting of the talents of the pupils, and where we are told of Mary McCracken superintending the making of a harp.

Drogheda, where Bunting had lived as a child, and where his brother Anthony had been organist for many years, was the next scene of a Harp Society effort. It is pleasing to know that the society started there in January 1842, two years before Bunting's death, and he must have been cheered by news of it.

Father Thomas Burke, O.P., of Drogheda, was organiser; Hugh Fraser, teacher of fifteen pupils. A German scholar called Kohl, travelling in Ireland in 1843, was entertained by Father Burke at a musical recital, of which he has given a vivid description:

> The first person who came forward, [writes Kohl], was an Irish declaimer, a man from among the people, I know not whether a gardener, a carpenter,

a ploughman, or a broken farmer, but I was told he knew a countless number of old Irish songs and poems. He came in, and thus addressed me: "I am come out of friendship for him" meaning the priest. "He told me that there was a foreigner here who wished to hear some of our old Irish poems, and I will gladly recite to him what I know . . . . Our fore-fathers have handed down to us a great number of poems from generation to generation, and very beautiful they are if you could only understand them. How beautiful is the song of the glittering Spring, which is but three miles distant from our town, or that of Cuchullin, the Irish Champion, who went to Scotland. Shall I begin with the story of Cuchullin?"

So he related the story of Cuchullin's strife with his own son, whom he slew unwittingly. Then a harper was introduced who played 'Brian Borou's March' and the traveller listened in rapture, and says:

When Moore mournfully sings,

> *The Harp that once through Tara's halls*
> *The soul of music shed*
> *Now hangs as mute on Tara's walls*
> *As if that soul were dead.*

We must not understand him literally. Many harps still thrill all through Ireland, and although the Harpers' Society of Belfast was lately dissolved, yet another has been founded at Drogheda, of which the Clergyman whose guest I was is the soul and president. His whole room was full of harps, and comprised many new ones.

To this account of Kohl's the present writer would add the evidence of a cousin, who died lately at a very advanced age. In the middle of life she opened a ladies' school at Drogheda, and was delighted on arriving in the town to hear of an old harper who rendered ancient Irish music in an exquisite fashion. She invited him to the school to play for her pleasure and for the pupils, and finally induced him to give her and her sister some lessons. This must have been one of the survivors of the Harp Society.

Kohl's description of the priest's room full of harps recalls a visit we paid to the Rev. Monsignor O'Laverty, P.P. of Holywood, the learned historian of the diocese of Down. The monsignor was as great an enthusiast as Dr MacDonnell would have desired to follow in his footsteps. He was instrumental in starting the making of harps in Belfast, and boldly advocated the introduction of the instrument into National Schools, instead of the squeaky harmonium and tinkling pianos so often found.

Through his enterprise and advocacy, and the support of the Gaelic League and Feis Ceoil Committees, the Irish hand harp is not obsolete, and even in London it is occasionally heard as an accompaniment to song at the concerts of the Folk Song and Irish Literary Societies. Is it not recorded in the preface of this book that it was through the medium of an Irish harp that the grandson of Edward Bunting was discovered to be resident near London? An expedition in quest of an instrument for a concert led finally to the threshold of Dr Louis MacRory, and to the custodianship of his grandfather's precious relics.

CHAPTER VII

EDWARD BUNTING—AN INTRODUCTORY MEMOIR (continued)

THIRTEEN YEARS HAD ELAPSED BETWEEN THE PUBLICATION OF BUNTING'S first and second collection. The latter, appearing at the end of 1809, was not to be followed by the third and final volume till the year 1840; but we are not to rashly conclude that his enthusiasm in the subject had waned. We have seen that his efforts were never rewarded by a due financial return, and that his published airs were pirated or lavishly borrowed from; so, whilst he continued in his work of research and collection, this was done at his leisure and as a labour of love, in the intervals of his necessary occupation as organist and teacher.

The great musical festival of 1813 must have helped to spread his fame to Dublin, and in a few years' time he went to reside there. There were two reasons which decided him to this step. His elder brother Anthony, for whom he had a warm attachment, had for some years been resident in the capital, and the lady who was now to be his wife had also left Belfast, and with her mother was conducting a ladies' school in Dublin.

Bunting, as we have seen, had been something of a spoiled youth, and a popular dining-out bachelor. He had lived an unsettled and roving life of necessity in connection with his teaching work and music-collecting. Though early left an orphan, a home was provided for him with the McCracken family from his early youth. The last glimpse we get of his life as a bachelor is from the pen of Petrie, and at an era which Charles Lever has very well described in one of his military novels. It was in Paris in 1815, while the allied sovereigns occupied it after the fall of Napoleon at Waterloo:

On this occasion, [*writes Petrie,*] his portly, well-fed English appearance procured him the honour of being harmlessly blown up, by a mass of squibs and crackers being placed under him as he was taking a doze on a seat in the Boulevards, by a crowd of mischievous Frenchmen, who, surrounding him, followed up the explosion with roars of laughter and exclamations of "Jean Bull!" Here, too, he made intimacies with many of the most eminent musicians, whom he no less delighted by the beauty of the Irish airs which he played for them than he surprised them by the assurance which he gravely gave that the refined harmonies with which he accompanied them were equally Irish, and contemporaneous with the airs themselves. "Match me that," said Bunting proudly to the astonished Frenchmen, as, slapping his thigh to suit the action to the word, he rose from the pianoforte after delighting them with the performance of one of his finest airs.[1] . . . Led by his love for music, and particularly of the organ, which was at all times his favourite instrument, he passed from France into Belgium, where from the organists of the great instruments at Antwerp and Haarlem he acquired much knowledge, which it was our good fortune to have often heard him display on our own organ at St Patrick's.

Four years later, on 20th January 1819, he wrote to Mrs Chapman, a widow, lady principal of a school at 18 Leeson Street, Dublin, and asking the hand of her daughter, Miss Mary Anne Chapman, in marriage.

This family had formerly been resident in Belfast, where Mrs Chapman also had kept school. It is advertised in the *Belfast Newsletter* of 1819-1820 as having been located at he corner of Curtis Street, near York Street.

As Petrie, in the *University Magazine*, says Mrs Chapman had removed to Dublin some time previous to this, it may have been that her daughter remained some little time in Belfast conducting the older establishment, whilst her mother was launching the new enterprise. A brother was already in Dublin, a fellow of Trinity College, and this gave the family a status and educational connection.

About the very time when Mrs Chapman was leaving Belfast, the

---

1. The great Catalani, delighted with Bunting's performance of some of the Irish airs, took a diamond ring off her finger and presented it to Bunting. It is now in the possession of his granddaughter, Lady Deane.

wife of Bunting's brother John was advertising the most fashionable ladies' school in the town as being removed from 67 Donegal Street to a building in Donegal Place, with an outlook on the castle and into a fine garden situated at the angle of Castle Street.

Of this brother John we hear very little, save that he was also engaged as a music-teacher. There may have been some rivalry with Edward in the musical line, and at the same time between the school-teaching ladies. At any rate, Mrs John Bunting, who had been a Miss Ash, with good local connections, nourished exceedingly. Little medals awarded at her school have been handed down inscribed with the names of the grandmothers of present-day citizens.

The granddaughter of Edward Bunting informed the present writer that her mother never spoke of any uncle but Anthony, to whom they were all attached. Uncle John and his triumphant school-teaching wife may not have been friendly. We must, however, not stray away in conjecture.

The fact remains that Mrs Chapman had been in Belfast, removed to Dublin, and that for the sake of her daughter Edward uprooted himself from his old familiar surroundings in the town which he had come to as a child prodigy; through her gentle and benign influence, moreover, he did what was more difficult, in breaking away from habits and modes of life in which he was becoming confirmed.

The Harp Festival had proved the turning-point of his youth, providing him with an ideal and aim to work for, and now that the aim was accomplished, and a position of ease assured, a new stimulus was given by his love for his chosen wife. Succeeding in winning her hand, a new life opened up before him. Petrie, who seems to have received Bunting's own confidences on this matter, deserves to be quoted here:

> Hitherto, it should be observed, he had, for a period of more than forty years been living at little cost with the respectable family of the M\^{c\}Crackens at Belfast, to whose house he had been invited when he arrived there at the age of eleven, "getting and spending" as he pleased, but certainly not saving. He had now to commence house-keeping on

his own account. To begin the world, as we might almost say, to earn his bread in a new locality where he was comparatively little known, and where he would have to contend with the professors of his art of high powers and established reputations, and that at an advanced period of life, when the mind is as indisposed to form new friendships or associations as the public is to reciprocate them. Yet he was not unsuccessful. Through the influence, chiefly of his northern connections, he soon got into an extensive practice as a teacher in the higher circles, and was appointed organist of St Stephen's Chapel, and thus toiling daily, and without rest, he was enabled to support a growing family in respectability, and had the happiness to leave them able, if required, by the exercise of their own talents, to provide for themselves.

To the difficulties commented upon by Petrie we may add the fact that the newly-married couple, elderly husband and young wife, at first resided with Mrs Chapman. Bunting had not known since his early childhood the loving rule of a mother. The rule of a mother-in-law would naturally have been all the more irksome, and he was a man who, by his own avowal, suffered from irritability of temper. After a brief experiment the joint housekeeping was abandoned, and Mr and Mrs Edward Bunting removed from 18 Leeson Street to a home of their own at 28 Upper Baggot Street. Later on they resided at No. 45, in the same street. An intimate glimpse into the happiness of his married life is given us in a letter written to Mary McCracken, which we may quote apart from the correspondence later on which deals with his publication work.

It is dated 29th December, 1820, when his heart was still tender with rejoicing over his first-born child, the only son, little Anthony.

We cannot live for ourselves alone and I hope I shall grow better every day, at least as to those notions of propriety which all sensible folks practise and which I never did, to my shame be it spoken, till now.

I for the first time received the Sacrament at Patrick's Cathedral on Christmas Day with my lady. She seems happy now to what she did during her mother's superintendence of the household, in consequence of my altered behaviour perhaps. My little darling son, she and I take the greatest delight in. He is grown handsome. All the people are delighted with him. I intend to be in Belfast on Thursday per day mail so I shall soon see you all once more, hearty and well. I am with true affection ever yours sincerely,

E. BUNTING.

Thus did he open his heart about his home happiness, and his resolve to try to live in worthiness of it, to the friend who had been as a sister by his side since earliest youth.

Another letter is necessary to this life narrative, as it alludes to the fact that the links were not all broken with Belfast as regards musical work. He writes again to Mary McCracken:

Dec. 27th 1827.
28, Upper Baggot St.

I received an unsought letter from the Trustees of George's Church (where a new organ price one thousand pounds has been put up lately), to be their organist with a salary of from ninety to one hundred pounds a year, for which situation above twenty candidates started and canvassed the Parish. My appointment is dated 1st December and the duty is twice per week, Wednesday and Fridays and Sundays also. They would not allow me a deputy at present so that I could not go to Belfast to you.

I am indebted for this place to the Attorney-General, who sent for me and spoke to me so kindly and friendly, that I was nearly overpowered with all my old recollections of the Joy tribe, from your dear, dear, departed mother, till the present time, they have been an honour to Ireland from their first introduction into it, and friendly beyond my deserts have they been to me one and all of them since I was twelve years of age, now a period of forty years.

The Attorney-General alluded to was Miss McCracken's cousin, Henry

Joy, who shared the enthusiasm of his relatives for Irish music and antiquities. It was natural that he should extend a helping hand to Bunting.

St George's Church is a large Georgian building on the north side of Dublin, near Mountjoy Square, then a very fashionable quarter, and here we must picture to ourselves Bunting busy on Wednesdays and Fridays and Sundays, with a good deal of teaching amongst fashionable young ladies eager to become accomplished pianoforte players.

His allusion to Belfast would lead us to think that previous to this he went up north at intervals and continued to give sets of lessons. However, this was now impossible, as he could not leave a deputy. In Baggot Street the darling little son Anthony had two sisters to play with. With their support as his main object in life, expensive music publishing schemes were, for the time, unthought of.

Tom Moore, soaring to exalted altitudes in society on the wings of poetry and song, may have at times given him twinges of irritable envy. That poet had gone on at intervals between the years 1807 and 1834, publishing his sets of Irish melodies up to the tenth, and from Bunting since 1810 there had come nothing. The volume, whose advent had been hailed by the Belfast banqueters, was now almost lost in oblivion.

CHAPTER VIII

EDWARD BUNTING—AN INTRODUCTORY MEMOIR (continued)

Bunting, however, was destined to renew his labours and to spend the last years of his life in furthering the great aim which had inspired his youth.

There was now rising in Ireland a new school of antiquarian scholars men who were to achieve great things in the realms of Irish language study, and of historical research. Amongst them the old musician was accorded recognition as historian and scribe of the last harpers, as one who had enquired into the character and antiquity of Irish music, the origin and development of the instruments. We are not told how or when Bunting made the acquaintance of John O'Donovan and George Petrie, but as he was accustomed to pursue investigations in Trinity College and the Royal Irish Academy, we may almost with certainty assume that Whitley Stokes was the connecting link.

This remarkable man lived till the year 1846, and his talents and patriotism were renewed in his descendants, in his son Dr William Stokes, and his grandson and grand-daughter, Margaret and Whitley Stokes.

The old veteran, Dr MacDonnell, was well in touch with the new school. In 1834, when John O'Donovan went to Ulster in connection with the Ordnance Survey at County Down, he called on Dr MacDonnell in Belfast in order to see a manuscript journal of the Irish Confederate War of 1641, by a Friar O'Mellan. He had previously investigated a copy of it made by a Mr McAdam, but as this was somewhat incorrect, Dr MacDonnell gladly showed him the original which was then in his keeping, though the property of Lord O'Neill. O'Donovan writes:

> The Doctor has promised me he will write to Lord O'Neill to whom
> the copy belongs and request of him to send it down to Mr Petrie where
> it will be properly translated and elucidated . . . I am very anxious to

preserve this fragment, as it forms a continuation of the *Annals of the Four Masters.*

We may here digress to state that a translation of this historical document, very fully annotated, is to be found in that admirable miscellany *Old Belfast* by E. M. Young, M.R.I.A. Amongst the events chronicled in it is the death of Bunting's ancestor, Patrick Gruamach O'Quinn. He was killed in an attack of the English forces on Dungannon in July 1641, when the Irish were weakened by the absence of a large part of their army. They had been despatched by the Commander Phelim O'Neill to Doe Castle in Donegal to meet and greet the great Owen Roe O'Neill, who was returning from the Low Counties to take the lead in the Irish War.

Dr MacDonnell in his letters to Bunting makes several references to "Dunnevan," as he spells the name, and once the third volume of the ancient music is embarked on, is constant in his advice that this great scholar and others like him should be referred to.

Writing in October 1836, however, the doctor seems to think that any plan of publication by Bunting is so indefinitely in the future, that he must not hope to see it realised. "I am," he writes, "so old and you so indolent." However, at the date Thursday, 16th August, 1838, we find a letter from Mr J. Sidebotham, a solicitor of 26 Hatton Gardens, London, from which we learn that Bunting was at last prepared to issue his final and monumental work. Sidebotham offers his assistance "in superintending the publication of the proposed works, correcting letter proofs, etc" on Bunting's terms, and in proportion to whatever the financial success of the publication might turn out. He urges haste.

> Let me entreat you to lose no more time. I am really alarmed when you bring to my recollection that it is twenty-eight years since you and I were so agreeably associated together in bringing out the first Volume (*i.e.* that of 1809, really Bunting's second).

He also recalls their visits to Skarrat "the pewter-puncher," as he calls the engraver of the music plates, and the "glorious repasts or breakfasts," which they shared.

Mr Sidebotham subsequently engaged the same engraver, Skarrat, to produce the plates of the new work; and from this point we have a constant correspondence amounting to scores of letters, from which we can only give typical selections. The delays, anxieties, impatience of Bunting are evident from Sidebotham's replies, which, with unfailing good humour and gaiety, still urge him on and keep him informed of all the doings of the pewter-puncher, his excuses on account of other work when payment is delayed, his grand achievements when ready money is forthcoming, rushing in with the plates wet.

Bunting gets an idea that Skarrat may pawn the plates to raise money. Sidebotham relieves this unfounded fear by going and looking at them where they are carefully stored.

We learn that the plates were sent to Ireland in parcels of *The Lancet*, and from a letter of Skarrat (2nd May, 1839) the following:

> When you let me know how much each plate is to contain of the Irish character, I will get the estimate and let you have it without delay . . . I must learn from a writing engraver what his charge will be for the Irish character, for these I cannot accomplish.

This passage is interesting as suggesting the mode by which it was likely intended to publish the Gaelic poetry collected by Lynch in 1802. We find among the MSS. certain of the song words copied in an exquisitely clear Gaelic script, which an engraver could have copied. The prospect of expense, or the success of Moore with his songs in English, or the coldness between Dr MacDonnell, the McCrackens and the unlucky Patrick Lynch, prevented the carrying out of such a design of publication. It would have ante-dated Hardiman's *Minstrelsy* by many years, and giving words and music together would have eclipsed in importance that work or any of that character which has since appeared.

Dr MacDonnell's letters of the same period are extremely interesting, but can scarcely have given poor Bunting as much satisfaction as those of his musical friend. The doctor urged him to extraordinary effort, to leave no stone unturned, no point uninvestigated, particularly as regards "the essential differences between the music of different nations *with the causes of those differences*," and having alluded to investigations, which led to Greece, Rome, Egypt, the Holy Land, he says:

> Sir William Jones has traced something in Persia and the thread of this ends at Benares in the Sanscrit tongue *where it should undoubtedly be followed by you into Thibet*, and if nothing can be made out there or in China we are at the end of our tether.

Thibet, the *terra-incognita*, which is only now being opened up to explorers would seem to have been very much out of the way of the elderly music master in Upper Baggot Street, Dublin, but Dr MacDonnell was advising a library and not a geographical exploration, and knew what he was talking about.

Something would seem to have been made out in China, for a learned reviewer of Bunting's work writing in the *University Magazine*, January 1841, says:

> The few Chinese Melodies which have been communicated to the public have a character so singularly old Scottish that they might well pass as Melodies of the Highlanders of Albin. Is it accidental, or the result of a common Scythian origin of the Scotch and the Chinese or Tartar race?

In such investigations Dr MacDonnell goaded on Bunting. In his letters to his old friend Mary McCracken, he confides all the trouble and weariness that the effort was costing him and his patient wife. The doctor was most triumphantly delighted to find that Mrs Bunting was so competent, and that, with her and Anthony to depend on, the work could still go on even if he was "dished and deserted" by Petrie and Ferguson. Some such catastrophe he seems to have feared might result from Bunting's irritable temper: but these, his collaborateurs, were amongst the most amiable of men, and genuinely enthusiastic about what they had undertaken.

George Petrie, LL.D., is described in Lady Ferguson's life of her husband as:

> Perhaps most generally known by his researches on the Round Towers of Ireland and his essay on Tara Hill. His charming personality, his kindness, his gentleness and refinement endeared him to all who had the privilege of his friendship. It was characteristic of him that among them, he was ever spoken of as "dear Petrie." He was beloved as a father by the younger men, being their senior by many years. He loved Ireland and rendered her native music enchantingly on his violin, but he played only to a sympathetic audience.

Petrie was indeed the disciple and successor of Bunting as a collector of Irish airs, and used his violin to capture the elusive melodies sung in the cottages of Aran Islanders of Irish-speaking natives of other remote parts of Ireland. We are informed on the authority of Dr W. H. Grattan Flood that he was undoubtedly author of the biographical article on Bunting in the *Dublin University Magazine*, which we have quoted from so frequently.

He must have been a delightful companion, charming away with his conversation and his violin strains, the irascible moods of his friend, and giving him his due of praise and veneration as an incentive to this last work.

Samuel Ferguson, who provided the interesting introductory article on "The Harp and Bagpipe" and who edited "The Lives of the Harpers" from O'Neill's diary and other sources, was at the outset of a distinguished career as poet and scholar. He was born in 1810, in the house of his maternal grandfather, High Street, Belfast, and educated at schools in that town. It is pleasing to believe that the atmosphere of historic research and of Irish musical revival, created in the years succeeding the Harpers' Festival, must have helped the growth of his youthful genius. At twenty-two years of age he made his mark with a poem 'The Forging of the Anchor', contributed to *Blackwood's Magazine*, and at twenty-four, in the *Dublin University Magazine*, made certain translations from the Irish, in which he attained his highest mark as a lyrical poet. He had also written his historical tales *Hibernian Nights Entertainment*, had been for some years a member of the Royal Irish Academy, and was called to the Bar in 1838, the very year that Sidebotham was arranging for the engraving of Bunting's plates.

Amongst his Dublin friends was Henry Joy, a lawyer already referred to, who had contributed to the learned 'Essay on the Harp' in Bunting's 1809 volume. With Dr William Stokes, son of Whitley Stokes, he was from an early period of his residence in Dublin on intimate terms.

Like Petrie, he was noted for benign temper, and with such helpers the way was smoothed for Bunting.

Ferguson took in hand the rugged accumulations of Bunting's learned research, the simple and humorous narrative that Blind Harper O'Neill had dictated to Tom Hughes, and put all into concise literary shape. That he was reasonably proud of his work for Bunting is proved by the fact that when in May 1848 he became engaged to Mary, the daughter of Robert Guinness of Stillorgan, his first gift to his betrothed was a volume of the ancient music.

But to return to Bunting's preparations for it. Just when it was the eve of publication there was a visit to Belfast, where his two daughters accompanied him. We learn this from a little note from his wife, scribbled on one of Sidebotham's letters, in which she announces the arrival of proofs, rejoices that the end is now in view, and sends her love to "my dear girls."

They were now growing up, bright attractive girls in their teens, and it was likely on the occasion of this visit that Sarah Bunting won the affection of her future husband, Mr MacRory.

They stayed at the house of Francis M‘Cracken, the bachelor of the family for whom Mary kept house. During the visit Dr MacDonnell wrote frequent little notes which would lead us to believe that he was detained in the house through ill-health or much occupation. He got the loan of *Lynch's Journal*, which he had never read before, and invited

Bunting and the ladies to meet Sam Ferguson. Finally, when Bunting went away he left behind on his dressing-table two little slips of paper (careless man) which contained a Scotch version of the lamentation of 'Dardrae',[Deirdre] and the doctor sent it after him, reminding him of the occasion on which he had taken it down many long years ago. But amidst the papers relating to this period, nothing is more touching than the tone of the letters in which he unburdens his heart to his old friend, Mary McCracken, and confides the foreboding that he may never live to see the work finished, and his doubts (only too truly realised) that his family would not gain financially by all the labour. Death was indeed approaching, and doubtless he had felt some warnings of the fact, but a few short years remained which were to see his last work launched amid a chorus of approbation from all discerning critics.

CHAPTER IX

EDWARD BUNTING—AN INTRODUCTORY MEMOIR (concluded)

THE 1840 VOLUME OF *THE ANCIENT MUSIC of IRELAND* WAS, AS WE HAVE SEEN, briefly described by Thomas Moore as "a mess of trash." This rash judgment has most unfortunately found acceptance in some quarters, and is quoted, for example, in the account of Edward Bunting given in the admirable *Compendium of Irish Biography*, by the late Alfred Webb.

It is most regrettable and amazing that the poet, whose name and fame is associated so intimately with Irish music, should have shown so little appreciation of this monumental work, in which the result of the life-long labours of Bunting are chronicled and illumined by the discerning gracefully written essays of George Petrie and Samuel Ferguson.

At a meeting of the Irish Folk-Song Society, held in Dublin in the autumn of 1908, and presided over by its president, Lord Shaftesbury, the relatives and descendants of Edward Bunting were present, and had the pleasure of listening to a learned discussion on the characteristics of Irish music between Rev. Professor Bewerunge of Maynooth and Mr Brendan Rogers, the latter in referring to the methods and style of the Irish harpers, paid tribute to the absolutely faithful record preserved by Edward Bunting. His object was not to attain instant popularity by a display of his own talents, but, to quote the words of Mr Henry Joy, one of his earlier collaborators "to restore a page of the history of mankind."

The contents of the volume may be briefly summarised. There is first a preface dealing with the sources from which he gleaned the music, the Harpers' Festival, his visits to old Hempson of Magilligan, his journeys through the country.

While forming these collections, [he writes,] the Editor had an opportunity of rendering himself thoroughly acquainted with the genius and habits of the old people of the country. His plan would have been imperfect had he not resorted to the artless modulations of the aged heads of families, and of females taught by their parents to sing to children on the breast, or at the milking of the cow. In these excursions, especially in the remote parts of Tyrone and Derry in Ulster, and of Sligo and Mayo in Connaught, he has had the satisfaction of procuring old music and experiencing ancient hospitality, at the same time, among people of manners so primitive and sincere as could leave no doubt on any mind of the perfect genuineness of everything about them. Had he gained nothing else on these occasions but a knowledge of the worth and warm heartedness of his poor countrymen, a knowledge so little sought after by those who might turn it to the best account, he would have been well repaid for all his toil. But his acquaintance with the humours and dispositions of the people, has, he conceives, enabled him to preserve with a fidelity unattainable to any stranger, however sincere and honest in his notation, the pure, racy, old style and sentiment of every bar and note in his collection.

There follows a learned disquisition on the characteristics of Irish melody, and the second chapter deals with the method of playing and musical vocabulary of the old Irish harpers. This includes, what should be of extraordinary interest to Gaelic students—a complete vocabulary in the Irish language with translation, of everything connected with the instrument. The vocabulary is an exhaustive one of several hundred words.

The third chapter by Samuel Ferguson, M.R.I. A., 'On the Antiquity of the Harp and Bagpipe' is prefaced by a superb plate of the old harp in Trinity College, Dublin, usually spoken of as Brian Borou's. A learned enquiry into the origin of this harp by George Petrie, follows with further full page illustrations. There is then given a history of the various efforts to revive the Irish harp, and extracts from the lives of the harpers, largely drawn from the O'Neill *Autobiography*, and introducing incidentally Samuel Ferguson's translations from the Gaelic 'Farewell to Alba', and the 'Lament for the Sons of Usneach'.

A classification and history of the airs included in the volume follows, which goes far to prove the great antiquity of some of them, distinguishing these whose origin is obscured in the mist of ages from others attributed to bards whose names live in history, which again are separated from the modern compositions of Carolan.

The Irish names of the hundred and fifty melodies are next given, in Irish character, parallel with an equivalent in Roman type, and in English translation.

An index giving the English title and source of every air published, whether recorded from the harpers or taken down from a rural singer, with the date of the year in which it was recorded.

The Irish cry or caoine, for example, was taken from three separate sources, from "O'Neill, the Harper," from "Hired Keeners at Armagh," and from a "Manuscript over a Hundred Years Old."

A solid foundation of scientific research was therefore laid for all who came after.

It is satisfactory to know that the importance of the work was recognised in certain quarters, *The Athenæum, Literary Gazette,* and *Tait's Magazine* published highly appreciative notices, and in September 1840 Bunting wrote to his daughter Sarah (afterwards Mrs MacRory) when on a visit to Belfast, to go to Dr MacDonnell and borrow *Chamber's Edinburgh Journal,* with a long paper in it about a young man who wrote down Irish tunes in 1792. This was written by Robert Chambers,[1] himself a collector of old Scottish folk-songs, so the appreciation all the more welcome.

We close with regret Mr Bunting's volume because we believe that with it we take leave of the genuine Music of Ireland. It must not be regarded as a Musical publication alone, but as a National Work of

---

[1] Mrs Alice C. Bunten, daughter of Robert Chambers, writes: "My father was an enthusiastic lover of music, and my earliest recollections are dancing with my sisters round the room, while my father played the flute accompanied on the piano by my mother, who was also celebrated for her taste in music. We were brought up on the old Scottish songs, and nursery jingles, and my father made a collection of them, which he published for private circulation, called *Scottish Songs prior to Burns.*"

the deepest antiquarian and historical interest. Were we to institute a literary comparison, we could say that Moore's *Irish Melodies* had about them all the fascination of poetry and romance, Bunting's collections all the sterner charms of truth and history. When we hear Sir John Stevenson's *Irish Melodies* played by a young lady on the pianoforte, or even on the pedal harp, we do not hear the same music, which O'Cahan, Carolan and Hempson played. It is as much altered as Homer in the translation of Pope. For the true presentment of this music to modern ears we require the old sets as preserved in the volumes of Bunting and "The Irish Harp" played by an Irish harper.

The anonymous author (whom we have seen to be George Petrie) wrote in his biographical article in Bunting 1847:

> Of the success of this work as a pecuniary speculation we are not in a position to speak. We believe, however, that its sale, though not equal to its deserts has not been inconsiderable . . . but it was not for such reward that Bunting toiled, and its publication was, for the very few years which he survived it, not only a matter of the greatest happiness and consolation to him, but it excited him to devote the leisure of those years to the re-arrangement of the old airs and to terminate his labours by leaving behind him a complete uniform and he trusts very nearly perfect collection of Irish music. And thus with the ruling passion strong in death, he departed this life, as we trust for a better on the 21st December, 1843, aged 70 and was interred in the Cemetery of Mount Jerome.

It may be added that Bunting's death occurred very suddenly, the weariness of which he complained in his letters to his life-long friend, Mary McCracken, was a fore-warning of heart failure, which overtook him on that December night, when, taking his bedroom candle in hand, he was about to go upstairs and retire to rest. Overcome with faintness, he was obliged to seat himself on the stairs, and there suddenly expired.

Petrie concludes with a description of his appearance and an appreciation of his character, valuable as coming from such a source:

Edward Bunting was in size above the middle stature and he was strongly made and well-proportioned. His somewhat English face was also symmetrical and its expression manly and independent, full of intelligence and character, and must in youth have been eminently handsome. And though his manners might be found fault with as occasionally rough and unpolished, in appearance at least he was always the gentleman. [Note Petrie's impression of the characteristic Northern bluffness, acquired by Bunting in Belfast.] His mental qualities were naturally of a higher order and remarkably extensive, for though they had never received culture, or been applied in a systematic way to any study but that of his art, there were few departments of knowledge, in which he did not take an interest and learn something. He had a fine perception of, and an enthusiastic love for, the beauties of Nature, and a high appreciation of the charms of Poetry and of all the fine Arts, though in most of them his subject was circumscribed. In short, he was in everything a lover of beauty, and it was this sentiment that enabled him to appreciate so truly, and free from professional prejudice, the excellence of our Native music, and that marked his own musical performance with a charm which the more powerful and brilliant execution of great instrumentalists could hardly equal.

Strong in his attachments, he was an affectionate husband, father, brother, and friend; but as his temper had been spoiled by indulgence, and want of control in early life, it was sometimes necessary for his friends to bear a little with this infirmity, which, however, to those he loved, was never more than a passing cloud upon the sunshine of his genial nature, and hence his friends were not numerous. But that he was susceptible of the warmest and most lasting attachments is abundantly proved by the fact of his residence in friendship with the McCracken family for a period of forty years, and that that friendship was never broken or interrupted till his death, twenty years after. Let us also add his attachment to ourselves, which, though lot of so very long a standing, could hardly have been of a kindlier nature.

Thus writes Petrie, a man who had done much to brighten Bunting's last years, and who followed in his footsteps as a collector of Irish traditional music.

Bunting's elder brother, Anthony, survived him for some years, and, having been left childless by the death of his only daughter Susan, was of great assistance to the widow and orphan family.

Edward's only son, called after this kind uncle, Anthony, was a young man of brilliant promise, articled to a great engineer MacNeill, who built the Drogheda Viaduct.

From a letter of Sidebotham's, written in 1840, we learn that even then young Anthony had embarked in his career. The London lawyer had been asked to send him certain scientific instruments addressed to Anthony Bunting, Lough Swilly (Donegal), which is "a queer address," writes Sidebotham, "except there be a town of that name as well as an arm of the sea."

This young man was in a position to support his mother and sisters, but was unfortunately cut off by death in the prime of youth and promise.

An effort to have the name of Mrs Bunting placed upon the civil pension list, in recognition of her husband's research work, was of no avail, though a great rally of admirers of his genius forwarded the application; but a happy and comfortable home was provided before long for the wife who had sustained the last labours of Bunting, and who had taken a heavy share in them.

Her daughters are described in a letter of Mr Orr's, a Belfast man resident in Dublin, as having been very good-looking and charming.

The elder, Sarah, married Mr MacRory, a member of a well-to-do Belfast family. He resided in Rutland Square, Dublin, and there Mrs Bunting lived till her death some years later. Before she passed away she had the happiness to see her other daughter, Mary, married to Mr Wright. The descendants of these families it is who, inheriting the papers of Edward Bunting, placed them in the hands of the present writer. It may be said in conclusion, that his love of Irish music has also come down as a heritage to the fourth generation.

CHAPTER X

THE HARP IN ANCIENT IRELAND

To appreciate the character and importance of the music of the harpers, prefaced and published by Bunting, it is necessary to understand the place which the harp took in the social life of Ireland for a very lengthened period.

In his 1809 and 1840 volumes, Bunting gave a great deal of space to learned articles dealing with the history of the instrument as known to other races and nations. The opinions of scholars, historians, poets, and travellers in different ages are quoted to show that Irish musicians were at all times acknowledged to be supreme as harpers. The most convincing quotation is from Giraldus Cambrensis, who accompanied the early Norman invaders to Ireland and wrote an account of the country, with the express object of proving its barbarity and need of a civilising and Christianising influence.

But even this hostile critic could not find language too complimentary to express his opinion of the Irish harpers, and in Bunting's 1809 volume he is quoted in translation as follows:

> The attention of this people to musical instruments I find worthy of commendation. Their skill is beyond comparison superior to that of any nation I have seen. For in these the modulation is not slow and solemn, as in the instruments of Britain to which we are accustomed, but the sounds are rapid and precipitate, yet at the same time sweet and pleasing. It is wonderful how in such precipitate rapidity of the fingers, the musical proportions are preserved, and, by their art, faultless throughout. In the midst of their complicated modulations and most intricate arrangement of notes, by a rapidity so sweet, a regularity so irregular, a concord so discordant, the Melody is rendered harmonious and perfect whether the chords of the *diatessaron* (the fourth) or *diapente* (the fifth) are struck together; yet they always begin in a soft mood and end in the same, that all may be perfected in the sweetness of delicious sounds. They enter on, and again leave their

modulations with so much subtlety; and the twinklings of the small strings sport with so much freedom under the deep notes of the bass, delight with so much delicacy and soothe so softly that the excellency of their art seems to lie in concealing it.

To this is added in Bunting's preface:

This description so perfectly answers to the airs now published, that it strengthens the conclusion that they have not suffered in the descent, but have come down to us in the very forms in which we wish now to transmit them to those who shall succeed us.

An Italian historian of music, Vincentio Galilei, in a work printed at Florence in 1581, is also quoted as saying:

This most ancient instrument was brought to us from Ireland [as Dante says], "where they are excellently made and in great numbers, the inhabitants of that island having practised on it for many many ages . . . . The Harps which this people use are considerably larger than ours and have generally the strings of brass, and a few of steel for the highest notes, as in the Clavichord. The musicians who perform on it keep the nails of their fingers long, forming them with care in the shape of the quills which strike the strings of the spinnet.

More enthusiastic even than these opinions of foreigners are the allusions of ancient Irish poets, chroniclers and tale-writers, to the beauty of music, and its effect upon its hearers.

The subject is very fully dealt with in Eugene O'Curry's work on the *Manners and Customs of the Ancient Irish*. Dr W. H. Grattan Flood's *History of Irish Music* abounds in quotations and testimonies.

The musical skill of the Irish, as exhibited on the harp in particular, is, moreover, acknowledged in the fact that the harp has come to be the heraldic emblem of Ireland, and that its outline was stamped on our coinage by the English sovereigns from the time of Henry VIII. till the union; some say that in a rude form it appeared from the time of King John.

Urchins playing pitch-and-toss in our streets, still demand before spinning the coin, " Head or harp." Britannia with her trident now appears on the reverse, but all the same, the memory of the harp that was in use so long still lingers.

Before coming to the memoirs of the last harpers, and the record of their gathering at Belfast, let us restore clearly in our minds the historical figures of the ancient harpers of Ireland. Eugene O'Curry in his lectures on the *Manners and Customs of the Ancient Irish*, relates this anecdote, which is embodied in a tale and poem attributed to MacLiag, a famous poet of the tenth century, who was attached to the Court of the great King Brian Borou. It illustrates the fact that the harper was distinct from the poet, and frequently in attendance on the latter.

On one occasion MacLiag was travelling from Lough Riach, in County Galway, to visit King Brian at his palace of Kincora on the Shannon. He was attended by his usual retinue of learned men and pupils and by Ilbrechtach, a harper, who had previously been harper to Flann MacLonan, predecessor of MacLiag, as poet to King Brian's tribe of the Dal-Cais. The path of this procession lay over the high and dreary range of mountains called Sliabh Echtge, separating the counties of Galway and Clare. As they sat to rest on the side of Ceann Crochan, one of the hills of the range, MacLiag looked out over the prospect and said:

> "Many a hill and lake and fastness is in this district, and it would take great learning to know them all."

To this Ilbrechtach, the harper, said:

> "If it were Flann MacLonan that were here, he could name them all and give the origin of their names besides."

> "Let this fellow be taken and hanged," said MacLiag.

The harper begged a respite till next morning, and he was granted it. When morning came they saw the form of his dead master, MacLonan, approaching, who pleaded with MacLiag, saying that he would relate the names and origin of every notable place in the mountain range, if the life of the condemned harper was spared.

His request was granted, whereupon he recited a poem of one hundred and thirty-two lines, commencing:

Delightful, delightful lofty Echtge.

and followed by the history of the mountains, the warriors and tribes, who had made it their hunting ground including the famous Finn MacCumhaill and his band. Giving the names of peaks, lakes, rivers, fords, woods, he concluded with a eulogy of the Dalcassians of Clare. The poem goes on as if composed by the ghost of MacLonain, describing how he had been killed by a party of robbers.

O'Curry cannot decide whether MacLiag thus recited and introduced a poem by MacLonan, or whether the the whole composition was his own. I cannot help thinking that we have here an example of a primitive drama, which was recited in the palace of Kincora. The story of the quarrel with the harper, through jealousy of his former master, his condemnation to death, his deliverance by the appearance of the dead poet's ghost, and the recital of the poem which ingeniously led up to praise of King Brian's royal clan, all give scope for a dramatic recital in which different parts could be taken by the members of the bardic suite. If the poetical part was the work of MacLonan, MacLiag all the same would have won applause for his artistic skill in introducing the descriptive poem by the dead bard, who had been high in favour with King Brian's father, and who would be lovingly remembered by the old men present.

Such dramatic dialogues in verse frequently break the course of the old historical narratives. *The History of the Wars of the Gael and Gall* describing the course of events that led up to the battle of Clontarf, contains several, notably a disputation between Brian and his elder brother, Mahon, who was King before him. Mahon had made peace with the Danish invaders, but Brian, with a band of followers, waged unceasing war against them. At last he arrived in the presence of his royal brother, and their conversation is related in verse, Mahon beginning:

> *Alone art thou, Brian at Banba*
> > *Thy warfare was not without valour*
> *Not numerous hast thou come to our house*
> > *Where has thou left thy followers?*

And Brian answers:

> *I have left them with the foreigners,*
> > *After having been cut down, Mathgamhain,*
> *In hardship they followed me over every plain,*
> > *Not the same as thy people.*

And so he continues describing his warfare against the Danes and reproaching Mahon for his complacence.

Such dialogue passages were without doubt recited in dramatic style, possibly chanted, to the accompaniment of the harp, in the manner of the Welsh Penhyllion chanting. Otherwise for what purpose was the harper associated with the bardic suite? Not merely, I would conclude, as instrumentalist, though he would be frequently called on to render strains of music, whilst even the bards of the company sat silent and entranced. And now comes my point of argument, for I have not been digressing far in thought from the Harpers' Festival, where Bunting gathered his great store of ancient melody.

Many of the bardic lays have come down to us, of indisputable authority in regard to their authors and period of composition. O'Curry mentions and quotes from over a dozen poems of MacLiag, this bard of King Brian Borou who died in 1015, and several by his predecessor MacLonan. Half a dozen other bards of the ninth and tenth century could be mentioned, whose personality is as well authenticated as that of the Elizabethan dramatists, and whose works have come down to us.

If the store of lyrical poetry has been preserved for over a thousand years, what of the harp airs, which accompanied them, and which won for Ireland the fame of supremacy in music? If the words of MacLonan and MacLiag survived, is it too daring to suggest that the strains played by Ilbrechtach, the harper, still vibrate upon the winds of the world? Of the composers of the music played at Belfast, the names have only in a few instances been rescued. "Very ancient, composer unknown." "Remarkable, old." Such are the notes affixed to a large majority. Reference to the *Autobiography* of Arthur O'Neill, now first published will show how far tradition and hearsay went.

Carolan, the modernist, poet, composer, and harper, was universally admired and fresh in the memory of all.

The name of Thomas Connellan, born about 1640, was still associated with his compositions 'The Dawning of the Day', 'Golden Star', 'The Breach of Aughrim', 'Molly St George', 'Bonny Jean', and his younger brother William Connellan got credit for 'Lady Iveagh', 'Saebh Kelly', 'Molly McAlpine'. Cornelius Lyons, a contemporary of Carolan, was known as arranger of variations in modern style of such ancient airs as 'Eileen Aroon' and 'The Coolin'. Tradition was hazy as to which of two harpers Murphy had composed the fine song 'Lord Mayo', and the figure of Rory Dall O'Cahan, harper to Hugh O'Neill, was gathering about it a fog of uncertainty.

Whatever was to be gleaned from tradition through the oldest harpers living Bunting set down for futurity.

Eugene O'Curry's investigations are worthy of extended repetition. He quotes an eight-line poem by Cormac MacCuilennain, King and Bishop of Cashel, who died in the year 903, which is sung to an old air, now popularly known by the title 'For Ireland I would not tell who she is', and adds:

I cannot say that these particular verses were written to that particular air. I adduce it only as an interesting fact, that a fragment of a lyric poem ascribed to a writer of the ninth century and actually preserved in an MS. book, so old as the year 1150, presents a peculiar structure of rhythm exactly corresponding with that of certain ancient Irish musical compositions, still popular and well known, though traditionally as of the highest antiquity, one of which is the air I have named . . . . Many such instances could be adduced of ancient lyric music still in existence in minutely exact agreement with forms of lyric poetry peculiar to the most ancient periods of our native literature.

He then goes on to refer to the four-lined Ossianic lays, of which a great number have been preserved and published. He had frequently heard his father sing these, and before the time of his birth there had lived in his native place—in County Clare—a school-master, Anthony O'Brien, who was famous for his knowledge of the Ossianic chants. It was this man's custom to row out into the bosom of the Shannon in a boat with some companions, whilst the labourers from the fields on either shore flocked down to listen. O'Curry assumes that the air to which the lays were sung, had been associated with the poetry since the time of its composition.

He then refers to the *Book of Ballymote*, compiled from older books in the year 1391, and containing a tract on versification giving specimens of all the poetic measures, known to, or practised by the ancient Irish. From these he selects three of the largest and most complicated kind of verse. The first with a stanza of sixteen lines of an intricate character fits admirably to an air known as 'Buachaill Cael dubh', or 'Black Slender Boy'. A second of eight lines goes to the air 'Sean O'Dwyer an Gleanna', and to this same air can be chanted the dialogue between Queen Meave and the Champion Ferdia, in the old Red Branch epic tale of the *Tain bo Cuailgne*. The same subject is touched on and illustrated in a form more readily appreciated by the general reader, in Dr Sigerson's splendid volume, *Bards of the Gael and Gall*. This book consists of specimen translations from Irish poetry, from the most ancient times till the end of the eighteenth century, in which the metre of the originals is marvellously preserved and the peculiarities of Gaelic verse construction are illustrated. In his introduction he writes of the poets of Ireland:

Their artistic skill which enabled them to produce such admirable effects, in gold, silver and bronze work, and later in illuminations, was most fully displayed in the art of versification.

They made it the most refined and delicate instrument of artistic structure, which the ingenuity of human intelligence could invent to charm without fatiguing the ear, by the modulation of sound. They avoided in Gaelic the tinkle of repeated words regularly recurring at the ends of lines. They had echoes and half echoes of broad and slight vowels, and of consonants, differentiated into classes so that it was not necessary even to repeat the same letter, and these echoing sounds, now full, now slender, rising, falling, replying, swelling, dying, like the echoes at Killarney came at varied intervals, not merely at the close, but within and between the lines. They constitute Word Music.

And to this "Word Music" of the bards surely the string music of the harp kept rhyme and time, echoing, rising, falling with the intricate metre. And the race which treasured the poet's words for a thousand years, would as fondly preserve the marvellous melodies.

When the Belfast harpers faltered in their answers regarding the airs they played, and could not attribute them to the Connellans or Rory Dall himself, we may be sure they had come down from "beyond the mist of years."

Dr Grattan Flood in writing his *History of Irish Music*, explored the old annals to some purpose and found notes in every century of famous harpers and makers of melody.

Thus in 1357 the death is recorded of "Donlevy O'Carroll, an excellent musician and a noble master of melody, the person that was best in his own art in Ireland," and in 1361 died " Magrath O'Finn, Chief Professor of Siol Murray in music and minstrelsy."

The fame of Carrol O'Daly, composer of 'Eileen Aroon', is rescued from oblivion by the romance of his courtship by song of the lady of his heart. He died in 1405. 'The Song of Blooming Deirdre' was composed in 1409 for the marriage of the sixth Earl of Desmond.

The air which Moore has made known in his 'Rich and Rare Were the Gems She wore', is an old Irish one, to a song about 'The Coming of Summer'. It was copied and preserved by a Benedictine Monk of Reading about 1230.

Bunting recovered it from the singing of a Father O'Donnell, a priest in Belfast, and it was played for him by Hempson on the harp.

The investigation of the age of the music, is a subject that opens up wonderful possibilities. O'Curry's and Dr Sigerson's method of matching ancient metres with ancient melodies is one that might profitably be pursued by the Gaelic revivalists in Ireland; for as you shall see when we come to consider the Gaelic folk-songs collected by Bunting, many of the noblest, most heart moving of these melodies, have been degraded by association with unworthy lyrics.

This will be a proper place to introduce Bunting's conclusions with regard to the peculiar characteristics of Irish music, as he held that its peculiar excellence arose from the fact that the harp was the instrument most practised and honoured, from a very early date.

The 1840 volume published as *The Ancient Music of Ireland* has in the first chapter an account of the characteristics of Irish melody which we quote in full as follows:

Irish Melodies may be distinguished as to their minor characteristics, into two classes, those namely which are marked by the omission of the fourth and seventh tones of the diatonic scale or one of them, such as the air of 'An Chuaichin Mhaiseach' ('Bonny Cuckoo'), and those which, although also quite Irish in their structure, are not so characteristic, such as the air of 'Ciste no Stor' ('Coffers nor stores').

These subordinate distinctions have been often observed, and arguments derogatory to the antiquity of our best music have been very confidently advanced on their authority, for it has been urged the only assignable characteristics of genuine Irish melody being those of omission, we must refer the more elaborate class of airs, in which such omissions do not occur, to a less National and more modernised school.

Having thus assumed that the airs of the first class are the more ancient, and seeing that such performances are more likely to have drawn their origin from a defective instrument, such as the ancient bagpipe which was incapable of properly producing either of the omitted tones, these reasoners go on to argue in like manner against the antiquity of the Irish harp; for, say they, if the tunes proper to the pipes or to the six-stringed Cruit, be older than those which can only be performed on the harp, we must of necessity conclude that the latter instrument is of proportionately more recent introduction here than the former; and thus both the antiquity of our national instrument and the genuineness of those airs of which it is so peculiarly worthy are impugned on common grounds.

These conclusions, gratifying as they may be to nations which have no genuine music of their own to boast of, spring from the fundamental error of considering the omission of the tones of the fourth and seventh to be the grand characteristic which really makes all Irish melody, and which truly distinguishes it from that of other countries. Now the fact is that these omissions *are not* the true tokens of our ancient and National Music. They occur in some airs, not in all; and yet all are equally characteristic, all equally Irish, and some marked by the uniform presence of both these tones are the most Irish and the most ancient of all. The feature which in truth distinguishes all Irish melody, whether proper to the defective bagpipe or suited to the perfect harp, is not the negative *omission*, but the positive and emphatic *presence* of a particular tone; and this tone is that of the sub-mediant, or major sixth; in other words the tone of E in the scale of G. This it is that stamps the true Scotic character (for we Irish are the original Scoti) on every bar of the air in which it occurs so that the moment this tone is heard we exclaim "That is an Irish melody."

If ever the symmetrical relation of musical vibrations should be determined, and a great step has already been taken in that direction by the inventor of the Kaleidophone (*an instrument designed to make sound vibrations produce visible forms*), we may expect to find some exact mode of accounting physically for this phenomenon; but in the present state of musical science, we are unable to do more than assert the fact, that peculiar and deeply delightful sensations attend the intonation of this chord when struck in a sequence of musical sounds, sensations which thrill every ear, and may truly be said to touch the "leading sinews" of the Irish heart.

There are many hundred genuine Irish airs, some of them defective in the fourth and seventh, some supplying the place of the latter by a flat seventh, and others, again, perfect in all their diatonic intervals; yet let even an indifferent ear catch the strain of any one of them, whether performed by the best orchestra or by the meanest street musician, and it will at once feel thrilled by this searching tone of the emphatic major sixth, and in that touching and tingling sensation will recognise the proper voice of the Land of Song.

The Irish school of Music is, therefore, not a school of omissions and affected deficiencies drawing its examples from the tone of a barbarian bagpipe, but a school of sweet and perfect harmony, proper to a harp of many strings and suited to its intricate and florid character to cultivated ears and civilized assemblies.

Having illustrated this theory by two selected airs, 'What is That to Him?' and 'Kitty Tyrrel', he proceeds:

Such, in the Editor's opinion, is the grand characteristic of Irish melody, a characteristic which pervades alike the defective class of song and pipe tunes, such as the first in the above examples and the perfect harp lessons represented by the latter.

Independently of these particular features, Irish Melody has also its own peculiarity of structure and arrangement, but this is more observable in the very old class of airs. These airs are for the most part in a major key and in triple time: the modulation of the first part of the melody may be said to consist of the common cadence; the second part is generally an octave higher than the first; it begins with the chord of the tonic and proceeds to the dominant, with its major concord; it then returns to the tonic from which it progresses to the tone of the sub-mediant with the major harmony of the sub-dominant, or to the sub-mediant with its minor concord; but the harmony of this peculiar note is most frequently accompanied by the major concord of the sub-dominant; the conclusion of the air is generally a repetition of the first part of the tune, with a little variation. This constitutes the structure and modulation of three-fourths of our song and harp airs, and the main features of such an arrangement—namely, their being principally in a major key and triple time, the rise of an octave in the second part and the repetition of the first part at the conclusion with the modulation as above, are markedly observable in the composition of our most ancient melodies. Various harmonies dependent on the taste or science of the musician might be adapted to these old airs, but it is presumed the above will be found the most correct and suitable. The most ancient, it may be observed, will be found more easily harmonised than those of a more modern date, a certain indication of the purity of their structure.

It will be observed that the tones of the dominant and sub-dominant, with their corresponding concords and modulations above described, agree in a remarkable manner with the *diapente* and *diatesseron* of Cambrensis. Would it then be too much to surmise that that writer was himself acquainted with these peculiarities in the structure of Irish melody which have so long eluded the search of modern musicians, and that the famous account of Irish music in the twelfth century, which he has given us, is actually a scientific description of the modulation of a genuine Irish tune as preserved to the present day?

Irish song music being thus carefully adjusted to one standard of arrangement, a conjecture may be hazarded as to the character of the original melody on which the whole school has been founded.

'The Young Man's Dream' and the air of 'The Green Woods of Truagha' might be suggested as answering more nearly to the Editor's conception of such a standard than any others with which he is acquainted. The latter melody is of great antiquity, as is proved both by its structure, and by the fact of its being known by so many different names in different parts of the country. Thus it is known in Ulster as

'The Green Woods of Truagha', in Leinster as 'Edmund of the Hill', in Connaught as 'Colonel O'Gara', and in Munster as 'More no Beg', with a variety of other aliases.

Examples of songs then follow and he concludes:

These specimens may be considered as the skeletons of most of our song airs. But it would be impossible to assign any similar model for harp tunes which are strongly resembling the vigorous productions of the modern German school, but which from the predominance of the major sixth or sub-mediant with its suitable harmony still sound equally Irish with the most characteristic of the defective class.

From these considerations, grounded on the structure of the airs themselves, we may conclude that the comparative antiquity of the two classes of airs (both being now proved equally genuine) may be determined by the comparative antiquity of the instruments to which they are adapted, and if, as shall presently appear, the harp and the bagpipe be both found to be of immemorial use in Ireland, we shall be entitled to claim for the ancient Irish school of Music the credit of a very elaborate, artful and refined style of composition.

CHAPTER XI

THE HARP FESTIVAL OF 1792
CONTEMPORARY DOCUMENTS AND DESCRIPTIONS

H AVING GIVEN A GENERAL SURVEY OF THE LIFE OF EDWARD BUNTING, IT remains for us to enter into a detailed account with regard to his work and achievement, in preserving a faithful record of the *Ancient Music of Ireland*. It will be seen, that he worked on lines of strict archaeological research, sought as far as possible to ascertain the antiquity of the musical forms and instruments, and that, beyond any worker in the same sphere, before or since, he has maintained the links uniting our national music with the native language.

The circular issued a few months previous to the Harp Festival, namely, at the end of the year 1791, for the purpose of soliciting funds, gives us in brief an insight into the minds of the organisers of that historic gathering.

It has been reprinted in Bunting's 1840 volume, but one of the original circulars, yellowed with age, lies before us as we write, and seems to bring us into intimate touch with the enthusiasts who drafted, issued and dispersed them amongst the well-to-do and enlightened men of town and country, from whom financial support was expected.

BELFAST, *December* 1791.

Some inhabitants of Belfast, feeling themselves interested in everything which relates to the honour, as well as the prosperity of their country, propose to open a subscription, which they intend to apply in attempting to revive and perpetuate the ancient Music and Poetry of Ireland. They are solicitous to preserve from oblivion the few fragments which have been permitted to remain, as monuments of the refined taste and genius of their ancestors.

In order to carry this project into execution, it must appear obvious to those acquainted with the situation of this country that it will be necessary to assemble the Harpers, those descendants of our Ancient Bards, who are at present almost exclusively possessed of all that remains of the Music Poetry and oral traditions of Ireland.

It is proposed that the Harpers should be induced to assemble at Belfast (suppose on the 1st July next) by the distribution of such prizes as may seem adequate to the subscribers; and that a person well versed in the language and antiquities of this nation should attend, with a skilful musician to transcribe and arrange the most beautiful and interesting parts of their knowledge.

An undertaking of this kind will undoubtedly meet the approbation of men of refinement and erudition in every country. And when it is considered how intimately the spirit and character of a people are connected with their national Poetry and Music, it is presumed that the Irish patriot and politician will not deem it an object unworthy his patronage and protection.

By the spring of the following year the project had received substantial support, as we may see from the following report in the *Belfast Newsletter*.

At a meeting of several subscribers to the scheme for assembling the Harpers by public advertisement in Belfast, the 23rd April, 1792, it was agreed; 'That a Committee of five subscribers be appointed to forward and receive subscriptions to circulate by advertisement in different newspapers and other ways the period and objects of the meeting, and to regulate and conduct the subordinate parts of the scheme; that Mr H. Joy, Mr Robt. Bradshaw, Mr Robert Simms, Doctor Jas. Macdonnell, be that Committee. That a Committee be now appointed as judges for appreciating the merits of the different performers on the Irish Harps, who may appear at Belfast on Tuesday the 10th day of July next. That the following ladies and gentlemen be appointed to that Committee: Rev. Mr Meade, Rev. Mr Vance, Mr Rainey Maxwell, Mr Robert Bradshaw, Mr Henry Joy, Doctor Jas. MacDonnell, Mr Thos. Morris Jones.

Honble. Mrs Meade, Honble. Miss de Courcy, Mrs M⁣ᶜKenzie, Miss Catherine Clarke, Miss Grant, Miss Bristow, Mrs John Clarke, Mrs Kennedy.

That the premiums be adjudged in proportion to the fund raised, in the following proportions: 1st premium £——— [1] 2ⁿᵈ, ditto ; 3ʳᵈ, ditto; 4ᵗʰ, ditto; 5ᵗʰ, ditto; with smaller gratuities to others in aid of their expenses. That the airs to be performed previous to the adjudication of the premiums be confined to the native music of the country the music of Ireland. In order to revive obsolete airs, it is an instruction to the judges on this occasion, not to be solely governed in their decisions by the degree of execution or taste of the several performers, but independent of these circumstances, to consider the person entitled to additional claim, who shall produce airs not to be found in any public collection, and at the same time deserving of preference, by their intrinsic excellence. It is recommended to any harper who is in possession of scarce compositions to have them reduced to notes: that the Rev. Mr Andrew Bryson[2] of Dundalk be requested to assist, as a person versed in the language and antiquities of the nation, and that Mr William Weare, Mr Edward Bunting and Mr John Sharpe be requested to attend as practical musicians. That notification of the meeting on 10ᵗʰ July, and an invitation to the harpers be published in the two Belfast papers and in the National Journal and in one of the Cork, Limerick, Waterford, Kilkenny, Galway, Sligo and Derry Papers.

The first circular would lead us to believe that those inspiring the enterprise were as much concerned about the preservation of ancient

---

[1.] No sum is mentioned.

[2.] Rev. Andrew Bryson was minister at the Presbyterian Church of Fourtowns, between Dundalk and Newry. He was succeeded in the care of the same church by his son and grandson. The Presbyterian community being sparse in this district, the Brysons had leisure for study and literary work. It was to the minister Bryson of the day that Charlotte Bronte's Irish uncle brought a copy of *Jane Eyre* for inspection, tied up in a red cotton handkerchief.

Gaelic poetry and tradition as about music, and that they expected to find in the harpers, custodians of the relics of ancient traditional literature.

They were assuming that the harpers were the successors of the Irish professional bards, and in this respect were destined to be disappointed.

O'Curry and other writers, who have since thrown light on the customs and educational systems of ancient Ireland, make it plain, that the bard was distinct from the harper. Just as in the present day, a lyrical poet is rarely found to be a singer of his own compositions, the professional poets of the bardic schools were concerned with the making of poetry, and with the recital of famous poems and tales, handed down from previous generations.

To perfect the Belfast Festival, the country Shanachies should also have been summoned to recount Ossianic lays and hero tales.

On page 184 you will read in Arthur O'Neill's *Autobiography* how the advertisement took effect. He happened to be laid up with rheumatism, after a bad wetting, at the house of a friend and patron, Captain Westenrae, of Lough Sheelin. His fingers being stiff he was unable to play, and to pass the time, desired to be read to. The newspaper was brought, and it happened to be the *Belfast Newsletter*, and in its columns stood the following advertisement:

National Music of Ireland.

A respectable body of the inhabitants of Belfast having published a plan for reviving the ancient music of this country, and the project having met with such support and approbation as must insure success to the undertaking; *performers on the Irish Harp* are requested to assemble in this town on the 10th day of July next, when a considerable sum will be distributed in premiums in proportion to their merits.

It being the intention of the Committee that every performer shall receive some premium, it is hoped that no harper will decline attending on account of his having been unsuccessful on any former occasion.

Robert Bradshaw,

Secretary and Treasurer.

Belfast, 26th *April* 1792.

A letter from Dr MacDonnell followed, urging O'Neill to be present in Belfast without fail. The doctor had a special interest in this harper, who had spent some time in his father's house in Glenarrif, giving lessons on his instrument to the boys of the family. We may be sure, however, that he sent out many letters of invitation and enquiry to different districts, and through the medium of the advertisements in the other papers mentioned got into communication with harpers and their patrons. We read, for example, in Bunting's anecdotes of one O'Shea, a County Kerry harper almost eighty years of age, "an enthusiast in everything connected with Irish feeling; extreme debility alone prevented him attending the Belfast meeting."

Even in our own day of railway travelling the journey from Kerry to Belfast was found to be a difficult matter, by a blind piper who turned up as a competitor at a feis ceoil gathering in the Ulster capital. He came all the way from Darrynane, the seat of Daniel O'Connell's descendants in Kerry. Having mislaid the paper bearing the address of the people in Dublin, who were to be wired to to meet and assist him on his return, the Belfast Committee[3] were for a time in a dilemma what to do with him. Ultimately a scrap of paper was found with the Dublin address, and he was put in the charge of John Cash, a Wicklow piper, who had the gift of sight.

The Committee at this same feis had to deal with another difficulty, which we find referred to in Harper O'Neill's account of the Granard competitions. The expense and trouble of travelling far, to attend competitions, came very hard on the musicians who were not prize winners. A subscription for their benefit was necessary, so that even

---

3. Dr Sinclair Boyd, first President of Belfast Gaelic League, deserves to be mentioned here, for his efforts to revive the Irish pipes, and his thoughtful attention to the old pipers.

the unsuccessful lost nothing by attendance.

No uncertainty as to this matter of expenses stood in the way of the harpers in 1792, yet only ten attended. Their names are given in the newspaper reports of the day with that of a Welshman, Williams. This Welsh harper Bunting describes (1840 vol.) as

> a good performer, who died on shipboard shortly after this date. His execution was very great; the contrast between the sweet expressive tones of the Irish instrument and the bold martial ones of the Welsh had a pleasing effect, as marking the difference of character between the two Nations.

The scene of the gathering was the ball-room of the Exchange Rooms, a building which stood at the junction of Donegal Street and North Street on the site of the present Belfast Bank.

The names of the Irish harpers present, with age and place of birth, we give from Bunting's list (1840 vol.) in preference to that in the Newsletter report, which differs slightly:

Denis Hempson, blind, from Co. Derry, aged 97 years or more, exponent of the old style of playing with long crooked nails.

Arthur O'Neill, blind, from Co. Tyrone, aged 58, afterwards instructor to the Belfast Harp Society.

Charles Fanning from Co. Cavan, aged 56. The most brilliant performer, but a modernist in style.

Daniel Black, blind, from Co. Derry, aged 75.

Charles Byrne,[4] from Co. Leitrim, aged 80, had the use of his eyes, and as a boy had acted as guide to his blind uncle, a harper contemporary with Carolan.

Hugh Higgins, blind, from Co. Mayo, aged 55.

---

4. Sometimes called Bereen, see O'Neill's *Diary.*

Patrick Quin, blind, from Co. Armagh, aged 47, one of the youngest harpers.

William Carr, from Co. Armagh, aged 15, the only juvenile competitor.

Rose Mooney, blind, from Co. Meath, aged 52.

James Duncan, from Co. Down, aged 45.

The character of the music played by them will be dealt with in the next chapter.

Besides Bunting's description and references in the prefaces to his publications, contemporary allusions of the festival will be found in Wolfe Tone's *Autobiography*, Arthur O'Neill's *Life* (which is now printed for the first time in full), the files of the *Northern Star* and the *Belfast Newsletter*.

The *Newsletter* report was reprinted in a book, now scarce, *Belfast Politics*, issued by Henry Joy in 1794, and from it we quote:

National Music of Ireland, 13th July 1792.

The number of Harpers that were present in our Exchange rooms on Wednesday last, and who are to continue to assemble in the same place for three days longer were ten, a sufficient proof of the declining state of that simple but expressive instrument and of the propriety of holding our every lure to prevent the original music of this country from being lost. As a principal motive in this undertaking was to revive some of the most ancient airs now nearly obsolete, their dates and authors perhaps for centuries unknown, pains will be taken to reduce to notes such of those that have been played on this occasion as may lead to a general publication of the best tunes. No one that remembers the exquisite finger of Dominic will hesitate to confess the capability of the Harp of Ireland, and how worthy it is of preservation. By such means alone can our National airs be saved from oblivion. Wales and Ireland have a National Music, while England has none; if she had, it would not, like that of the two first countries, be only in the hands of a few itinerant minstrels.

A list of the harpers present follows, but differs slightly, as to age of performers, from that preserved by Bunting. 'Dominic' here referred to was a harper not long passed away, whose surname was Mungan. He was in the custom of visiting the north during the Assize Circuits. A full account of him will be found in O'Neill's *Life*.

We have already quoted in an introductory biography Bunting's account of the impression made on him by the proceedings and particularly by Hempson's playing. Wolfe Tone picked out Fanning as the best performer, and he was the first prize-winner through his rendering of 'The Coolin' with elaborate variations.

In addition to the newspaper descriptions there is very fortunately available a letter written by a Belfast lady at that time in a gossipy and familiar fashion to a friend. This letter was published in that admirable publication, *Old Belfast*, by Mr R. M. Young. His father, the Right Hon. Robert Young, has made a special study of all matters relating to Bunting and the Musical Festival and published in the *Ulster Archaeological Journal* and in the *Irish Folk-Song Journal*, vol. II, 1905, a great deal of information, which has been a guide to us in our research and our study of the Bunting's manuscript.

The letter we have referred to goes on as follows:

And so my friend did not wish to come to the review, neither did I, and yet I went. We had a very agreeable day; indeed the review was over by three o'clock. When the Volunteers came into town, they were joined by the Gentle-men of the Town and neighbourhood, with the emblematick Paintings and plays. They then marched through the principal streets; this march terminated in Linen Hall Street, where the Volunteers fired three great feus de joys. They then went into the Hall as many as it would hold, and made their declaration, held their debates, and settled the affairs of the Nation; it was eight o'clock before they got to their dinners. There were a number of publick dinners through the town, but the grandest was the celebration Banquet at the Donegal arms; there they had all the grand toasts, celebrated songs, etc., and paid half a guinea each man. There were a number of Dublin gentlemen here;

among the rest was the celebrated James Napper Tandy, that I suppose you often heard of. I suppose there never was such a number of people in Belfast at once; the grand Review was nothing to it . . . and so you must have an account of the Harpists too. I was hearing them one day. I like them very much. The Harp is an agreeable soft musick very like the notes of a Harpsichord; would be very pleasant in a small room. There were eight men and one woman all either blind or lame, and all old but two men. Figure to yourself this group, indifferently dressed, sitting on a stage erected for them in one end of the Exchange Ball Room, and the ladies and the gentlemen of the first fashion in Belfast and its vicinity looking on and listening attentively, and you will have an idea of how they looked.

You can't imagine anything sweeter than the musick; every one played separately. The money that was drawn during the four days that they were here was divided among them according to their merit. The best performers got ten guineas, and the worst two and the rest accordingly. Now how do you like the poor old Harpers?

The only point calling for remark in this letter is the reference to "the celebrated James Napper Tandy," the only one of the Dublin visitors mentioned, though they included Wolfe Tone, John Keogh, and Whitley Stokes. Tandy was, however, immensely in favour with the populace. Tone, in his *Diary*, refers to him as "The Tribune," likely thinking of the Roman Tribunes of the plebs, champions of popular rights. To this we may add this note by Bunting (1840 vol.).

It may be interesting to the reader to know something of the personal appearance of these last representatives of a class so famous in song and history. They were in general clad in a comfortable homely manner in drab-coloured or grey cloth of coarse manufacture. A few of them made an attempt at splendour by wearing silver buttons on their coats, particularly Higgins and O'Neill. The former had his buttons decorated with his initials only; but O'Neill had his initials, surmounted by the crest of the O'Neills, engraved on silver buttons the size of a half-crown. Some had horses and guides when travelling about the country, others their attendants only who carried their harps. They seemed perfectly happy and contented with their lot, and all appeared convinced of the excellence of the genuine old Irish music, which they said had existed for centuries, and from its delightful melody would continue to exist for centuries to come. The Editor well remembers the anguish with which O'Neill contemplated the extinction of the old strains, which he said had been the delight of the Irish Nation for so many years. He called them with tears coursing down his aged cheeks, "*The dear, dear sweet old Irish tunes!*"

As to the general character at the harpers' playing Bunting preserved a vivid recollection, and published at the end of his life a detailed account.

The second chapter of the 1840 volume opens with a remonstrance against the generally accepted idea of the characteristics of Irish music. What is there published in a condensed and toned-down form, we find a rough draft of, among the manuscripts. In this Bunting speaks his mind more vehemently than his literary co-editors sanctioned him to do in print. We think it well to reproduce the rugged and unedited phrases of Bunting himself.

The world have been too apt to suppose our music of a highly plaintive and melancholy character, and that it partook of our National feeling at the state of our country in a political view, and that three parts out of four of our tunes were of this complaining nature. Now there never was anything more erroneous than this idea. In the year 1792 when the meeting of Harpers took place at Belfast the Editor being selected to note down the tunes was very much surprised to find that all the Melodies played by the harpers were performed with so much quickness, that they did not bear the least comparison with the manner in which he had been accustomed to hear them played on the flute, violin, etc., by the Professors of those instruments, who universally performed them so slow that the melody was nearly lost, and they were sung by the better class of people in the same drawling sleepy style.

The fact was the tunes were played with a great degree of animation at this meeting, quite different from the common adopted mode, which made them assume a new character and approached nearest to the national manners of the Irish, a spirited, animated and highly lively style, which certainly and in truth accords more with the natural character of the Irish than the drawling dead, doleful and die-away manner in which all our airs were and are in many instances played and sung to this day by our public performers and singers (for instance in 'Savourneen deelish').

The Editor has often been complimented on his style of performing Irish airs on the pianoforte, but he claims no merit superior to other players on that instrument than that of playing the melodies quicker and in humble imitation of that animated manner peculiar to the old harpers. The Editor has taken pains to point out the time of the airs at the head of each tune in this collection, which when attended to will place the Irish Tunes in their proper positions hereafter . . . . It may be well to remark however that such is the purity and elegance of our melodies, that let them be played slow or quick they serve the purpose of either grief or most joyous music.

Throughout, Bunting's decided preference for the airs when rendered by the harp, is evident. The voice even of traditional singers tends to dwell on and lengthen out notes. The flute and violin easily imitate the sostenuto effects of the singer, but the harp is at its best when rapid, rippling passages are played. Something of the gaiety and spirit of Irish music has, without doubt, passed with the decline of the harpers.

The last sentence, in which he admits that the same air can speak grief or joy was not printed. It suggests very interesting experiments. Take, for example, the melody made known to fame in Moore's 'Let Erin Remember the Days of Old'. In march time, it suggests the spirited tread of an army going hopefully to battle: sung slowly by the dragging voices of a choir it might be the dirge for the slain after defeat. In its original form, before Moore handled it, it is the tune of the 'Maidrin Ruadh', or 'Little Red Fox', imitating in quickest possible measure, the gallop of the hunt, and with a spirit of reckless jollity. Another air occurs to me which is popular in the north as 'My Love, Nell', and in other parts of Ireland the refrain is:

> My love, Dan, was an Irishman,
>> From the County Cork came he.
> Oh, I weepit' and I wailit as the big ships sailit
>> To the shores of Americee.

There is no weeping and wailing in the music which is remarkable for its jaunty comicality, but of late years the very same air has been popular at Dublin concerts, sung to a slow, sorrowful, almost heartrending chant, 'Farewell to Cork'.

In view of the fact that Giraldus Cambrensis was struck by the rapidity of Irish harp music in his day it is interesting to have this evidence that the same style was sustained by performers at the Festival of 1792.

CHAPTER XII

THE LAST HARPERS

Amongst this group of harpers, mostly old and blind or lame, Bunting was instantly attracted by the appearance and performance of the oldest of them, Denis Hempson, whose style of playing had characteristics shown by none of the others. In his person there survived the most perfect link with the ancient harpers of Ireland. He was absolutely untainted by the modern school of composition, and regarded the airs of the famous Turlogh O'Carolan with scorn.

To this old man, then well over ninety, and destined to live till his hundred and twelfth year, Bunting instantly attached himself; coaxing, admiring, and humouring, following him to his home on the northern coast, always patiently listening and recording, till he had drained him of his store of music.

Let us realise the personality of Denis Hempson with his environment, and the historical background of his long career.

He was a native of the district of Ulster, planted by the London companies in the reign of James I., and ever after mapped as County Londonderry. Anciently it had been the tribeland of the O'Cahans, the most powerful and loyal of the sub-tribes of the regal O'Neills. When an O'Neill was inaugurated as chief on the flag-stone on the mound of Tullahoge, the O'Cahan of the day stood by his right hand and took a leading part in the ceremony.

Hugh, the last O'Neill that had the title of chief, made his final stand after years of warfare in the wild glen country of this part of Ulster at the end of Elizabeth's reign.

You will read later on of an O'Cahan of this country, Rory Dall, a famous harper, who was honoured by this great O'Neill.

It was an O'Cahan, a woman harper, who first taught Denis

Hempson[1] to play, and when he had acquired the art, his instrument was made for him in his native County Derry by a skilled harp maker, Cormac Kelly of Ballinascreen.

The Londoners had made a new settlement here called Draperstown, which still stands prim and clean on the verge of a mountainous country, where the Irish speech, the old traditions, the old music, still linger. Even into that Puritan-looking town, designed for a stronghold of Anglicism in Ulster, the reflex of the Gaelic tide has crept. The present writer has sat in the schoolhouse there to listen to children's voices singing in Irish, whilst their companions fingered the graceful harp. How delightful it was to see this in a district associated with old native culture and music.

When Denis Hempson was a boy he must often have sat to listen to tales of the great wars in Ireland. The old men of his early days could have taken part in the great rising of 1641. From his tribeland there sailed to the Scottish shore the Irish swordsmen of Alastair MacDonnell to share in the rising of Montrose. The Colonists, among whom he lived, fled with their families to take shelter behind Derry walls during the famous siege, and the native tribes had rejoiced as Lord Antrim's men came marching to the music of the pipes, and the news flow round of the coming of King James to Ireland. After that there was to be mourning for the defeats of Aughrim and the Boyne. In that central district of Ulster, Edward Bunting recovered a lament for Aughrim. This song was a new one when Hempson was a child. Later, when as a harper, he wandered through Ireland and Scotland, the poets of the Gael, in allegorical song, were sending forth tidings of a royal exile, and prophesying the return of an absent lover to a beautiful mourning bride.

At last it was Hempson's lot to sit in the hall of Holyrood, and play his harp in the presence of the hero of these stirring Jacobite songs, Charles Edward, the young Chevalier.

And in old age, after years of wandering, he came to settle on the

---

[1] He was known in Magilligan as O'Hampsey, and the name has been anglicised as Sampson.

sea coast of his native territory at Magilligan. Here he was patronised and protected by a man who had taken a leading part in the stirring political events of 1782. Hervey, Earl of Bristol and Bishop of Derry, one of the most picturesque figures in the gathering of the Irish Volunteers, an advocate of Catholic emancipation, liberal-minded, a patron of the arts and noted connoisseur.

He had a passion for architecture, and designed a stately country residence on the steep cliff of Down Hill, overlooking Magilligan strand. The Bishop had travelled abroad to the most noted beauty spots of Europe, yet no wonder that he chose Magilligan for a residence. It is an enchanted land.

The River Bann, famous for salmon and all manner of fish, comes to the sea some miles westward of the Giants' Causeway, flowing past low sand-dunes to a long strand. Across it are steep cliffs, on the high plateau of which is the Bishop's residence. At its foot the strand continues in a long sweep out at right angles to the land, looking like a golden pathway over to the dark mountains of Innishowen, ten miles away. But the barrier is broken over there by a channel through which the ships can sail into the sheltered waters of Loch Foyle, that often lie glass-calm, mirroring the hills of the coast.

There St. Columcille steered his currach with its prow turned from Derry, and in later years thither he returned from Iona, and going up to the green mound of Drumceat, on the banks of the Roe, made intercession and peace between the king of Ireland and the Bardic Order.

This is history; but the legends that hover about those waves and strands have also to do with poetry and song. Where the Bann comes down by the sandhills, King Lir's lonely daughter, in her swan shape, once floated and sang; and, again, on the strand at the mouth of the river, the skeleton of a great sea-monster once lay bleaching, the wind shrilling through its bones made such music that it lulled asleep a woman who came that way, flying from the love of one whom she did not desire. He, following, found her asleep, and heard the wind music, and, wishing to imitate it, fashioned out of the bones a harp, and with it made music to win her love. "This," says the legend, "was the first harp ever made in Ireland." The castle on the cliff, that looks down on the strand where it was made, treasures the harp of one of the last minstrels, old Denis Hempson of Magilligan.

I had almost forgotten the most beautiful of all the legends of the place, for the surge that roars for miles on the great strand is one of the famed magical waves of Ireland, that used to roar and resound when the shield of Ireland's king was smitten in battle.

To this beautiful place Edward Bunting hastened as soon as possible after the Harp Festival of 1792 lest the old man's treasury of music might perish with him. His note-books are full of airs taken down from him, and the information given about them is always carefully noted. Then we have a record of the wonderful age attained by a large proportion of persons in the district.

Referring to the invaluable *Belfast Newsletter* files, we find a very prosaic piece of information about Magilligan to add to all the history and poetical legends about the place. A regular trade was carried on between Belfast and this beautiful sand-dune land at the mouth of Lough Foyle. We find, in the advertisement columns regular announcements of the coming auction of Magilligan rabbit skins. So we may make bold to imagine that when Edward Bunting, organist in Belfast, wanted news of the old harper, to hear if he was still alive and well, he went over to the auction mart where the rabbit skins were being disposed of, and met some countryman carter from Magilligan. The fur, we understand, was used in the manufacture of "beaver" for hats then fashionable.

A very full account of Hempson is published in the 1840 volume of Bunting, of which we now reproduce the following:

Denis O'Hampsy or Hempson, with whom the Editor of this collection was many years ago struck as a model of the old Irish school, was born shortly after Carolan, in the year 1695. He had been in Carolan's company when a youth, but never took pleasure in playing his compositions. The pieces which he delighted to perform were unmixed with modern refinements, which he seemed studiously to avoid; confining himself chiefly to the most antiquated of those strains which have long survived the memory of their composers and even a knowledge of the ages that produced them. Hempson was the only one of the harpers at the Belfast meeting, in 1792, who literally played the harp with long crooked nails, as described by the old writers. In playing, he caught the string between the flesh and the nail; not like the other harpers of his day, who pulled it by the fleshy part of the finger alone. He had an admirable method of playing *Staccato* and *Legato*, in which he could run through rapid divisions in an astonishing style. His fingers lay over the strings in such a manner, that when he struck them with one finger, the other was instantly ready to stop the vibration, so that the Staccato passages were heard in full perfection. When asked the reason of his playing certain parts of the tune or lesson in that style, his reply was: "That is the way I learned it" or "I cannot play it in any other way." The intricacy and peculiarity of his playing often amazed the Editor, who could not avoid perceiving in it vestiges of a noble system of practice that had existed for many centuries; strengthening the opinion, that the Irish were, at a very early period, superior to the other nations of Europe, both in the composition and performance of music. In fact, Hempson's Staccato and Legato passages, double slurs, shakes, turns, graces, etc., etc., comprised as great a range of execution as has ever been devised by the most modern improvers.

An accurate portrait of Hempson, when above one hundred years old, was inserted in the Editor's former collection, and is given here in miniature. The following account of him, communicated in a letter from the late George Sampson, the historian of Londonderry, was originally published by Miss Owenson, now Lady Morgan, in her admired novel, *The Wild Irish Girl*. Were the writer still alive, the Editor is satisfied he would approve of his memoir being transplanted into a work to which it is so peculiarly suited, and where it will be handed down with the minstrel's favourite music.

3rd July 1805

I made the survey of the man with two heads (in allusion to an enormous excrescence or wen on the back of his head) according to your desire, but not till yesterday, on account of various impossibilities; here is my report:

Denis Hempson, or the man with two heads, is a native of Craigmore, near Garvagh, in the County of Londonderry. His father, Bryan Darragher (blackish complexion) Hempson, held the whole town land of Tyrcrevan; his mother's relations were in possession of the Woodtown (both considerable farms at Magilligan). He lost his sight at the age of three years by the small-pox; at twelve years old he began to learn the harp under Bridget O'Cahan; "for," as he said, "in these old times, women as well as men were taught the Irish harp in the best families, and every old Irish family had harps in plenty." His next instructor was John C. Garragher, a blind travelling harper, whom he followed to Buncranagh, where his master used to play for Colonel Vaughan; he had afterwards Loughlin Fanning and Patrick Connor, in succession, as masters. "All these were from Connaught, which was," as he added, "the best part of the kingdom for Irish harpers, and for music." At eighteen years of age he began to play for himself, and was taken into the house of Counsellor Canning, at Garvagh, for half a year; his host, with Squire Gage and Doctor Bacon, joined and bought him a harp.

He travelled nine or ten years through Ireland and Scotland, and tells facetious stories of gentlemen in both countries; among others, that, in passing near the residence of Sir J. Campbell, at Aghanbrach, he learned that this gentleman had spent a great deal, and was living upon so much per week for an allowance. Hempson through delicacy would not call, but some of the domestics were sent after him. On coming into the castle, Sir J. Campbell asked him why he had not called, adding, "Sir, there never was a harper but yourself that passed the door of my father's house." To which Hempson answered, "that he had heard in the neighbourhood his honour was not often at home"; with which delicate evasion Sir J. was satisfied. He adds, "that this was the stateliest and highest bred man he ever knew; if he were putting on a new pair of gloves, find one of them dropped on the floor (though ever so clean), he would order the servant to bring another pair." He says that in that time he never met but one laird who had a harp, and that was a very small one, played formerly by the laird's father; and that when he had tuned it with new strings, the laird and his lady were so pleased with his music, that they invited him back in these words: "Hempson, as soon as you think this child of ours (a boy of three years of age) is fit to learn on his grandfather's harp, come back to teach him, and you shall not repent it"; but this he never accomplished. He told me a story of the Laird of Strone, with a great deal of comic relish. When he was playing at the house, a messenger came, that a large party of gentlemen were coming to grouse, and would spend some days with him (the laird). The lady, being in great distress, turned to her husband, saying, "What shall we do, my dear, for so many, in the way of beds?" "Give yourself no uneasiness," replied the laird; "give us enough to eat, and I will supply the rest; and as for beds, believe me, every man shall find one for himself" (meaning that his guests would fall under the table).

In his second trip to Scotland, in the year 1745, he was at that time, by his own account, nearly fifty years of age: being at Edinburgh when Charley the Pretender was there, he was called into the great hall to play; at first he was alone, afterwards four fiddlers joined; the tune called for was, 'The King Shall Enjoy His Own Again': he sung here part of the words following:

> *I hope to see the day*
> *When the Whigs shall run away,*
> *And the king shall enjoy his own again.*

I asked him if he heard the Pretender speak; he replied, I only heard him ask, "Is Sylvan there?" On which some one answered, "He is not here, please your Royal Highness, but he shall be sent for." He meant to say Sullivan, continued Hempson, but that was the way he called the name. He says that Captain Macdonald, when in Ireland, came to see him, and that he told the Captain that Charley's cockade was in his father's house.

Hempson was brought into the Pretender's presence by Colonel Kelly of Roscommon and Sir Thomas Sheridan. He played in many Irish houses; among others, those of Lord de Courcy, Mr Fortescue, Sir P. Bellew, Squire Roche; and in the great towns, Dublin, Cork, etc., etc., respecting all which, he interspersed pleasant anecdotes with surprising gaiety and correctness.

General Hart, who was an admirer of music, sent a painter to take a drawing of him, which cannot fail to be interesting, if it were only for the venerable expression of his meagre blind countenance, and the symmetry of his tall, thin, but not debilitated person. I found him lying on his back in bed, near the fire of his cabin; his family employed in the usual way; his harp under the bed clothes, by which his face was covered also. When he heard my name, he started up (being already dressed) and seemed rejoiced to hear the sound of my voice, which, he said, he began to recollect. He asked for my children, whom I brought to see him, and he felt them over and over; then with tones of great affection, he blessed God that he had seen four generations of the name, and ended by giving the children his blessing. He then tuned his old time-beaten harp, his solace and bed-fellow, and played with astonishing justness and good taste.

The tunes which he played were his favourites; and he, with an elegance of manner, said at the same time, "I have not forgotten the airs you used to ask for," which were 'Coolin', 'The Dawning of the Day', 'Ellen a Roon', 'Cean Dubh Dilis', etc. These, except the third, were the first tunes which, according to regulation, he played at the famous meeting of harpers at Belfast, under the patronage of some amateurs of Irish music. Mr Bunting, the celebrated musician of that town, was here in 1793, the year after, the meeting, at Hempson's, noting his tunes and his manner of playing, which is in the best old style. He said, with the honest feeling of self-love, "When I played the old tunes, not another of the harpers would play after me." He came to Magilligan many years ago, and at the age of eighty-six married a woman of Innishowen, whom he found living in the house of a friend. "I can't tell," said Hempson, "if it was not the devil buckled us together, she being lame, and I blind." By this wife he has one daughter, married to a cooper, who has several children, and maintains them all, though Hempson (in this alone seeming to doat) says, that his son-in-law is a spendthrift, and that he maintains them; the family humour his whim and the old man is quieted. He is pleased when they tell him, as he thinks is the case, that several people of character for musical taste send letters to invite him; and he, though incapable now of leaving the house, is planning expeditions never to be attempted, much less realised; these are the only traces of mental debility. As to his body, he has no inconvenience but that arising from a chronic disorder. His habits have ever been sober; his favourite drink, once beer, now milk and water; his diet chiefly *potatoes*. I asked him to teach my daughter, but he declined; adding, however, that it was too hard for a young girl, but nothing would give him greater pleasure if he thought it could be done.

Lord Bristol, when lodging at the bathing-house of Mount Salut, near Magilligan, gave three guineas, and ground, rent free, to build the house where Hempson now lives. At the house warming, his lordship with his lady and family came, and the children danced to his harp.

It will be satisfactory, to such as take an interest in the simple annals of the harpers, and venerate any vestiges of the bardic system to learn, that the close of Hempson's long life of one hundred and twelve years (he died in 1807) was rendered comfortable by the humanity of the Rev. Sir H. Harvey Bruce, from whose hand he was often literally fed. The day before his death, upon hearing that this gentleman had come to his cabin, he desired to be raised up in his bed, and the harp placed in his hands. Having struck some notes of a favourite strain, he sunk back unable to proceed, taking his last adieu of an instrument which had been a companion, even in his sleeping hours, and was his hourly solace through a life protracted to the longest span. His harp is preserved in Sir Henry's mansion, at Downhill, as a relic of its interesting owner. It was made by Cormac O'Kelly, about the year 1700, at Ballynascreen, in the County Derry; a district long famous for the construction of such instruments and for the preservation of ancient Irish melodies in their original purity. It was with great difficulty the Editor was able to procure the old harp music from Hempson. When asked to play the very antique tunes, he uniformly replied, "There was no use in doing so, they were too hard to learn, they revived painful recollections." In short he regarded the old music with a superstitious veneration, and thought it in some sort a profanation to divulge it to modern ears.

Thus concludes Mr Sampson's account of the Magilligan harper.

Hempson was a contemporary of the famous Turlough O'Carolan of whom many anecdotes are related in Arthur O'Neill's *Memoir*; an outline of his life may be fitly included here, as his music was so much in favour with performers at the Belfast festival. Goldsmith in his youth saw him and has recorded his impression in an essay on the last of the Bards. Perhaps when he in his turn started out to tour through Europe, with no other means of support than his flute, he had in mind the wandering minstrel, who was such a welcome guest in the country gentlemen's homes in Western Ireland.

Bunting writes of Carolan:

He was born in the year 1670 at Nobber, or, as some assert, at a neighbouring village in the County Westmeath, and died at the age of sixty-eight in the year 1738. Early deprived of his sight by the small-pox, the inhabitant of a country recently desolated by a civil war and add to these his propensity to dissipation, we must wonder at the proofs he has given of the depth and versatility of his talents. Some idea of the fertility of his invention may be formed from this circumstance, that one harper who attended the Belfast meeting in 1792, and who had never seen Carolan, nor been taught by any person who had an opportunity of imitating him had acquired upwards of one hundred of his tunes, which he asserted constituted but an inconsiderable portion of them. As an instance of the facility with which he committed tunes to memory as well as of the astonishing ease with which he could produce new melodies, take the following fact vouched for by the *Monthly Review*. At the house of an Irish nobleman where Geminiani was present, Carolan challenged that eminent composer to a trial of skill. The musician played over on his violin the fifth Concerto of Vivaldi. It was instantly repeated by Carolan on his Harp, although he had never heard it before. The surprise of the company was increased when he asserted that he could compose a concerto himself at the moment, and the more so when he actually played that admirable piece ever since known as *Carolan's Concerto*. He composed as one who knew him well reported upon the buttons of his coat, taking them as representative of lines and spaces . . . .

Dr Grattan Flood corrects this story, stating on the authority of O'Conor of Belnagare, that Geminiani never met Carolan, but having heard of him tested his powers by sending over to Elphin a Concerto having certain mistakes purposely inserted. This was played over for Carolan who remarked in Irish: "Here and there it limps and stumbles," and, taking his harp, he suggested improvements. These were noted and sent to Geminiani then in Dublin, who pronounced him a genius. Dr Grattan Flood in his history of music gives an admirably concise life of the bard with an account of his various compositions. He writes in conclusion:

It seemed like a design of Providence that in the year 1738, Carolan stricken with illness found himself at the hospitable mansion of his old patroness Madame McDermott at Alderford near Boyle. His illness was of short duration and he died after a last performance on the Harp, crowning a life of song with a wild and touching *Farewell to Music* on Saturday, March 25th, 1738.

Charles O'Conor briefly yet expressively wrote as follows in Irish, which may be translated "Turlough Carolan the talented and principal Musician of Ireland died. May the Lord have mercy on his Soul, for he was a moral and religious man."

Dr Grattan Flood goes on to quote Hardiman's description of the funeral:

> On the fifth day after his death upwards of sixty Clergymen of different denominations, a number of gentlemen from the surrounding counties and a vast concourse of country people assembled to pay the last mark of respect to their favourite bard. All the houses in Ballyfarnon (on the border of Co. Sligo) were occupied by the former and the people erected tents in the fields around Alderford House. The Harp was heard in every direction. Old Mrs MacDermot herself joined the female mourners who attended to weep as she expressed herself "over her poor gentleman," the head of all Irish Music. The funeral was one of the greatest that for many years had taken place in Connaught.

So far as Dr Flood is quoting Hardiman, he continues to say:

> O'Carolan was buried in the east end of the old Church of Kilronan adjoining the vault of the MacDermots. From a letter written by Charles O'Conor the following extract is of interest: "In my pensive mood at Kilronan I stood over poor Carolan's grave, covered with a heap of stones; and I found his skull in a niche near the spot, perforated a little in the forehead that it might be known by that mark . . . ." Although no monument marks the grave of O'Carolan yet the late Lady Louisa Tighe got the cemetery enclosed, and had an Irish designed gate surmounted by a central cross. Over the arch of the gateway is the inscription:
> *Within this Churchyard lie the remains of Carolan the last of the Irish Bards who departed this life March 25th, 1738. R. I. P.*

A fine portrait of Carolan was executed from life by order of Dean Massey of Limerick about 1720 of which engravings are familiar.

Through the exertions of Lady Morgan a subscription was raised for a monument to him, which took the form of a white marble bas-relief, in which he is represented as playing on the harp.

It is placed in a prominent position in St Patrick's Cathedral, Dublin, not far from the monument to Dean Swift, who, by the way, was Carolan's contemporary and translator of one of his well-known songs, 'Pleraca na Ruarcach' [Pléaráca na Ruarcach] or 'O'Rourke's Noble Feast'. The skull of Carolan underwent strange vicissitudes, and Dr Grattan Flood asserts that it is at present in Belfast in possession of a Masonic Lodge, and made use of in some part of the ceremonial of the Order. It is to be regretted that in the city so famous for its veneration for harpers, the relic of such a famous bard should be used in such a way.

CHAPTER XIII

THE LAST HARPERS (continued)

CHARLES FANNING, THE FIRST PRIZE-WINNER AT THE THREE GRANARD balls, and at the Belfast festival, was evidently a brilliant and showy performer and skilled in rendering variations.

Arthur O'Neill (see that harper's *Life*) had visited him in his father's home, spending three weeks there. He had an evident liking for him mingled with pity and scorn that he did not sufficiently maintain the dignity of his calling. He dictated the following biographical notice, the original of which is among our MSS.:—

Charles Fanning was born in the County of Leitrim in the Province of Connaught. His father, Loughlin Fanning, was a decent farmer and played well on the harp. Charles was principally instructed by Thady Smith, a native of the County of Roscommon, and a tolerable performer on the harp. Charles Fanning in consequence of his performance on the Harp, became much respected. He never taught any, but merely was an amateur and principally supported himself by the private emoluments arising from his profession. (Note *O'Neill's contradictory definition of an amateur. He had, perhaps, confounded the words professor and professional, and had heard that amateur was the negative of the latter. Ed.*)

On his first arrival into the County of Tyrone he got acquainted with a Mrs Bailie of Terrinaskea in that County, who played on the harp very well. Charles married her kitchen maid, for which Mrs Bailie was greatly disobliged, as she frequently had him at her table, and had him introduced to genteel Company. She fell out with him and he was not received as usually. Charley and the wife boxed now and then.

He visited Mrs Bailie generally at three months a time in his professional way. His wife was discharged and was generally sneaking after him everywhere. He went from Mrs Bailie's to Derry, and got himself introduced to the Bishop, who seemed to like him well, otherwise he would not keep him. I, Arthur O'Neill, went to Derry where I met Charley, and when I asked him how he was Charley replied that I might "blow a goose-quill through his cheek," meaning he was so poor and thin, and this time he had the wife and one or two children to support.

After he left the Bishop's he rambled about the Nation awhile. I next heard he fell in with a Mr Pratt of Kingscourt in the County Cavan. He lived a couple of years there and had a house and a garden and four acres of land and the grazing of four cows in the demesne. He had a letter from Mr Pratt, that he would give him a lease of his concern; but on Mr Pratt's death his brother's son, who was his heir, refused giving the lease and turned him out. Charles consulted Counsellor (now Judge) Fox with his case, who gave an opinion in his favour, and said he would make it good.

Charles gave Fox the letter, but in consequence of some private influence as he believed, he never could get it from him again, and it is generally believed he was betrayed. He then rambled as usual. I saw him often afterwards, who told me the above story about Mr Fox. I next heard of his being in Belfast in 1792, at the time of the celebration of the French Revolution, where I met him. He got the highest prize for his performance on that occasion.

Fanning and O'Neill had met in three competitions previous to the Belfast gathering, namely, at Granard, an account of which will be found in the blind harper's *Life*. He handsomely acknowledges the ability of his rival, saying, "Fanning deservedly always got the first prize." The story of the lost letter and the lease will cause many to wonder whether the Counsellor, who behaved so shabbily to the poor harper, could possibly have been the "Noble Fox" made famous in the ballad of 'Willie Reilly and his own Colleen Bawn'. Of James Duncan, O'Neill related:

This gentleman was descended of respectable parents in the County of Down, and was taught to learn the Harp only as a qualifying branch of his education for which instrument he had a partiality. He was principally instructed by a Harry FitzSimmons, professor of the Harp, under whom he made a very considerable proficiency. His embarrassment in life was the chief cause of his becoming an itinerant harper for some years. He was deeply engaged in a law-suit with some of his family, and the emoluments arising from his performances were the principal means of defraying the expenses of it. The law-suit terminated in his favour, and he obtained his property in the possession of which he lately died. I met him in Belfast in 1792 on the occasion already mentioned, and his gentlemanly conduct induced me to form an uncommon opinion of him. I was much grieved when coming to Belfast afterwards, I made his part of the country with the intention of calling on him when I was informed of his death. He was an excellent performer, but knew very little of ancient Irish Airs. He played a great variety of modern airs very well.

Though he does not here mention it, it will be seen by reference to O'Neill's *Life* that he had also met Duncan at the third Granard ball and kept company with him.

Rose Mooney, whom Bunting notes as "blind, from the County Meath, aged fifty-two," had been competitor and thrice third prize winner at the Granard balls. O'Neill's *Life* contains many anecdotes of her and her maid Mary, and he adds a brief memorial note, in which he says that she had been a pupil of Thady Elliot, a disreputable drunken fellow, given to coarse drollery. He tells of one occasion on which he, the highly respectable and cultivated harper, encountered him.

I was entertained at a Mr Preston's near Navan, and the same Thady Elliot was there at that time to offer his usual services; but Mrs Preston dismissed him for two reasons; one was to pay me a compliment and not to suffer him to intrude on me, and the other was that she was much prejudiced for his conduct, as he would endeavour to show his wit no matter in what company. I know nothing more about Thady, but I understand he died one day of an Innishoen (Epilepsy) in the County of Meath, where he was born. But to return to Rose Mooney, I never heard much about her only as an itinerant Harper, until I was informed that she and her maid, Mary, were in Killala at the time the French landed there. How she and her maid (and the Devil's own maid she was) finished their career, is not well known, but it is generally imagined, that when the rebels forced open the loyalists' spirit stores, Rose and her maid went in to some of them, where the impression Thady Elliot gave Rose in her early days had such an effect that it is thought she kicked the bucket as her tutor did. Rose was at one time much respected, but it is certain that her maid was the principal cause of her falling into dis-esteem as she would and did sacrifice her mistress's reputation for a glass of whiskey.

Hugh Higgins, a native of Tirawley, County Mayo, was blind, and fifty-five years of age at the time of the Harp Festival, is referred to in O'Neill's *Life* as a gentleman harper, and as "my dear deceased friend," from which we may gather that he was a man of respectable character, for O'Neill called no one friend who was not a credit to the calling of which he was so proud.

Higgins played an adventurous part in helping another blind harper, Owen Keenan, out of bonds. The incident occurred in Omagh, my native town, and I can readily picture all that happened. Arthur O'Neill, who states that Keenan was his earliest teacher of the harp when resident in Augher, County Tyrone, gave a full account of the incidents. Samuel Ferguson condensed his narrative as follows:

Owen Keenan (born about 1725) was another of the reckless turbulent class. Still there is a good deal of adventurous interest, if not genuine romance, in the various escapades and frolics in which he was engaged.

Being often at Kilymoon, the residence of Mr Stewart near Cookstown, in the County of Tyrone, he became enamoured of a French governess, who resided with that family, and blind though he was contrived on one occasion, like another Romeo, to make his way to her apartment by a ladder. Mr Stewart, justly offended, had him committed to Omagh gaol on a charge as is presumed of housebreaking. There was at that time a very good harper, also blind, called Higgins, who was of a respectable family, in Tyrawley, County Mayo, and who travelled in a better style than most others of the fraternity; he, hearing of Keenan's mishap, posted down to Omagh, where his appearance and retinue readily procured him admission to the gaol. The gaoler was from home, his wife loved music and cordials, these harpers, too, knew how to humour the amiable weaknesses of one who had been once a beauty. The result may be imagined. The blind men stole the keys out of her pockets, while oppressed with love and music, made the turnkeys drunk, and while Higgins stayed behind like another Orpheus charming Cerberus with his lyre, Keenan "marched out by moonlight merrily" with Higgins' boy on his back to guide him over a ford of the Strule (*the river flows close under the gaol walls*). He took his route direct to Kilymoon again, scaled the walls once more and finally after commitment for "the ladder business" as O'Neill calls it, and a narrow escape at the County Assizes carried off his Juliet and married her.

Keenan after his marriage emigrated to the States where his French wife proved unfaithful.

This is the most interesting anecdote recorded of Hugh Higgins.

Daniel Black from the County Derry was blind, and sang to the harp. He chiefly frequented the house of a Mr Heyland, Glendaragh, near Antrim. No anecdotes are given relating to him. Bunting visited him in 1796 shortly before his death, which occurred when he was about eighty.

Patrick Quinn, one of the youngest harpers present at Belfast, belonged to Portadown, County Armagh. His master had been Patrick Linden of the Fews [Pádraig Mac Giolla Fhiondáin], County Armagh, "a distinguished performer and poet." Arthur O'Neill tried to secure the presence of Linden at the Harp Festival, and gave him clothes to attend in. Linden had met O'Carolan in his time, and was acquainted with certain of the poets who had written the Gaelic words of famous Ulster songs. How he disappointed O'Neill will be read in the *Memoir*.

Quinn was the only harper present at Belfast who attempted to play 'Patrick's Day', and was very proud of having "fixed it," as he said "for the harp." He was selected to play at the Carolan Celebration in the Rotunda, Dublin, 1809, and was afterwards patronised by Bernard Trotter, who engaged him to appear at entertainments given at his residence in Clontarf. Quinn sat in an arbour with his harp and delighted the guests. Miss Trotter took a sketch of him amid these picturesque surroundings. Returning to the north Quinn was so proud of his performances that he refused ever after to play the violin at wakes and merry meetings, though he had previously made considerable earnings in this way. Quinn was about forty-seven in 1792, and was blind.

Charles Byrne, who was about eighty at the time of the Harp Festival, is without doubt the Charles Bereen mentioned in O'Neill's *Memoir* as a competitor at the Granard "Balls." Bunting in his notes 1840 remarks that he was not distinguished as a performer, but had an extraordinary fund of songs and anecdotes. O'Neill, moreover, tells us that Bereen in his youth had acted as guide to his blind uncle. The latter we take to be the Bereen, for whom O'Carolan had such an antipathy, and concerning whom an amusing anecdote is recorded by O'Neill. He was a native of County Leitrim, and from a letter, preserved among our manuscripts, we learn some further particulars regarding him. The letter was written by a Mr O'Reilly, belonging to near Scarva, County Down. His sister was the lady referred to by Dr MacDonnell as the last person who received harp lessons through the medium of Irish. It would seem that Charles Byrne had been her instructor, and that she had made a portrait sketch of him.

The Reillys of Scarva were a particularly hospitable family. An account of a visit to their house is preserved in a scarce little volume, *Biography of the Blind*, published in Belfast in 1821. The author, a blind artisan called James Wilson, with literary taste and some writing capacity, was encouraged and helped to bring out *The Lives of Famous Blind Men from the Time of Homer Onward*. In the Preface he tells the story of his own life and struggles from the day when, as an orphan child, sick with smallpox, he was put ashore at the Port of Belfast. The philanthropists of that town had a particular tenderness for that form of human affliction, and we understand, from Wilson's biography, how the fortunes of the Harp Society became associated with a charitable effort to relieve the blind. In the account of his life Wilson tells how his Belfast friends had him taught upholstering, when an attempt to teach him music was unsuccessful. In the pursuit of his trade he went to Scarva. He goes on to say:

> The first of my literary acquaintances of any respectability was John Lushington Reilly of Scarva, to whose family I was warmly recommended by a lady who introduced me as a lover and composer of poetry. In this gentleman's house I was employed for some time, and during my residence there, I was not treated as a common workman, but was highly entertained by Mr & Mrs Reilly, who had the goodness to read to me by turns, whilst I was at work, and in their absence a person was appointed to supply their place; here was a fine library where I first met with Spenser's *Faerie Queene*. When I left home I did not expect to remain at Scarva beyond three or four weeks at farthest, but such was the partiality of that worthy family for me, that I was detained there for nearly three months. On taking leave of my benefactors Mrs Reilly observed that I ought not to be tired of them as they were not tired of me.

Such was the hospitable home in which old Charles Byrne was a welcome visitor. Though he was not blind, he was very likely read to also, if not entirely taken up with singing and reciting his own store of songs. The letter already referred to follows:

SCARVA, 16*th* *April* '40

L. B. LAND.

SIR,— Doctor McDonnell expressed a wish that I should let you see the enclosed slight sketch of Charles Byrne, a native I believe of Connaught, who for many years visited this house and the neighbourhood about Xmas, and was the "last Minstrel" I can remember regularly visiting this country. He could speak Irish and sing in that language, and my sister, who made this sketch, used frequently to adapt English words to some of his tunes, and altho' I may have some of his tunes amongst my papers, I have not at this moment any idea of where to look for them, else I should be most happy to send you anything of the kind in my power, according to Doctor M'Donnell's wish.

The sketch I send, though very slight, is very like, and brings the old man strongly to my mind. Should it be any use to you in your proposed work I should be glad, but hope you will have the goodness to return it when you have done with it. I remain, with great respect your obedient servant,

J. M. REILLY.

P.S. Since I wrote the above Mrs Reilly has found one of the songs I alluded to and which I hope you will also return.

Of William Carr, aged 15, the only juvenile Harper present at Belfast, we have no account further than that he played 'The Dawning of the Day'.

This completes the list of harpers who attended the festival. Bunting lost sight of none of them, as we learn from his song indexes, of airs taken down from one or other for several years after. Most remarkable is the fact that whilst O'Neill tells us that Rose Mooney perished miserably as a victim to drink during the French invasion at Killala in 1798, Bunting notes an air and Carolan's 'Planxty Charles Coote' as having been taken down from "*Rose Mooney the Harper in 1800.*"

Of other harpers, who were not present, from whom he afterwards got songs, we hear of Patrick Linden of County Armagh (Quinn's master), who gave him 'Miss Hamilton', the composition of C. Lyons, harper to the Earl of Antrim in 1702, and also 'Sally Kelly', by Thomas Connallon, composed about 1660. Several airs were given by D. O'Donnell, harper, County Mayo, in 1803. Catherine Martin of Meath is mentioned as a good performer, who confined herself to modern compositions by Parson

Stirling of Lurgan. Bunting did not collect any of these.

In addition to preserving the music of the harpers an attempt was made to secure their traditions and the technology of their art. Bunting made notes of everything that was told him of the history of the airs, and published particulars in his later volumes. In the 1840 publication he included a lengthy list of musical technical terms in Irish. These the great scholar, Eugene O'Curry, alludes to scornfully as apocryphal. A knotty problem is thus propounded which it is beyond one's skill to pronounce on. Bunting was so eager to be assured of accuracy in his antiquarian research that it is hard to conceive of him as being hoaxed into giving much of the space in his last and greatest collection to the publication of a worthless vocabulary containing several hundreds of Irish words.

It is therefore necessary to give his own account of how they were accumulated, and this takes us back to the Festival of 1792. In his 1840 Preface he writes:

> The Irish Harpers, when assembled in Belfast in 1792, uniformly made use of technical terms designating the several notes of the instrument and their various combinations, shakes, moods, etc., which, although admirably characteristic and descriptive in themselves, are altogether unlike the language of modern musicians, a language which is well-known to have been invented at a comparatively recent period by the continental nations. Had the Irish derived their knowledge of music from nations making use of the continental vocabulary, they would have received the terms of Art employed by these nations into their own language, either by adopting them absolutely, or by translating them into corresponding Irish phrases. The contrary is invariably found to be the case. Thus that combination of notes termed a shake by the modern musicians is by the Irish dominated barluith signifying activity of the fingers; a beat again is termed 'barluith beal anarde' or 'activity of finger ends striking upwards' and a run of execution 'Sruith-mor' or 'the great stream.' In like manner, the principal *times* have their independent and native designations, such as 'Cuigrath', 'dirge time'; 'Cumbradth',

'lamentation time'; 'Cruaidhchlesadh', 'heroic time'; 'Phuirt,' 'lesson time'; corresponding to the modern terms, Adagio, Larghetto, Andante, and Allegro. So also of the chords, moods, keys, etc.

The following collection of these native terms of art was procured from the most distinguished of the Harpers who met at Belfast in the year 1792.

Their vast importance in establishing the antiquity of the country's music was first pointed out to the Editor by Dr James MacDonnell of that town, who zealously assisted in forming the collection.

The Harpers whose authority were chiefly relied on were, Hempson, O'Neill, Higgins, Fanning and Black . . . . Although educated by different masters (through the medium of the Irish language alone) and in different parts of the country, they exhibited a perfect agreement in all their statements referring to the old traditions of the art as their only authority, and professing themselves quite at a loss to explain their method of playing by any other terms.

A general vocabulary of Irish musical terms, so far as the Editor has been able to collect them from the remaining authorities, will be found annexed. Both collections are no doubt imperfect; for the sources of written information on the subject are equally difficult of access and of interpretation, and with respect to the traditionary statements of the Harpers themselves, it must be recollected that Irish music has been on the wane, at least since the reign of Elizabeth, and that as the Belfast meeting was in fact, the expiring flicker of the lamp that once shed its lustre over Christendom, the Editor cannot be expected to have done more than catch some straggling rays, which are still, however, brilliant enough to show how illustrious an instrument the Irish harp has been in former ages.

We may add that in taking down Irish terms or names of songs Bunting spelt phonetically in English character. His rough notes show evidence of a keen ear for accent, but complete ignorance of Irish methods of spelling. These notes were deciphered in Irish character by skilled scribes, such as Patrick Lynch, who was in or near Belfast from 1794 or 1795 up till 1803.

At a later date Cody, tutor to the Belfast Harp Society from 1808 to 1813, was helpful.

At the actual time of the Harp Festival the Rev. Andrew Bryson of Dundalk had been invited to be present "as a person skilled in the Irish language and antiquities;"[1] but we have no record of his having attended, and nothing among the Bunting papers to prove the presence of an Irish scholar. The atrocious spelling of the list of airs published in the *Northern Star* newspaper would seem to show that neither Bryson, nor any one else competent to write Irish, was present. Who then took down in Irish the list of technical terms supplied by the harpers in 1792, which forms the basis of the list published in 1840?

Definite evidence is forthcoming in a letter of Dr MacDonnell's among the manuscripts undated and unsigned, but evidently written with a number of others when Bunting was preparing his last publication and likely when he was on a visit to Belfast.

Finerty, who is referred to as copying for Bunting, was, without doubt, Tomas O'Fiannachtaig [Tomás Ó Fiannachta of Ballinscreen], whose name appears on the title page of a translation into Irish of two of Maria Edgeworth's short tales, published in 1833, by the Ulster Gaelic Society. The book is dedicated to the Marquis of Downshire in a letter signed by R Bryce and E. S. McAdam as secretaries. Finerty was, in fact, the successor of Lynch and Cody, for the lovers of the Irish music in this northern town never neglected the language. The Doctor writes:

[1.] Members of the scholarly Bryson family were instrumental in saving some unique Irish tales and poems. A collection of Gaelic poems and tales transcribed by one of the Brysons was inspected by Dr Douglas Hyde in the College Square Museum, Belfast, and from it he copied a very remarkable version of *Deirdre* which has been published in Berlin, and which Dr Hyde quotes from in his *History of Irish Literature*. In the spring of 1911, Dr Hyde lectured in Dublin on a hitherto unknown Ossianic manuscript which he had unearthed. The copyist was Bryson of Belfast, and the Irish was in the dialect of Co. Antrim, where the home of the Bryson family is situated near Glenwherry and in view of St Patrick's Slemish.

If an air had twenty names, I would preserve them all in order to facilitate the identification of the tune. When you go to Dublin get some person to collect all the musical terms extant in any Irish lexicons or vocabularies; and after comparing them deliberately, with such as you have already taken down yourself; and with those which I committed to writing long ago (without a proper knowledge of the sound or sense), and which I sent to Finerty yesterday, you will then be able to see more distinctly whether they be worth printing, and how they will bear upon the general subject. The really technical words will not be found numerous in any dictionary. You should be beside Finerty while he is writing for you. What can be the reason that one particular air is so associated in the mind with another, that if you are endeavouring to recollect one, the other will often come into your mind instead of it, and *vice versa*, thus, when I want to hum over 'Scots wha hae' I often hit upon 'For aid lang syne', and instead of 'Ellen I roon' I find 'God save the King' coming up instead of 'A lovely Nun to a Friar came' I get the Scotch air 'An gint thou wert mine thing'.

From this letter we learn that the doctor was responsible for making Bunting publish the vocabularies, that he had himself taken down a number of them "long ago, without a proper knowledge of the sound or sense," and that Bunting had also taken some down which he was advised to compare with words extant in Irish dictionaries. The doctor's own list had been sent to Finerty, a competent Irish scholar, and Bunting was told to be with Finerty for consultation, whilst revising the spelling of these rough lists.

Taking this letter side by side with what we have quoted with regard to the 1792 Harpers being the authority for the vocabulary, we cannot but assume that Dr MacDonnell and Bunting had taken down this information from the harpers named, and had carefully preserved their notes.

The following letter, however, refers to material for the musical vocabulary having been sought out at a much later time. It is undated, but was written during Bunting's visit to Belfast.

> DEAR BUNTING,— Since hearing from you, I have learned from Pat Byrne, a harper, that all harpers prior to O'Neill, having taught only through the medium of Irish, must have had names for all the strokes or chords on the harp. The strings which are octaves to the sisters he said had others, which he said were called 'Gilli ni fregragh ni Havlai' the servants of the answers to the sisters. He says that Miss Reilly of Scarvagh is the only person whom he knows now living who was taught to play through the Irish language, and he will endeavour to collect from her some technical terms he spent a day with me and I brought Alexander Mitchell to hear him. I hope you will soon report some progress of your own to me. I met with an old man from Connaught, called Thadeus O'Flynn, from whom I took down the words of some songs and traditional tales. I found that this person had visited Mr Hardiman, and therefore I shunned copying any of the pieces that had been printed in Hardiman's two volumes. I wish you to be acquainted with Mrs Colonel Garner, the niece of Mr Halliday who is now in Dublin, and has a great enthusiasm about all Irish affairs. She is acquainted with my sons, and has a taste for both music and poetry. I hear a report that the Queen has ordered a copy to be made for herself of *The Annals of the Four Masters*. I hope Mr Donnevan may be employed about that I should prefer his, as far as I can judge, to all others. Your friend, Mary, is going on with her old capers—if she does not get to a good berth in the other world, there can be no good in good works.— I am, Dear Bunting, your sincere friend,
>
> J. MacDonnell.

The reference to Miss Mary McCracken is in relation to her extravagance in acts of charity. As long as any sufferers, widows, or orphans of the United Irishmen survived, she considered it her duty to support and succour them.

We next come to the most interesting of the 1792 harpers, Arthur O'Neill, whose *Biography* has been fortunately preserved, and is now for the first time published.

CHAPTER XIV

MEMOIRS OF ARTHUR O'NEILL
INTRODUCTORY AND FIRST JOURNEY

The name of Arthur O'Neill stands out pre-eminently in connection with the Harp Festival.

Hempson had been the best and most reliable performer in the genuinely ancient style, but O'Neill carried in his memory the greatest store of recollections and of traditions with regard to the harpers and composers of preceding generations. Moreover, he became a permanent resident in Belfast in 1808, when the first Harp Society was founded, and Bunting had opportunities of prolonged conversation. He retired on a little pension collected for him through the exertions of Dr MacDonnell, when the society fell through in 1813.

During his residence in Belfast he had dictated his *Memoirs* to a scribe, whom, by a letter of Bunting's we find to have been one, Tom Hughes, a clerk in the confidence of the McCracken family.

O'Neill's *Memoir* has never been published, but in preparing material for the 1840 volume, it was largely availed of by Samuel Ferguson for information and anecdotes.

As a testimony of O'Neill's good faith and reliability, Dr James MacDonnell wrote the following letter for publication. The original is among our MSS., carefully pinned into the front of the stoutly-bound manuscript of the *Memoir*.

My Dear Mr Bunting,— In compliance with your request, I furnish you with some particulars of my acquaintance with Mr Arthur O'Neill, the Irish Harper, from whom you procured some information prior to your first Publication.

My Father, who had a great fondness for Music, selected O'Neill as the most proper person he then knew to teach his children, and he lived in our house for two years, in this capacity; but my Father's death in 1780 put an end to this study, which we found very difficult, on account of the Teacher being blind. At that period, almost all Harpers were blind, this profession having been humanely reserved as a provision for the sons of reduced Gentlemen, who happened to be blind, a calamity then much more common than at present, owing to improvements in the treatment of small-pox. During the two years he lived in the house he was treated as a poor Gentleman—had a servant—was a man of strong natural sense, pleasing in his manners, and had acquired a considerable knowledge of the common topics, so that he acquit himself very well in mixed society, when encouraged to converse. He had, according to the customs of these itinerant musicians, travelled several times all over Ireland, and became thereby acquainted with several of the principal Families, who were in the habit of entertaining such persons; among these were some Protestant families, but the Harpers frequented mostly the homes of old Irish families, who had lost their titles, or were reduced more or less in their estates. These they would visit once in two or three years, and remain from a week to a month in each house, and it was generally a day of rejoicing among the young and the old, when one of these itinerants appeared. As to the character of O'Neill, I found him a perfectly safe companion, a man of veracity and integrity, not at all addicted to boasting, or pretending to anything extraordinary, he never affected to compose or alter any tune, but played it exactly as he had been taught by his Master, 'Hugh O'Neill,' for whom he expressed always great veneration.

I think, therefore, you may rely with the greatest confidence upon any information he gave you, as to the technical names of the strings and parts of the harp, and names of the different notes, or strokes upon the harp. He was as incapable as he would have been uninclined to have invented these terms, which I think of great consequence as connected with the literary History of Music; and if in the course of human events your singular ingenuity, zeal and success, in discovering those ancient airs, shall be the means of preserving O'Neill's name also from oblivion, it will always gratify me to remember that I was the means of introducing you to each other.— And I am, Dear Bunting, most sincerely yours,

J. MacDonnell.

Nov 8th '38, Belfast.

A portrait sketch of Arthur O'Neill appears among the plates published in the 1809 volume to illustrate the introductory article on the Harp.

It is in simple outline on a page which includes illustrations of Grecian and Egyptian manipulators of various stringed instruments. Two characteristic sketches, from which this little picture was derived, are among our manuscripts. In one O'Neill is represented as asking, "How does my coat fit me, Mike?" And it will be seen that our harper was very particular about his dress. At one of the Granard festivals he lost his chance of the largest money premium through looking better dressed and less necessitous than his rival, Fanning. Mr John McCracken was, without doubt, the artist of these sketches, as all the plates in the 1809 volume are stated to be from his drawings.

On the break up of the first Belfast Harp Society, O'Neill retired to his native district on his pension of thirty pounds a year. This was, as already stated, in 1813. He died at Maydown, County Armagh, 29th October 1816, at the age of eighty-eight. His harp is preserved in the museum of the Belfast Natural History and Philosophical Society, College Square North, an institution which is in process of being acquired by the municipal authorities. On the occasion of the celebration of the centenary of the birth of Sir Samuel Ferguson, an exhibition was held in the Municipal Art Gallery, consisting of relics and manuscripts of the poet. On this occasion O'Neill's harp was given an honoured place in a glass case along with the MS. of Ferguson's essay, in which many of the old harper's anecdotes were included.

Along with it was an exquisitely carved model facsimile of the so-called harp of Brian Borou, which O'Neill had restrung and played on in Limerick.

Arthur O'Neill's last resting-place is said to be in the Churchyard of Eglish, which is between Armagh and Dungannon in County Tyrone. Accompanied by the Rev. W. T. Latimer, a well-known Ulster historian and antiquarian, resident at Eglish, my sister visited this churchyard and a careful search was made for the harper's grave. Mr Latimer states that according to tradition it was somewhere about the middle of the churchyard, near to a broken gravestone. Neither on the occasion of my sister's visit nor at any time since has he been able to find the broken stone, and surmises that the fragments have been carried away, and with them the last landmark indicating the whereabouts of O'Neill's grave. That it had not been marked by a headstone Mr Latimer concludes from the following lines in a poem entitled 'Exile Musings', written by Patrick Mallon, a native of Eglish, in 1871.

> *Oft have I searched your graveyard*
> *To scan the tombstones old,*
> *Where Friar prayed and fathers famed*
> *Lie in your sacred mould,*
> *And Harpers sweet whose magic notes*
> *Throughout the land were known*
> *Neglected sleep in tranquil grave*
> *Without a cross or stone.*

Considering that his own grave is thus unmarked, O'Neill's description of the grave of Carolan in the following *Memoir* will have added pathos and significance!

BIRTH, EDUCATION, AND FIRST JOURNEY
THROUGH IRELAND

I was born (1737) in Drumnistad in the County of Tyrone. My Father and Mother were named O'Neill,[1] their father and mother's names were O'Neill, and my Great Grand-father and Great Grandmother's names were O'Neill, and as far as I can learn their Ancestors both male and female were all named O'Neill, and at this day I have not a relation, either male or female, from the first to the last degree, to the best of my knowledge, but are all of the name of O'Neill.

In consequence of which there is a family pride amongst the O'Neill's, both rich and poor, of the County of Tyrone, conceiving themselves descended from Hugh, Con and John O'Neill of the Tyrone family, who were in no manner allied with the O'Neill's of Shane's Castle,[2] in the County of Antrim.

At the age of two years I was diverting myself with a pen-knife which pierced my right eye, but was not deprived of the sight of it immediately. I had a Grandmother who loved me to excess, and she, perceiving my eye in danger, sent everywhere for Oculists and Doctors to cure me. I had to submit to all their prescriptions, and the result was, that in their efforts to cure one eye, I unfortunately lost the sight of both, and I have now

---

[1.] Harper O'Neill was a true Clansman of the great Northern tribe, whose line of Chieftains gave sovereign over-lords to Ireland for many centuries with scarce a break. The dominance of the ancestor of the O'Neills lasted practically from the time of Con of the Hundred Fights in the second century to the rise of Brian Borou in the tenth century, when rivalry with the Southern tribe weakened the central regal authority of the country. It is most interesting to note in the harper's account of the Milesian gathering at Killarney, how the descendants of the Southern Clans hailed the presence of an O'Neill with delight. In the reign of Queen Elizabeth the old regal clan had given two famous men to Ireland in the persons of Shane O'Neill and the later Hugh O'Neill, who was favourably remembered in Munster, as was also Owen Roe O'Neill, leader of the Ulster army in the Irish War.

[2.] The Shane's Castle O'Neills of modern days, were not regarded as true representatives of even the Clandeboye Branch of the great Northern family. In this phrase the harper echoes popular opinion.

no doubt on my mind, that if it were not for quacking I would have the perfect use of both my eyes at present. But there is an old adage in the Irish language, the meaning of which is in English, "The Grandmother's pet is an unlucky pet."

When I was about ten years old I commenced learning to play on the Harp under Owen Keenan of Augher, who frequented my Father's house for about two years, to instruct me, and afterwards I attended him in Augher about a year, at which I was allowed to play tolerably.

When I was about fifteen years old I commenced as an itinerant musician. My first adventure was to Ballycastle, where I fell in with Squire Boyd, whom I attended backwards and forwards occasionally. From Ballycastle I went to Shane's Castle, where I was introduced by the agent, a Mr O'Hara, as an O'Neill. I remained here a few days, and was well pleased when leaving that place with the treatment I received from Charles O'Neill,[3] Esq., the then proprietor.

From thence I made my way to Downpatrick, and thence to Newry, Dundalk, and Navan, in which last place I met Thady Elliott, who treated me very affectionately, I being but young and he middle-aged, and universally known as a Harper.

On Christmas Day Thady was to play at the Roman Catholic Chapel of Navan. A humorous fellow took Thady to a public-house and promised to give him a gallon of whiskey if he would rattle up 'Planxty Connor'[4] at the time of the Elevation, which Thady promised to do.

Accordingly, when Mass commenced on Christmas Day, Thady as usual played some sacred airs until the Elevation, when, for the sake of the whiskey, and to be as good as his word, he lifted up 'Planxty Connor'. The Priest, who was a good judge of music, knew the tune, but at that solemn stage of the ceremony he could not speak

---

3. The Shane's Castle O'Neills were not yet ennobled at the time of the harper's first visit.

4. 'Planxty Connor', a merry dance tune by Carolan.

to Thady, so to show his disapprobation he stamped violently where he stood at the Altar, so much so that the people exclaimed in Irish, "Dhar Dhiah thaw Soggart a dhounsa," that is "By God, the Priest is dancing." However, after playing 'Planxty Connor' for some time, he resumed his usual airs; but when Mass was over Thady was severely reproved and dismissed.

A Harry Fitzsimmons, a harper, happened to be in a gentleman's house in that quarter, who came that day to Navan to hear Mass, where I met him.

On Elliott's disgrace I was applied to by the priest to succeed him in the chapel, which I declined, not wishing to supersede Thady, who was always very civil to me, but I recommended Fitzsimmons, who readily accepted the offer, borrowed my harp, and played during the remainder of the Masses. In the interim, Thady, to be revenged of him, went to his lodging, got a long staff, and, coming back to the chapel, he offered any one of the congregation half of the whiskey if they would tell him when Fitzsimmons was coming out. Some of them agreed to, but on the priest coming out one fellow cried in Irish, "Tage, Dhar Dhia, Shin eh" (*Thady, by God, there he is*); with that Thady began to lay about him furiously, and made one desperate clipe, which struck the chapel door; if the priest had got it he would not have said Mass for a long time. However, Thady, who was as great a devil as ever lived, was so much vexed with his mistake that he went to the chapel and made a public apology for his behaviour.

After staying for some time in and about Navan, I went towards Dublin, from thence to Carlow, then to Wexford, from that to Waterford, from that to Kilkenny, from that to Clonmel, from that back to Carrick-on-Suir, where I fell in with a gentleman who was blind, named Oliver Size, an excellent harper who lived in great repute in that country. Although an itinerant he dressed very gaudy, wearing scarlet, and gold and silver lace. He treated me uncommonly friendly. I remained some time in Carrick with a clergyman named Thewles. I crossed from Carrick over again to Kilkenny, and there became acquainted with the Protestant and Roman Catholic Bishops. The Protestant Bishop's name was Dr Morris, a native of the County of Tyrone, who knew my father and some of my relations there, and I believe it induced him to be more civil to me than perhaps he otherwise would.

I frequently played in his Palace, and on my leaving Kilkenny he gave me a recommendation to such of the Clergy of his own or other dioceses as he knew, but I scarce made any use of them. I next came to Clonmel again, then crossed the River Suir into the County Waterford, and went to Cappoquin, from that to Youghal, then to Cork, in which place nothing particular occurred to me, not being eighteen years old at that time.

Near Cork I went to a gentleman's named Coppinger[5] of great rank and consequence, who treated me as if I was the son of a Prince of Ulster.

From Cork I went to Kinsale, where I fell in with the great Baron De Courcy, who kept a harper. I did not meet him but played upon his harp, which was a very fine one. I forgot to mention that when I was in Cork I got acquainted with a gentleman of the name of Bowling, who lived in Mallow Lane. He was rich but miserly. He liked music, and had a harp in his house that was made in Belgrade;[6] though it was as large as mine it did not weigh more than twelve pounds.

Not a man in Cork could tell what kind of wood it was made of. I played on it myself and never heard anything like it. I would have given him any money for it, but he would not part with it. Indeed, at that time I had not much money, and was as childish as when I set out. I was fond of sweet things, such as raisins, figs, prunes, gingerbread, etc., of which I

---

5. This family is still prominent in Ireland. Professor W. Butler, M.A., writing in the *Cork Archaeological Journal* on 'Town Life in Mediaeval Ireland,' groups them with families of Danish descent, and says the first Coppinger appears on the list of Mayors in 1319.

6. The officers of the Irish Brigade had popularised Irish music and the harp. This instrument had evidently been brought from abroad by some one who had relatives in the Austrian service. Munster was more in touch with the Continent than any province in Ireland. (See note on Murtogh O'Sullivan).

and my boy used to have our pockets eternally crammed. At this time I am sure I had never tasted whisky.

I travelled the principal part of the County Cork without anything occurring worth relating. I spent one Christmas with a gentleman that lived in Berehaven, named Murtagh MacOwen Sullivan,[7] who lived in a princely style.

My boy came to me one morning when in bed, and desired me to bless myself. I asked him "Why so?" "Och, sir," says he, "there is a pipe of wine and two hogsheads of some other liquor standing up in the hall, with the heads out of them, and a wooden cup swimming in each, for any one that likes to drink their skinfull." I mention this merely to record the hospitality of the gentlemen of the Province of Munster, nor was this the only instance of it, as similar occurrences happened to me during the time I travelled through that country.

Lord Kenmare,[8] the principal proprietor of Killarney, the lake,

---

7. This was without doubt the famous Murty Oge O'Sullivan whose romantic history is dealt with in Froude's novel, *The Two Chiefs of Dunboy*, Harper O'Neill gives his name somewhat inaccurately; he was Murtogh, son of Murtogh, son of Owen. He had served in the Irish Brigade on the Continent, and fought at the Battle of Fontenoy, also with the young Chevalier in his forty-five campaign, and at Culloden. Froude, however, confuses him with another O'Sullivan, who was Prince Charlie's right-hand man. Returning to his native territory of Berehaven, at the mouth of Bantry Bay, Murty Oge acted as a recruiting agent for the Irish Brigade, exporting shiploads of Cork and Kerry men to fill its ranks. The abundance of wine in his mansion would be accounted for by his constant communication with the Continent. Puxley, a Revenue officer, was placed at Berehaven by the English Government to watch his proceedings. Constant feuds ended by O'Sullivan killing Puxley, and being afterwards killed himself. The date of his death was 1754. A fine lament in Gaelic by one of his followers called O'Connell is traditionally preserved, and was printed in the *Cork Archaeological Journal*, 1892, with an admirable biography of O'Sullivan.

8. Though Lord Kenmare assembled this Milesian gathering he was not himself a representative of any Irish clan. His family name was Browne, and his ancestor had acquired by purchase and by patent from Queen Elizabeth certain lands of the MacCarthymore. The heir of the first settler married a daughter of the great O'Sullivan of Beara, who defended the Castle of Dunboy after the defeat of Hugh O'Neill and O'Donnell at Kinsale, 1601. After this we do not find on the genealogical tree any marriages between the Brownes and the native Irish. The title of Viscount Kenmare was conferred by James II. on Sir Valentine Browne, a Colonel in his

and the surrounding country, took it into his head about this time to give a Milesian entertainment, that is, to entertain at Christmas every Milesian that could be found who bore the name of an Irish chieftain, which names are the O'Neills, O'Briens, McCarthys, O'Donoughues, O'Driscolls, O'Connors, O'Donovans, O'Sullivans, O'Connor Kerrys, McNamaras, O'Keefes, O'Meaghers, O'Learys, O'Callaghans, O'Connells, O'Mahonys, MacGillacuddys, and some others of the Milesian race, that my memory at present will not enable me to mention.

At the feast there were one or more of every name already mentioned present, except an O'Neill. This Lord Kenmare drew attention to. "Och," says my patron Murtagh MacOwen O'Sullivan, "upon my honour, I can soon fill up that gap for you, as I have now at my house a young blind man from the North who plays very well for his years, and from what I understand from his own lips he has a good claim to represent the O'Neills on this occasion." I was sent for accordingly, and without any ceremony, seated myself amongst them in the great hall. Hundreds of questions were asked me concerning my descent, and on my giving satisfactory answers, I was dubbed and deemed an O'Neill. They all said I had a good face.

When dinner was announced, very near a hundred of the O's and

---

army, and staunch adherent of his cause, who forfeited his estates on the Williamite revolution. His heir recovered the lands, but the title was not recognised in law till 1798, when the Browne of that time gave proof of his loyalty, on the French invasion of Bantry Bay. The French fleet were probably influenced in their choice of Bantry Bay as a landing-place, because of the old familiarity of French seamen with the place during the Irish Brigade recruiting era. Irish Jacobites of the South were, however, by no means favourable to the French revolutionists.

Kenmare's "Milesian Assembly," taking place a few years after Culloden, was very likely a Jacobite muster; the deference shown to the name of O'Neill, though only represented by a wandering harper, is significant of a certain national and political feeling. Those present had doubtless in mind Hugh O'Neill's league with the great Munster chieftains before the disaster of Kinsale. It is recorded to the honour of Munster that at a time when the English, by fomenting clan differences, found it easy to engage spies and informers against the different chieftains, no one could be found to inform on the military tactics of O'Neill during his march to the South. Such was the reverence for his regal name.

Macs took their seat. My poor self being blind, I did what blind men generally do, I groped a vacancy near the foot of the table. Such a noise arose of cutting carving, roaring, laughing, shaking hands, and such language as generally occurs between friends, who only see each other once a year. While dinner was going on I was hobnobbed by nearly every gentleman present. When Lord Kenmare hobnobbed me he was pleased to say, "O'Neill, you should be at the head of the table, as your ancestors were the original Milesians of this Kingdom." "My Lord," I replied "it's no matter where an O'Neill sits, let it be at any part of the table, wherever I am should be considered the head of it."

A universal burst of applause ensued, and my arm was almost shaken from my body by all present, and I believe it was in consequence of my reply to his Lordship, which they remarked, came by instinct to an O'Neill, and damn the O'Neill that ever was born, or ever will yet be born as well as myself, but was drank by all the Milesians then present. The gentleman who represented the O'Connor Kerrys after dinner took my harp and to my astonishment played a few tunes in the first style I ever heard by a gentleman of fortune. He afterwards shifted the harp into my hands, I played several tunes for which I received some compliments. But if King David came down to the hall of Lord Kenmare and played his best tunes for that set of gentlemen, they would have made him stop the best tune he ever played to drink to the real Irish. Harmony was lost whenever the Port and Claret began to box each other in decanters at all parts of the table. Then the cloth was removed, and the carpet was generally the bed for the principal part of the visitors. At that time, too, it was a common thing to drink a dram in the morning, to fulfil the old saying "The dog that bit you, a lock of his hair will cure you."

As I mentioned that a MacGillacuddy was one of the Milesians present, I was informed that once on a time, taking his seat in Dublin for the Stage coach, he gave in his name to a woman who kept the book, but she did not understand him and seemed confused. "Give me the book, my good woman," says he, "and I will enter it myself." "Thank you, Sir," says the female clerk, handing him the book, in which he entered the name of "Jeffrey MacShefferov MacGillacuddy." On looking it over she informed him that the children must pay half price, thinking that the length of his name would occupy the whole coach.

When I left Lord Kenmare I heard of the beauties of the Lake, which I witnessed in every sense except seeing them, and as far as my judgment, besides what I have been informed, the lake cannot be sufficiently described, but Garrick's,[9] the celebrated actor's, account came nearest to my imagination.

When I left the County Kerry my next tour was towards Limerick. I met a Counsellor MᶜNamara, then Recorder of Limerick, who invited me to his country house, about five miles from the City, called Castle Connell, where I was well received. In his house in Limerick, he had the skeleton of Brian Borou's harp,[10] and in consequence of the national esteem I held for the memory of its owner, I strung it, and then tuned it; it had not been strung for upwards of two hundred years before. It was made of cedar. Counsellor MᶜNamara requested

---

9. Garrick's description of Killarney. Mr W. J. Lawrence of Dublin, a well-known authority on the history of the drama, on being referred to wrote me: "Although I have a thorough knowledge of Garrick's life story, and have read not only all he wrote but everything of importance written about him, I never heard of his description of Killarney. He paid two visits to Dublin, the first in 1742 and the last in 1745. At the termination of each he returned at once to London. He never acted elsewhere in Ireland." Arthur O'Neill may have heard some other well-known actor's eulogy and have attributed it to Garrick.

10. An ancient and beautiful instrument, popularly known as Brian Borou's harp, is now preserved in the Library of Trinity College, Dublin. This was the instrument which was in Limerick during O'Neill's visit. The leading antiquarian authorities have not been able to decide as to its origin, but agree there is no evidence save tradition to connect it with the famous King Brian. Petrie, in Bunting's 1840 volume, wrote a learned dissertation and concludes that this was most likely an ecclesiastical harp of the 13ᵗʰ century, and the property of an O'Neill. Eugene O'Curry, in his *Manners and Customs of the Ancient Irish*, brings forward evidence to prove that the harp was likely one which is famous in ancient Gaelic song as the harp of Donogh Carbery O'Brien, a descendant and successor of King Brian. (*See* interesting references to it and translation of a poem in Dr Sigerson's volume of *Translations from the Irish Bards of the Gael and Gall.*)

me to tie it about my neck and play it through that hospitable city, which I agreed to, being young and strong.

The first tune I happened to strike on was 'Ellen Oge', now generally called 'Savoureen Deelish'. I played several other Irish tunes, and was followed by a procession of upwards of five hundred people, both gentle and simple. They seemed to be every one imbibed with the national spirit, when they heard it was the instrument that our celebrated Irish monarch played upon, before he routed the Danes at Clontarf, out of poor Erin. The Lord be merciful to you Brian Borou. I hope in God, I will tune your harp again in your presence in heaven, and if it should be the case, upon my honour and conscience I will not play the tunes of the 'Protestant Boys', or 'July the First'; but I would willingly play 'God Save the King', and that would be yourself, Brian. I understand that the Harp is now in the Museum in Dublin College.

When I left the county of Limerick, I went through the towns of Six Mile Bridge, Ennis, Gort, Athenree, Galway, Loughrea, Tuam, Ballinasloe. I then crossed over to Castlebar, Ballinrobe, Sligo, Leitrim, Carrick-on-Shannon, Roscommon. Then crossed Rousky Bridge, which divides Connaught from Leinster, through which the Shannon runs; then to Longford, Granard, Cavan, Enniskillen, Ballyshannon, Donegal, Mount Charles, then to Boylagh and the Rosses,[11] the wildest country I ever was in.

I passed through all these towns without anything happening worthy of notice, but was treated in the usual manner as well as itinerant harpers generally are. When at Boylagh I was invited by a gentleman, called Nesbitt, to go with him to a great wedding without my harp, for there were plenty of pipers and fiddlers. There was no expense spared to make it a grand wedding. The gentleman bridegroom's name was McGunnigall, and the lady's name, O'Donnell. There were as many people present as almost at any fair. All that wished to stay over night had to sit up, the

---

11. A barren rocky district on the west coast of Donegal. The land is periorated with lakes, the sea strewn with islands, a peculiar ragged appearance being given to the whole country. The blind harper could not, of course, get this impression, but would miss the shelter of a single tree, and be much impeded by the rough roads.

beds being occupied by scores lying *three-na-y'hela* (through other).

Mr Nesbitt and I sat up all night, and in the morning he made a remarkable breakfast for the remaining guests. He burned a large quantity of whiskey in a wooden bowl, put a pair of tongs across it when burning, and then he put some canes of sugar-candy on the tongs, which was soon dissolved into the whiskey, and then the party present drank of it with bread, for my part I never got a breakfast I liked so well, as at that time I began to be partial to that native cordial.

When I left Mr Nesbitt's, I was almost tired of rambling through the kingdom, and formed the design of going home to see them. I must remark that on my travels, described in this narrative, I was always sure to be well treated, when employed by any gentleman; to eat of the best, exclusive of drinking the best of liquors and wines, when I pleased, and the different gratuities I generally received were handed to me privately and genteelly. By the time I came to Dungannon, near my native place, I had some good clothes with some little money saved.

After this, my first journey, I rested myself with my parents for some time, improving myself in my profession. At this period, I was about twenty or twenty-one years of age (being now about sixty-seven), and it was in or about the year of 1760 I finished this my first tour.

CHAPTER XV

MEMOIRS OF ARTHUR O'NEILL
SECOND JOURNEY

AFTER REMAINING SOME YEARS WITH MY PARENTS AND FRIENDS IN AND about Dungannon, I felt an itching for rambling once more. The first place I went to was to a Colonel White of Redhill in the County of Cavan, with whom I remained seven years, sometimes with neighbouring gentlemen, particularly with a Mr Morris Thompson, who lived within a mile and a half of the Colonel's; with him I spent every Saturday night during that period. I spent my time very pleasantly between Colonel White and Mr Thompson. One Saturday night in particular, I recollect Mr Thompson was so fond of the tune of 'Past one o'clock' that we both *tête-a-tête* finished four bottles of good old wine, I playing the tune all the time, except when lifting my hand to my head.

I formed the idea of remaining with the Colonel during his life, he being a bachelor, and some said a woman hater. There was a fellow named William Saunderson, by origin a relative of Colonel Saunderson's;[1] this fellow conducted all Colonel White's domestic concerns, though no scholar. This fellow got jealous of me, as the Colonel was very fond of me, he was eternally tale-bearing to him. There was a Munster girl named Winnie Burke, a housemaid there, on whom this Saunderson pressed his attentions. She very prudently resisted him, and to mortify him the more told him that she preferred me. This so exasperated him the more, and he became so disagreeable to me, that I determined to leave the Colonel, much against his will.

During the time I remained with the Colonel I went to Colonel

---

[1.] This is the ancestor of the Unionist leader and orator, the late Colonel Edward Saunderson, whose statue has been erected in Portadown, Co. Armagh, in March 1910, in recognition of his political services, during the Parnellite era. It is interesting to find that in the eighteenth century, the Saundersons, who may be described as Cromwellian settlers, were patrons of the Irish harpers.

Saunderson, about two miles distant, where I spent about a month. On my return to Redhill there was a general report through the house that my room was haunted, which the Colonel himself told me; but I insisted on sleeping in the same room, which I did. I was not long in bed when I heard a strong and curious noise in the chimney. I bounced out of bed and groped to the place, thrust my hands up, and caught a large owl which had a nest in the chimney that by some means fell down. The owl lay quiet all day, but endeavoured to get up by night, making a frightful noise in the effort, which confirmed the superstitious servants that it must be a ghost. However, I secured the poor bird, and brought it down to the Colonel, who seemed so well pleased that he put fifteen guineas into my hand, saying that he would not for anything have it reported that his house was haunted.

When I left the Colonel I steered through the chief part of the County of Cavan, from one gentleman's seat to another, without carrying my own harp, as there was scarce a gentleman's house I touched at, but there was one. The harpers found in that country were Ned McCormac, James McGovern, Owen Clarke, Patrick Maguire, Simon Hunter, Phil Reilly, Francis Reilly, John Clarke, Ned Brady, Michael Duigenan, Nelly Smith, Kate Martin, Paddy Kerr, and Owen Corr. McCormac was by far the best harper of them all. In the County Tyrone I met three brothers, named Ned, James, and Frank McAleer, who all played very well on the harp, but Ned was far the best. He was very comical; he lived upwards of five years in France in the Irish Brigades, and would sometimes assume the title of the celebrated 'Leeriano from Paris,' as he could speak the French language very fluently. He was a slave to that pernicious beverage that generally leaves itinerants in that situation that they will either pledge their own or any gentleman's harp sooner than want it. Pox on you, Carolan, you must certainly have been half mulvardered when you composed your receipt for drinking whiskey, otherwise I am sure you would never have been a composer, as the effect of that cordial had so happy an effect on you that your ideas floated faster on you than they might have done, if there was no such liquor to be had.

At one time, when poor Ned McAleer assumed the name of 'Leeriano,' he went to a Counsellor Stewart of Baillieborough, in the County Cavan, which time Harry Fitzsimmons, the harper, was there. Leeriano was announced. He was ordered to play in the hall as a specimen, where there were some tailors then at work for the servants. Leeriano began to play some Irish tunes, jigs, reels, etc. Mrs Stewart, after some time, came from the parlour to the hall, and told him she was much disappointed, as some of her own countrymen could excel him. McAleer, chagrined, started up and exclaimed, "Madam, as you were pleased to order me to play in the hall, I played you tailors' and servants' music, which would otherwise be different." "Damn your soul, you trumping rascal," says one of the snips, bouncing off the floor, and was going to destroy poor McAleer with his goose, and if it was not for some interference, he was determined to avenge the mighty insult. Fitzsimmons knew McAleer, who undeceived Mrs Stewart respecting his foreign descent, and was probably jealous with him, as McAleer was much the best performer.

When I left the County Cavan, I rambled into the County of Tyrone, where I fell in occasionally with different harpers. The first and best who claimed my attention was poor Paddy Ryan, my dear lamented friend, next to Hugh O'Neill (hereinafter mentioned).

His father was a Munster man, and an excellent performer, and indeed Paddy was not inferior to any man I ever heard on the harp. He was not blind, and, exclusive of what I knew and was informed of him, he was pregnant with sentiments of honour and unlimited friendship to every person, which he evinced to me in a particular manner. He was destitute of the low ideas of jealousy common amongst itinerants; he took pains, and taught me several tunes, which, however, I now forget. I met my old master, Owen Keenan, who was glad to see me; I also met Hugh Quin, who was taught by Con Lyons. He was a gentleman's son, and as such conducted himself, and was one of the best of Lyon's pupils. He was not blind. I met a John McCrory, a blind harper, who was a middling player. I met my namesake Peggy O'Neill, who played very decently on the harp. She played all Carolan's Planxtys extremely well.

I met a Charles Byrne, I who was taught by his uncle on the harp. This man had many advantages, not being blind. He was a good player. He had an excellent memory, and could recount all the little incidents that happened to him during the time he led his blind uncle through the kingdom. I heard him sing a good many Irish songs in an agreeable style and pleasing voice.

Arthur Short was the next and last harper I met in the County of Tyrone at this time. He was not quite blind. The first specimen I heard of his abilities was at my father's house. He was but an indifferent performer. This man was very peevish, he generally travelled without a guide. I was informed he was about a hundred times married, The harper who competed at the Granard and Belfast Festivals, sometimes called Berreen. (*See* Biography in Chapter XIII.) but never heard how many children he had. I was informed he had one son who was a performer, beyond the common.

I knew and met Hugh Higgins[2] in all my peregrinations. He supported the character of a gentleman-harper, was uncommon genteel in his manners, and spared no expense in his dress. He travelled in such a manner as does and will do credit to an Irish harper. Hugh was born in a place called Tyrally, in the County of Mayo, of very decent parents; his mother's name was Burke. He lost his sight at an early period, and was bound to learn the harp, on which my dear deceased friend made such a proficiency as to rank him one of the best I ever heard.

When I left the Counties of Cavan, and Tyrone, I formed a notion of going into the County of Roscommon in Connaught, to see my dear friend Hugh O'Neill. We met by appointment at a Mr McDonnell's of Knockrantry in that county, who saw an immensity of the first company to be had.

There was at this time, which was about thirty years ago, a patron, or kind of a meeting not unlike a fair, held in that quarter, and Mr McDonnell's house was full of company when I met Hugh there. Amongst the rest of the guests there was a young nobleman from Germany, named the Marquis of Devianne. I was curious to know the cause of his coming to Ireland, and

---

2. A competitor at Belfast Festival, 1792 (see Chap.XIII.)

was informed he fell in love with a beautiful lady in his own country; but his parents not approving of the match, they diverted his attention from it by sending him over to this kingdom, to take possession of an estate, in the County Roscommon in right of his mother. From what I myself could guess, and from what an accomplished countryman of my own told me, he was one of the most finished and accomplished young noblemen he ever saw.

Hugh and I played our very best tunes for a long time. The Marquis was at a loss how to call for the tune of 'Past one o'clock', or 'Thaw me ma Cullagh naur dhourska me', which he heard played somewhere before. He perceived me going towards the door, and followed me, and informed me that there was a man that made boots for him whose name was Tommy MacCullough, and it was like the tune by saying, "Tommy MacCullagh made boots for me". In the broad way he pronounced it, it was not unlike the Irish name of it. I went in with him and played it, on which he seemed uncommonly happy, and informed the company all round it was his choice.

This young nobleman was some time afterwards afflicted with that ugly disease the small-pox, and Roderick O'Connor,[3] the then

---

3. The O'Connors were the kingly family of Connaught. At the time of the Norman invasion Roderick O'Conner was Ard-righ of Ireland. Harper O'Neill is not ironical in his allusion to the regal title and the little palace. Lady Morgan in her *Memoirs* tells of a dinner-party at which she met the O'Connor of her day, " as legitimate a representative of the supreme Kings of Ireland as any sovereign on or off his throne at this moment in Europe," who behaved with great coolness towards another guest, the Honourable Mr Ffrench, M.P. Pressed by Lady Morgan for an explanation, he poured forth a history of wrong and robbery wrought by the Ffrenches. "But when," said Lady Morgan, "did this happen? Lately?" "Well, not very long ago, in the last years of the reign of Queen Elizabeth." The title of O'Connor Don is still retained, and the late holder of it played a somewhat prominent part in politics. In 1895 the Royal Society of Antiquaries of Ireland, making a western tour, was entertained by the O'Connor Don to a hospitable luncheon within the walls of Ballintubber Castle. The O'Connor Don on that day was jubilant over the fact that he had quite recently acquired this castle, which had been out of the possession of his family for a length of time, and it evidently delighted him, in his character of an Irish Chieftain, to feast upwards of a hundred guests within the ancestral walls. The marquee in which the luncheon was served was pitched inside the ruin.

nominal Monarch of Connaught invited the Marquis to his little palace at Cloonalis, where, notwithstanding every exertion of the faculty, he died at the age of about twenty-two or three of that disorder.

At this time I went no further into Connaught, and made my way home again through the County of Leitrim, where I met a John Sneyd, but a very indifferent harper. In consequence of his being a great thief, so much so that he got the nickname of "Long Glue-fingered Jack" (he being very tall), I avoided him.

I then made the best of my way to Charles Fanning's father's house, where I met father and son, with whom I remained about three weeks very happy, during which time I attended many weddings and haulings home, where the national customs were all supported with the usual conviviality incident to the circumstances and abilities of the parties.

I next came into the County of Cavan, and visited my old friend, Colonel White, who received me very well. My old enemy Saunderson was there also, who affected some friendship to me. I next visited my old haunts in that county, and taught some scholars there, one of the best of whom was a Biddy Reilly, who was blind, who played very prettily before I quit that county. I next came into the County of Tyrone, and made my way home to my parents, whom I found alive and well. My mother was curious to know whether I saved any money; but my father seemed well content, if I returned whole and clean.

I was, after this second return from rambling, almost stationary between the Counties of Cavan and Tyrone, so much so that I spent eighteen successive Christmas days at the house of a Philip O'Reilly of the County of Cavan, without meeting with any harper worth notice but some of those already mentioned.

I forgot to mention in its proper place, like many other of my mistakes, that when I was perambulating part of the County of Antrim I stopped at the Glenns, near which I called at the house of Michael

MacDonnell[4] and Elizabeth MacDonnell (otherwise Stewart), his wife. I was uncommonly well received, and they expressed a desire that their three sons, Randal, James, and Alexander, should be taught by me.

The hospitality, disinterested friendship, and other favours and attentions shown to me in their hospitable mansion called Vawl iska or Watermouth, was not exceeded in all my peregrinations through this kingdom.

Randal MacDonnell enjoyed all the sporting comforts that romantic country admitted, and without adulation (not caring a pin into whose hands these unconnected Memoirs may fall) he was uncommonly abstemious from the toys incident to the chase, fowling, etc. He made a tolerable proficiency for his time on the harp. James (the now senior doctor) made some proficiency also, but he then appeared to me to have a partiality for some other study, and which, I am now happy to be informed, ranks him amongst the class of his profession.

Alexander, the now junior doctor, made the best attempt of the three in my opinion, his juvenile years being much in his favour, and before I left him he played very handsomely. I cannot account how I acquired the friendship of the three gentlemen above named, as it always was, and now is, exercised towards me in the most unlimited manner.

Long before my starting into the musical world there were two performers on the harp that almost totally eclipsed every one mentioned by me heretofore. The first was Murphy, whose father was a hawker of his instrument, and an uncommon poor dhoul (or devil) of a player, and, as far as I can learn, both father and son were both born in Leinster. But as for the son's excellence, I never heard in my travels so much praise given to any harper by all the musicians that heard him. He was well aware of

---

4. The father of Dr MacDonnell was son of Alexander MacDonnell, son of Coll —a Voulin or Coll of the Mill— who had lands in County Antrim after the death of his famous father the Alastair or Sir Alexander MacDonnell, leader in the rising of Montrose, killed at Cnocnanoss, County Cork, in 1647. The doctor's father lived near Glenarrif, County Antrim, and had been twice married. Arthur O'Neill mentions his sons of two families.

his abilities, and never spared an opportunity of boasting of them. He was in France in the reign of Louis XIV., and Murphy's fame reached the ears of that great monarch, who sent for him, and was so well pleased with his performance that he rewarded him in a kingly manner, as he himself said. He came home in the dress and style of a great count. His father heard of his being in Dublin, and at last made out where young Murphy was in high company, who was so vexed at his father's shabby appearance, that he very dutifully kicked the poor old man downstairs.

Cornelius Lyons was the other great performer, and a very fanciful composer, especially in his variations to the tunes of 'Eileen Aroon', 'Calleena a voch a thoo Shorsha' ('Girls, did you see George?'), 'Green Sleeves', 'The Coolin', and several others.

He was a County Kerry man, and by all accounts he was a superior character to Murphy as a gentleman, and in his profession as good a performer. They were both acquaintances of Carolan's, who could never abide Murphy on account of his lofty impudence.

Carolan was one night in Castleblayney, in a public house, when Murphy strutted in, and made some acrimonious speech against Carolan, saying that his compositions were like "bones without beef."

"Damn me," says Carolan in a fret, "but I'll compose a tune before I quit you, and you may put what beef you please on the bones of it." With that he left his seat, and cautiously stealing behind Murphy seized him by the hair of his head, dragged, and kicked him through the room unmercifully. During which time Murphy's screeches could be heard at a great distance; Carolan saying to him all the time he was roaring "put beef to that air, you puppy." But for some interference he would not have left a drop in Murphy.

It was quite the reverse between Carolan and Lyons, who were on the most intimate footing, as Lyons admired Carolan and his works. By all I ever heard speak of him, he was gentlemanly, civil, good-natured, and obliging, to all descriptions, especially to brother harpers. Lyons was at one time at the house of Mr Archdall, in the County Fermanagh, at which time Carolan happened to be there, and Lyons heard him composing the tune of 'Mrs Archdall', and as Carolan could not see him, Lyons wrote down the music, as fast as Carolan composed it, which was but middling fast, as on the harp Carolan was no great performer. Mr Archdall and Lyons planned a joke, which terminated in the following manner.

There was an itinerant harper called Charlie Berreen,[5] that Carolan detested very much. Mr Archdall, knowing this to be the case, threw up the window where they were sitting, and exclaimed: "Upon my word, here is Berreen coming," which vexed Carolan very much. But upon the expostulation of Mr Archdall concerning hospitality, and the crime attached to the breach of it, Carolan consented to his supposed admission.

Lyons had a servant named McDermott, who could play exceeding well on the harp and a very humorous fellow. Lyons and McDermott went into the hall, Lyons took the harp, and McDermott placed himself behind his master to answer any question Carolan might put to the supposed Berreen, Carolan well knowing Lyon's voice.

Lyons began to play the tune of 'Mrs Archdall' in the poorest manner he could, to imitate Berreen, who was but a poor performer, and McDermott could well counterfeit his voice. Carolan began to prance and dance with madness about the parlour, and roared out to the supposed Berreen to know where he got the tune.

"Och," says McDermott, "I have that tune this ten years and upwards."

"You are a damned liar and villain," exclaimed Carolan, "and if it was the devil taught you, you have it only since last night."

There was a public stocks near Mr Archdall's house, and Carolan told Mr A____ that if Berreen was not immediately put into them, he would never come near his house, on which McDermott made a pretended loud and strong resistance, but was dragged to the stocks, on which he sat down, and a noise was made as of putting in his legs. But Carolan was not yet satisfied without beating the plagiarist, and made a great blow of his cane at him, which McDermott avoided. At last Carolan suspected he was deceived, and seemed so unhappy that Mr Archdall and Lyons had to explain the whole to him, on

---

5. The blind uncle of Charles Byrne, or Berreen, mentioned previously.

which he laughed, and seemed well satisfied, then shook hands, and thanked him for his usual good-humour.

The present Marchioness of Antrim's great-grandfather and Lyons were almost inseparable. His Lordship was both a wit and a poet, and delighted in the system of equality, where vulgarity was not too gross. At one time he and Lyons when in London heard of a famous Irish harper, named Heffernan, that kept a tavern there. His Lordship and Lyons went there, but beforehand they formed the following plan.

"I'll call you cousin Burke," says his Lordship. "You may either call me cousin Randal, or My Lord, as you please."

After regaling for some time, Heffernan was called up, who was by this time well aware of the dignity of his guest, by the talk and livery of his Lordship's servants. When Heffernan came into the room he was desired to bring in his harp, and sit down, which was done.

Heffernan played a good many tunes in a grand style, but his Lordship, wishing to astonish the landlord, called upon his cousin Burke to play a tune. The supposed cousin made many apologies, but at length took the harp and played some of his best airs; on which Heffernan exclaimed aloud: "My Lord, you may call him cousin Burke, or what cousin you please, but damn me but he plays upon Lyon's fingers."

What was extraordinary was that Heffernan never saw Lyons before. His Lordship undeceived Heffernan, and desired them to enjoy themselves together, and to challenge the world on the harp; he then retired to some other appointment.

In my travels I became acquainted with a Dominic Mungan, I may say I had known him since I was twelve years old. He was born blind in the County of Tyrone, and a real good harper. He was a Roman Catholic. I presume my following reason will plead an apology for mentioning his religion. He was a great economist, but would spend money as genteelly as any man occasionally.

He had three sons, Mark, John, and Terence, whom he educated in the first style. Mark was educated for a priest, and finished his studies in France, in the College of Lombard, where he obtained upwards of forty premiums for his translations of Greek into French. After he finished his studies he came home, but in consequence of his intense application he fell into a decay, and died in his father's house in Strabane.

John, the second son, was bred a physician, and practised in and about Monaghan, and the adjacent country, with good reputation. About five years ago as he was returning from the races of Middleton in Monaghan in his gig he was upset and smashed to pieces.

Terence, the third and youngest son, is now Bishop of Limerick, and was formerly Dean of Ardagh. He had a good delivery, sung well, and acquired great interest. He and a priest O'Beirne, who was Chaplain to Lord Fitzwilliam when Lord-Lieutenant of Ireland, were promoted to their present ranks of Protestant Bishops.

Now my reason for mentioning the Roman Catholic persuasion is this, that the doctor and the bishop both read their recantations; the doctor before and the bishop after their father's death. He in his lifetime used to travel the north-west circuit with his harp, and at one time, as he was playing for one of the Judges, he asked Dominic his reasons for not speaking to his son, the doctor, since he turned Protestant.

"My Lord," says Dominic, "I spared no expense on him when he was unable to provide for himself; and assure your Lordship, I am no bigot; but I think it was his duty to consult me before he changed his religion. It was not, however, for the sake of religion he did so, but he fell in love with a young lady who was a Protestant. She informed him she could not have him as he was a Papist, on which he read his recantation, and then demanded her hand, on which, to his mortification, she scornfully informed him that she would be sorry to marry a turncoat."

These anecdotes I merely mention when speaking of Dominick Mungan, without the slightest idea of offending the two bishops, more especially as these are well-known facts.

When Carolan died he left an only son and three daughters, and these lived in the County of Louth. The celebrated Dean Delany[6] delighted in Carolan so much, that he took young Carolan by the hand with the intention of opening a subscription for the purpose of defraying all expenses in reviving and recovering all his father's compositions.

Young Carolan was but a tolerable performer on the harp, and totally destitute of any talent for composition. However, the Dean never ceased until he obtained a subscription to the amount of one thousand six hundred pounds or thereabouts, on which young Carolan made some attempts to represent his father; but his productions were scandalous, as I often heard, and Master Carolan becoming tired of industry, after humbugging the good-natured Dean for some time, formed an acquaintance with another man's wife in Ballymahon in the County of Longford, took her to London, where I am informed he died, when the residue of the one thousand six hundred pounds was spent, or otherwise disposed of between him and his Dulcinea. There is an immensity of ancient Irish music lost in consequence of the attachment harpers latterly have for modern tunes, which are now chiefly in vogue, the national airs and tunes being confined to a few gentlemen in the different provinces I have travelled through; and, without the most distant idea of any view or interest, I here declare that if it was not in consequence of the unprecedented, and I may say truly inspired genius of a gentleman[7] of Belfast, whose name I will have occasion to mention hereafter, the compositions of Dibden, and some other modern composers would, in a very few years, be the means of annihilating our dear Irish music.

---

6. The Rev. Patrick Delany, born in 1686, educated at Trinity College, Dublin, became a friend of Swift's. In 1743 Dr Delany, then a widower, married Mrs Mary Delany, a widow of literary and social distinction. They lived at Delville Glasnevin, Dublin, till Dr Delany was appointed Dean of Down, when they went to reside in the north. Mrs Delany is described as "stitching at shirts and shifts for the poor naked wretches in the neighbour-hood," whilst cheered by the music of her Irish harper. This was the son of Carolan referred to by O'Neill. The Dean died in Bath, 1768, Mrs Delany survived till 1788.

7. Edward Bunting.

I again make bold to say, that when the gentleman I allude to will be no more, his laborious exertions, to recover and revive our dying Irish music, should record him and his memory in a manner much beyond what my poor abilities could attempt to dictate. I heard a few tunes of the gleanings of young Carolan played, which I thought tolerably decent, but when I heard them and the chief part of his father's works played by the gentleman I alluded to I imagined myself in a manner enchanted.

There was a harper before my time, named Jerome Duigenan, a native of the County of Leitrim (not blind), an excellent Greek and Latin scholar, and a charming performer. I heard numerous anecdotes of him, one of which happened when he lived with a Colonel Jones at Drumshambo, a representative in Parliament for the County Leitrim.

The Colonel went to Dublin at the meeting of Parliament, where he fell in company with an English nobleman, who brought a Welsh harper with him, who played very well. Having played some tunes before the Colonel, the nobleman asked him if he ever heard so sweet a singer. "Yes," replied the Colonel, "and that a man who never wears either linen or woollen."

"I will bet you a hundred guineas," says the nobleman, "you can't produce anyone that can exceed my harper." The bet being taken up, the Colonel wrote immediately for Duigenan to Drumshambo, to come with all speed to Dublin, and to bring his harp and his suit of cauthic, that is, a dress made of beaten rushes with something like a caddy or plaid of the same stuff.

Duigenan came post haste, and on his arrival in Dublin went to the Colonel's lodgings, who acquainted Jeremy and a great number of the members of the House of Commons with the nature of the bet.

The members requested it should be decided in the Parliament House before business commenced. The two harpers performed before the members, and it was unanimously decided in Duigenan's favour, particularly by the English nobleman who exclaimed, "Damn you, why don't you wear better clothes?" "Och," says Duigenan, "I lost my all by a law-suit, and my old nurse for spite won't let me wear any other clothes."

"Damn me, but you shall," says the nobleman, and then putting a guinea in his own hat he carried it round through the other members, who every one threw in a guinea each, so that the hat was nearly half full, and the sum was put into Duigenan's pocket . . . . Duigenan was in the full cauthic,[8] dress, and wore a cap of the same stuff, shaped like a sugar loaf, with many tassels. He was a tall, handsome man, and looked very well in it. Poor Jeremy contrived to spend the chief part of his money before he left Dublin.

I knew an Ackland Keane,[9] a blind harper, a native of Drogheda, who was taught by Lyons, and an excellent performer. He travelled the chief part of the continent as he informed me. He played for the pretender in Rome, from thence he travelled into France, and thence to Spain, in which last place he was uncommonly well received and treated. He might have been happy, if it had not been for his great attachment to drinking, by which means he lost all his consequence.

At first the Irish in Madrid dressed him like a Spanish Don, with a servant, and he was introduced to his most Catholic Majesty, and played for him. The King had some notion of settling a pension on him in compliment to the Irish; but in consequence of his turning out to be an irreclaimable drunkard, the royal promise melted away into oblivion. He then came to Bilboa. He always carried his harp himself.

He was tall, strong and athletic, and absolutely beat the post in expedition from Madrid to Bilboa. After staying some time, he embarked for Ireland, where I frequently met him.

I was informed by Gen. Campbell in Armagh that Ackland Keane

---

8. A material woven of the pith of rushes. A dress of straw used by the Kerry country people in rustic sports has been added to the collection of the National Museum, Dublin. Mr George Coffey, director of the Irish section aims at illustrating the folk-customs of modern days as well as pre-historic, and ancient life. This rush dress has a high conical cap, like that worn by Jerome Duigenan.

9. Echlin Keane, i.e., Ackland Keane or Echlin O'Cahan, the same person who is referred to in a later page as having been presented with the harp-key of Rory *Dall* O'Cahan.

died in Scotland.

I forgot to mention in its proper place that the Duke of Argyle[10] who lived in Queen Anne's reign, heard of the celebrity of Heffernan, the London tavern-keeper that played for Lord Antrim, and came to his tavern with a large company to hear him play. The Duke called for a Scotch tune, and Heffernan, being of a good Irish turn of mind, played him the 'Golden Star', which is a very plaintive Irish tune. His Lordship said it was too melancholy for a Scotch tune.

"Oh, my Lord," says Heffernan, "you must know it was composed since the Union." His allusion was to the Duke being the counterpart of Lord Castlereagh in planning the Union of Scotland, and that the 'Golden Star' was the most appropriate tune he could play for such lovers as would barter their country's honour for the temporary use of that tangeant but useful and corrupted metal. The Duke started up, and hastily quitted the tavern of the plain spoken Hibernian with his company.

I wish I myself may have an opportunity of playing the same tune for Lord Castlereagh.

I knew a Michael Keane, a blind harper, who was born in the County Mayo in Connaught. He was a decent performer. He left this country for America with a Governor Dobbs, of Castle Dobbs, in the

---

10. The Parliamentary Union of Scotland and England, which passed the English House in March 1707, had been opposed in Scotland by an extraordinary amalgamation of parties. Defoe, author of *Robinson Crusoe*, who was present and witnessed many of the scenes of mob violence and demonstration against the Union, writes: "It was the most monstrous sight in the world, to see the Jacobite and the Presbyterian, the persecuting prelatic non-jurors and the Cameronian, the Papist and the reformed Protestant parley together, join interests and concert measures together." Amongst Scottish peers promoting the Union were the Dukes of Queensberry and Argyll. The Duke of Hamilton, a Jacobite, vigorously led the opposition till his action was checked by a message from James, the Elder Pretender, who, anxious to conciliate his half-sister, Queen Anne, signified that he had no objection to the intended Union. Heffernan's innuendo in answering the Duke of Argyll, had reference to the fact that a sum of twenty thousand pounds had been sent from the English Parliament to be dispensed in softening opposition to the Act of Union.

County of Antrim, who was appointed to the Government of South
Carolina, previous to the American Independence. Keane returned from
America, and Sir Malby Crofton told this story of Keane, that when he
and some other officers were garrisoned at Fort Oswego, and had a party,
Keane was with them, and quarrelled with them, and beat them very well,
and took a Miss Williams from them all.

He left the Governor, and came back to his native country which
he longed to see.

I have heard of Riree Dhol O'Keane[11] (Blind Roger Keane). He
was born in the County of Derry, a gentleman of large property, and
heir to an entire barony in that county. He was titled by O'Neill 'Eriagh
Thee O'Caughan' before he inherited his estates, which were Coleraine,
Garvagh, Newtown, Limavaddy, Kilreagh, and several others.

He showed a strong inclination for the harp, and by the time he
came to his estate he was an excellent performer.

He lived in a splendid style in those days (James the Firsts' reign).
He took a fancy to visit Scotland, where there were a great many harpers.
He took his retinue (or suite) with him.

Amongst other visits (in the style of an Irish Chieftain), he paid

---

11. The O'Cahans were one of the most important clans of the North owing allegiance
to the O'Neills. The reference of the great harper, Rory O'Cahan, for the person of the
O'Neill, as a greater man than James, King of Scotland and England is comprehensible
to readers of old Irish historical literature. When Brian O'Neill, the last who was
acknowledged as a King in Ireland, died in battle against the Normans in the streets
of Downpatrick, his body was surrounded by the corpses of all the leading warriors of
the Clan O'Cahan. Their territory was in the present County Derry, on the borders of
Tir-Owen, a district confiscated and planted by the London companies. James, when
King of Scotland, had secretly encouraged and profited by the war waged by Hugh
O'Neill by Elizabeth. When he ascended the throne of England, it was expected that
he would show favour to the Irish Chief; these expectations proved vain, and the
lands of Ulster were confiscated and the great plantation took place. The mention of
O'Neill's name by the harper should have brought the blush of shame to the King's
face. Rory Dall died in Scotland at Castle Eglintoun about 1653.

one to a Lady Eglinton, and she, not knowing his rank, in a peremptory manner, demanded a tune, which he declined, as he only came to amuse her, and in an irritable manner left the house. However, when she was informed of his consequence, she eagerly contrived a reconciliation, and made an apology.

The result was that he composed a tune for her ladyship, the handsome tune of 'Da Mihi Manum' ('Give me your hand'), for which his fame reached through Scotland, and came to the ears of the gun-powder prophet, James I. of England, then the VI. of Scotland. O'Keane delighted him so much, that the crabbed Monarch walked towards him, and laid his hand upon his shoulder, which one of the courtiers then present observed to Roger. "What," says O'Keane somewhat nettled, "a greater man than ever James was, laid his hand on my shoulder." "Who is that?" says the King. "O'Neill, my liege," says Keane, standing up.

He composed several fine tunes in Scotland, particularly 'Purth Athol', 'Purth Gordon' (the Purths are uncommon fine tunes), Purth means a lesson in music. I played them once, but now forget them. Roger died in Scotland in a nobleman's house, where he left his harp and silver key to tune it.[12]

About forty years after a blind harper, named Echlin Keane (a scholar of Lyons, whom I often met, and an excellent harper), went over to Scotland, and called at the house where Roger's harp and key were, and the heir of the deceased nobleman took a liking to Echlin, and made him a present of the silver key, he being name-sake to its former owner; but the dissipated rascal sold it in Edinburgh and drank the money. Rory Dall was never married.

I knew a John O'Gara well; he was blind, and born in the County of Sligo, a very good performer. He was called "The Bawn of Cool-a-vin,"

---

12. Rory Dall's harp-key was seen by Dr Johnson, when on his tour with Boswell in the Hebrides he came to the home of MacDonnell of Sleat.

which, I was informed by Charles O'Connor,[13] the Irish antiquarian, had lost his estate by means of confiscation. He was offered part but declined; he then forfeited the whole. He was a man of good qualifications. I met him in Bantry.

I met a Ned Maguire. He was blind. He was a native of the County of Mayo. I was informed he played very well. I never heard anything particular of him, but that he was drowned in the Shannon at Limerick.

I heard of a Matthew Ormsby, who was born in the County Sligo. I heard he was a good performer, but so peevish a creature that there was no enduring him.

I knew Owen O'Donnell. He was born in the County of Roscommon. He was blind. He was a very genteel young man.

I knew Andrew Victory. He was born in the County of Longford, and was blind. I met him in several places. He played well, and dressed very well. He told me he was once in the County Roscommon, at the house of MacDermott Rowe, who says to him one day, "Thonum an Dhoul," "Where were you the day the battle of Culloden was fought?" (alluding to the name of Victory.) "Och, sir," says Victory, "it was well for the Duke of Cumberland I was not there, otherwise he would not have the honour of being called 'Billy, the Butcher'. "

I knew a Nelly Smith who was born in the County Cavan; she was

---

[13] Charles O'Connor of Belanagare. "He was direct ancestor of the present O'Connor Don," and was one of the most distinguished Irishmen of the eighteenth century. He was born at Kilmactrary, County Sligo, on the 1st January, 1710, and died at Belanagare, County Roscommon, 1st July 1791. He devoted his life to Irish studies, and to the elevation of his Catholic countrymen. He collected many famous Irish manuscripts, and wrote several works, the best known of which is his dissertation on the *History of Ireland*. Samuel Johnson wrote him two charming letters, which are preserved. The Rev. Mr Contarine, the uncle of Oliver Goldsmith, was a friend of his, and also he was a friend and patron of the harper, O'Carolan, and he declared that nowhere had Carolan's harp the same power as in his house. O'Carolan's harp is still preserved by the O'Connor Don at Clonalis. Charles O'Connor's valuable MSS., including the first part of the *Annals of the Four Masters*, were purchased by the Marquis of Buckingham, and afterwards by Lord Ashburnham, and, finally, the Government purchased them and presented them to the Royal Irish Academy, where they are now.

blind. I often heard her play, which was tolerably well.

In a former part of this narrative I observed that I was almost stationary after my return from Munster and Connaught, in and about the County Cavan, these many years last past.

A little before the rebellion of 1798 I formed the idea of opening a school, which I proposed to my dear deceased friend, Captain Summerville of Lough Sheelin, in the County Cavan, who readily consented to erect one near his own house, and also to get me three scholars, and to have me live entirely with himself, but by means of the subsequent disturbances and the captain's death the plan, of course, fell to the ground.

ILLUSTRATIONS

1. Anthony Bunting
(Edward Bunting's brother)

2. Edward Bunting

3. Mary Ann Bunting
(Edward Bunting's wife)

three miniatures reproduced by Charlotte Milligan Fox
in the Journal of the Irish Folk Song Society

4. Mrs McRory (Sarah Bunting)
(Edward Bunting's daughter)

from a miniature reproduced in the Journal of the Irish Folk Song Society

5. Edward Bunting

from the engraving by W. Brocas, Dublin 1811

6. Mary Ann McCracken

from a painting by Thompson reproduced in Journal of the Irish Folk Song Society

7. Henry Joy McCracken

*from a painting by Roland Spottiswoode taken from the
contemporary miniature employed for R.R. Madden's etching*

8. Dr James MacDonnell

bust by Christopher Moore sculpted 1844

9. **Arthur O'Neill** (1737–1816)

from an engraving by Thomas Smyth, Belfast

10. Patrick Murney
a Belfast Harp Society boy harper and friend
performing at Glenarm Castle, June 1838

watercolour by Lady Dufferin (Private Collection)

11. Patrick Murney
performing at Glenarm Castle, June 1838

pencil drawing by Lady Dufferin (Private Collection)

**12. The Headquarters of the
Belfast Harp Society,
Shore Road, Belfast**
from an engraving by Thomas Smyth

**13. Valentine Rennie
(or Rainey) ✝1837**
*from an engraving by
Thomas Smyth*

14. Sir Samuel Ferguson
*from frontispiece of vol ii of "Sir Samuel Ferguson in the
Ireland of his Day" (1896)*

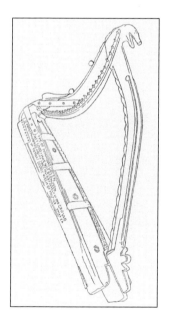

15. Denis Hempson's Harp
*from Bruce Armstrong's
"The Irish and the Highland Harps" (1904)*

16. Denis Hempson (1695-1807)
(Donnchadh Ó hAmhsaigh)

from Plate 2, Bunting's 1809 Collection

17. Arthur O'Neill

from Plate 4, Bunting's 1809 Collection
etched from an original drawing in Bunting MSS which was sketched
from life by Thomas Hughes while compiling O'Neill's Memoirs

18. Charles Byrne

sketched by Miss O'Reilly of Scarva,
16th August 1810

19. Patrick Quin (1745-1812)
Harper to the Irish Harp Society

etched from a painting by Eliza Trotter

20. Turlough O'Carolan (c 1670–1738)
(Toirdhealbhach Ó Cearbhalláin)

*from an old engraving commissioned by
Dean Massey of Limerick circa 1720*

The Celebrated Irish Harp Festival held in the Exchange Belfast on the 12th July 1792.

The following Harpers took part:—Art O'Neill, Denis O'Hampsaig, Cahal Fanning, Daniel Black, Cahal O'Beirn, Aodh O'Hagan, Padraig O'Quinn, William Carr, Rose O'Mooney, and Seamus Duncan.

Edward Bunting, James MacDonnell, Samuel Neilson, Wolfe Tone, Henry Joy M'Cracken, Thomas Russell, and many other patriots attended this Festival.

(From the original picture by John Carey, in possession of Francis Joseph Bigger).

21. John Carey's Watercolour reconstruction of the Belfast Harper's Assembly of 1792

*the original watercolour was commissioned by F.J. Bigger
and presented as a gift to Charlotte Milligan Fox*

CHAPTER XVI

MEMOIRS OF ARTHUR O'NEILL
THIRD JOURNEY

A T THE TIME I HEARD OF THE FIRST BALL IN GRANARD I WAS AT MY brother Ferdinand's at Glenarb in the County Tyrone, from whence I pushed toward the County of Longford without meeting with anything particular, only touching at some gentlemen's houses on my way. I met Paddy Kerr, the harper, who was going to Granard also. I remained in and about Granard before the ball commenced.

These annual Granard balls began in the following manner. A Mr James Dungan, a native of Granard, and a very extensive merchant, at that time residing in Copenhagen in Denmark, having heard in some manner that the gentlemen in Scotland encouraged annual meetings or competitions among Highland pipers, where premiums were awarded to the best performers, Dungan, through national ardour, anxious to preserve and support the original instrument of his own country, remitted to his friends in and about Granard a sufficient sum of money to defray the expenses of the three celebrated balls held there, in the years of 1781, 1782, 1783.

And it is to be lamented, [*says Dungan in a letter to his friends*], that persons placed in high situations, who have it in their power to do the most good by their rank and wealth for their own country, are, I am sorry to hear, the least disposed to do it—I will not attempt to say whether by habit or inclination. I am informed they know nothing of Irish music, or Irish misery only by the name, so great are their desires to support modern English music, and I consider my native country half a century behind Scotland in encouraging and rewarding the best performers on the bagpipe, which, if preferred to the wired harp, strongly evinces our taste. The Welsh harp is encreasing. The Scotch bagpipes are encreasing, but poor Erin's harp is decreasing. If I was amongst you it would not be the case. Farewell, my friends, and I hope you will amongst yourselves support what I make bold to dictate to you.

P.S. Why not make or establish a fund for the above purpose? I don't want you to imitate the Scotch but the ancient Irish. Adieu.

1781— FIRST BALL AT GRANARD

Harpers present

Charles Fanning	Hugh Higgins
Arthur O'Neill	Charley Berreen
Patrick Kerr	Rose Mooney

Patrick Maguire

They all played their best tunes. Charles Fanning got first premium, ten guineas, for 'The Coolin'. I got the second for 'The Green Woods of Truagh' and 'Mrs Crofton', eight guineas; and Rose Mooney got the third for 'Planxty Burke', five guineas. The Judges at the first ball were excellent, and there was some deliberation about the first premium between Fanning and me; but in consequence of my endeavouring to appear on this occasion in my very best duds, they decided in favour of Charley, who was careless in his dress, saying, at the same time, that he wanted money more than I did; however, I received many handsome verbal compliments, besides the eight guineas premium. To the best of my opinion there were there, at least, five hundred persons at the ball. It was held in the Market House of Granard. A Mr Burrowes was one of the Stewards, who was a tolerable judge of music, and who was so angry at the decision of the premiums, that he thrust his cane through one of the windows. Mr Patrick Reilly prepared the supper.

After this first ball I became a favourite in and about Granard, where I remained about four months, and my company much sought for. I will not attempt to say how I deserved such attention, only that I was then more cautious of avoiding inebriation than the other harpers, and kept as little of their company as possible.

On my way home from the County Longford, I made my way home, and stopped with Philip Keilly of Murrough, in the County Cavan. This gentleman was the original means, afterwards, of my coming to the Belfast ball, in 1792. With him I remained some months, and then came to Archdeacon Caulfield's of Castle Cosby, with whom I spent a very agreeable fortnight, without anything particular occurring; and from thence I visited all the gentlemen alternately hereinbefore named in and about the counties of Cavan, Armagh, Monaghan, and Tyrone, where I remained until the approach of the period of the second Granard ball in June 1782.

GRANARD, SECOND BALL

About the month of March I made my way again for Granard, and as usual touched again at all my acquaintances (gentlemen's houses).

I remained some time with a Rev. Mr Sneyd, Rector of Lurgan, County Cavan, successor to Parson Sterling,[1] the celebrated bag-piper, and composer of the tune 'the Priest of Lurgan'; from thence to Captain Fleming's of Bellville, County Cavan, where I remained about three weeks.

He was a Captain of Volunteers, a lover of music, uncommonly hospitable, but not a proficient in music; from thence to Lismore to Cosby Nesbitt's—he was a finished gentleman in every respect, with whom I remained a few days. I then went into the County of Longford, and went to see Captain Boyers of Mount Pleasant, with

---

[1.] Parson Sterling was a noted performer on the pipes, and composer as well. Lady Morgan in her Memoirs mentions another piper parson in the person of the Rev. Charles Macklin, nephew of the dramatist of that name. He lost a curacy through having used the pipes in the pulpit to play out his congregation. Dr W. H. Grattan Flood records in his *History of Irish Music* an instance of an English visitor to the Catholic Bishop of Kilmore being much surprised to see among the portraits of former bishops of the diocese, a picture of a piper in Highland costume. He was informed that this represented Bishop Richardson, who, being a skilled musician availed himself of this disguise in order to visit and console his scattered flock.

whom I chiefly remained until the ball was preparing, for he was one of the most comical geniuses I ever met. He knew something of music, and delighted in the harp, although he played very well on the violin.

Second Ball — Harpers present

Charles Fanning	Hugh Higgins
Arthur O'Neill	Ned MacDermott Rowe
Paddy Kerr	Rose Mooney
Pat Maguire	Kate Martin

Charley Berreen

who all played as usual their best tunes; but the premiums were reduced this year the first to eight guineas, the second to six guineas, and the third to four. Charley Fanning got the first, I got the second, and Rose Mooney got the third. Charles Fanning got the first for 'The Coolin' again; I got the second for 'The Green Woods of Truagh' and 'The Fairy Queen'. Rose Mooney got the third premium, but I do not remember for what tunes. Higgins got somehow huffed, and retired without playing a single tune.

A Major Smith, who knew nothing of music, was appointed one of the judges. He declared, "By heaven, they made me a judge, because they knew I knew nothing about it." The company at the second ball was more numerous than the first, and when all was over I just took the same route home, in a similar manner as described on my return from the first. Only on this, my second return, I stopped at a Peter Connell's of Cranary in the County of Longford. He could sing and compose well, and no end to his hospitality.

Mr Connell had a humorous servant, named Jack Hart, who sung both English and Irish songs, as well as Mr Owenson, the comedian, could.[2]

One day, taking his master's horses to be shod, he had to pass by Captain Boyer's door, and was accosted by the Captain. Hart was in the meantime singing the song of 'Speak O Yeough' with a chorus of 'Obber O Roo'. "Blast you come in," says Boyers, "until I give you a dram." On this Hart alighted, and walked into Boyer's house, who had at that time ten gallons of shrub in the house, and between singing and drinking, they never stopped, for the space of two days and two nights, and never parted, until the shrub was entirely finished. Mr Connell, in the meantime, imagined his man and horses to be lost, but when the shrub was out Hart brought the horses to the farriers to be shod, and returned home the third day. Mr Connell, of course, brought him to account for his conduct. Hart, without reserve, told him the whole story, and about the ten gallons of shrub. "Damn your body," says Connell, "did you finish it?"

"Damn me, if we didn't, with a little help," says Hart. "Why then, damn me, but I forgive you, and I never would, if you had left a single drop," says Mr Connell.

---

2. Mr Owenson, the comedian, was a popular Dublin actor, and for a time though disastrously Actor Manager in the National Theatre Music Hall and was in the height of his fame during the stirring Volunteer and Grattan's Parliament era of history. A Connaught man by birth, he studied under Dr Wargan of Westminster Abbey, returning to settle in Ireland in 1770. He was one of the first to introduce a pianoforte to an Irish audience, this was in 1785. His forte lay in singing old Irish songs in character, and he had a vast collection of them. His musical talent was inherited by his daughter, Sydney Owenson, author of *The Wild Irish Girl*, and other novels, and known to fame, and in society, as Lady Morgan. In her chatty journal there are many references to her father's traditional style of singing. His last appearance on the stage was in an operetta written by her in collaboration with Tom Cooke, entitled The *Whim of the Moment*, which was produced on 5th March 1807, the Lord-Lieutenant attending in state. In 1802, Owenson had been mainly instrumental in founding the Kilkenny Theatre, in which Thomas Moore later on graced the boards, and where he wooed and won his wife, Bessie Dyke, an actress in the theatre. He died in May 1812, and was passionately mourned by his daughter, who was distinguished by loyal affection to her family through all changes of fortune. Sydney Owenson had some correspondence with Arthur O'Neill, who is referred to in one of the notes to her novel, *The Wild Irish Girl*.

Mr Connell informed me afterwards that Boyers was very parsimonious only when seeing company, when he would spare no expense to entertain the guests.

Always on my return from Granard balls, I stopped at Counsellor Edgeworth's of Edgeworthstown,[3] where I was well entertained.

I taught two young ladies, Miss Farrel and Miss Plunket, who lived in that neighbourhood, to play on the harp. Miss Farrell played handsomely; Miss Plunket, middling.

I next came to a Cormack O'Neill's of Fardrum-hon in the County

---

3. Counsellor Edgeworth of Edgeworthstown here referred to was father of Maria Edgeworth, the famous novelist. None of her stories makes as interesting and romantic reading as her edition of her father's *Life*. It is largely an autobiography by Richard Edgeworth himself, in which he tells the story of his four marriages, and describes the eccentric wooing of his friend, Thomas Day, author of *Sandford and Merton*, a philosopher of the school of Rousseau. One of his ventures, when in search of a wife, was the adoption of an orphan girl Sabrina, whom he endeavoured to train according to his ideals. This incident has been dramatised recently in the successful play, *Mice and Men*.

Edgeworth was something of a scientist and inventor, anticipated the bicycle, and gave much attention to developing a system of transmitting news by semaphore signals. Before the days of telegraphy, with French Invasions threatening, his scheme was of practical importance. In 1798 Edgeworth and his numerous family, including his fourth wife, vacated the family seat on the approach of the insurgent forces. On their return home they found that though the house had been visited nothing had been stolen or even disturbed, Edgeworth's philanthropic efforts to improve the condition of the country had so endeared him to the peasantry. In advanced age he caught his last illness through over-exertion and exposure when investigating the bogs and swamps of the Midlands of Ireland, with a view to their reclamation.

In a letter to Lady Morgan, after the publication of her novel, *The Wild Irish Girl*, 1806, Mr Edgeworth wrote: "I believe that some of the harpers you mention were at the Harpers' Prize Ball at Granard near this place in 1782 or 1783. One female harper of the name of Bridget obtained the second prize. Fallen carried off the first. I think I have heard the double-headed man. My daughter published an essay on the subject of that prize in an obscure newspaper, of which we have no copy."

This letter is inaccurate, and therefore very likely Mr Edgeworth had not met old O'Neill during his visit to his house after the Granard balls, and his recollections were from hearsay. 'Bridget' is, of course, Rose Mooney; 'Fallon,' Fanning. O'Neill is not mentioned, but he possibly inspired Maria Edgeworth's newspaper article.

Longford. He was an eccentric genius, and kept a house not unlike an Academy such as dancing masters, music-masters, classical masters of modern languages, he having four sons and three daughters on whom he spared no expense. I next went to Felix O'Neill's of Edinbawn, and Toby Peyton's of Laheen, both in the County Leitrim, where nothing but hospitality occurred to me, next to Colonel Gore's of Woodford, and thence to Andrew O'Rourke's of Creevy of County Leitrim, where I got a letter from my friend, Hugh O'Neill, inviting me to come to him to a Mr Brown's of Cloonfad (at Churchland).

I accordingly came to him, and after some time he informed me that a Connor O'Kelly, a harp maker, was making one for him. As this O'Kelly was a very peevish man, he requested me to go and endeavour to keep him in temper.

While the harp was making, for fear of disappointment, I attended on Kelly, and by means of treats and jokes he contrived to finish it; but it had to be taken asunder, as when it was tuned the treble was thought too long. It had forty strings, thirty-five in general being considered enough. The harp was a second time put together, and turned out the best one I ever heard or played upon. It then only wanted varnishing to make it a nonsuch, and a Mrs Keane of Carrick-on-Shannon, a Japanner, wanted three guineas to varnish and burnish it, which Hugh declined. I, being well acquainted in Longford, informed her I could get it done there, and cheaper, which he agreed to. I took the harp then accordingly, and a Mr O'Sullivan finished it properly.

This O'Sullivan was like many other mechanics of merit, a harem-scarem good-natured fellow, with whom I spent a humorous time while he was finishing the harp.

When returning back to Mr Brown's where Hugh was waiting for me, I met a new married lady on the road, a Mrs Hamilton of Kill-ne-Carragh, who invited me to her house. I went to it, where I played several tunes. She was much inclined to detain me, but I was impatient to see Hugh, and never stopped till I came to him. He was impatient to try the harp, and when he got it into his hands he played the tune of 'Limerick's

Lamentation', or Tom Conlan's[4] stolen tune, which he called 'Lochaber No More' in Scotland. He was so well pleased that he exclaimed. "It answers my utmost fancy."

I remained at Mr Brown's with Hugh about a month, where nothing particular occurred to me, but I was highly entertained with hospitality and good nature.

I next rambled to Charles O'Connor's of Ballinagar, in the County of Roscommon, the celebrated Irish antiquarian, and, I may add, historian, who was one of the most learned men that Ireland has produced.

Hugh and I were invited there, and indeed we exerted our mutual abilities to please that worthy gentleman, with our best tunes and airs. Mr O'Connor was himself an excellent performer on the harp, and one of the best amateurs I ever heard. We stopped with him about a fortnight, and in consequence of the uncommon attention that was paid us by that gentleman, we only imagined it like a summer's day. I parted Hugh at Ballinagar.

I next came to Charles White's in the County Sligo, where as usual in that hospitable province I experienced the highest respect and attention. I remained a few days at this time, but often visited him from the year 1785 till 1795 as he was one of my greatest favourites. He died in 1795 and left an only son Robert White, the real counterpart of his father, whom I also visited until 1803, in which year he died.

I went to a Mr James Irvine's of Streamstown, County Sligo. I am totally at a loss how to describe that gentleman's manner of living at his own house and among his tenantry. He had an ample fortune. He was an amateur. He had four sons and three daughters, who were all proficient

---

4. Tom Conlan or Connellan, born about 1640 at Cloonmahon, County Sligo, composer of 'The Dawning of the Day', 'The Golden Star', 'Love in Secret', 'Bonny Jean', 'The Jointure', 'Molly St George'. The air of 'Limerick's Lamentation', known in Scotland as 'Lochaber No More', was often mistakenly attributed to him. He likely helped to naturalise it in that country, but the Belfast harpers, one and all, attributed it to one Miles Reilly, a Cavan man, who lived at the same time as Connelan.

William Connellan, a younger brother, was also a harper, and composed 'Lady Iveagh', 'Saebh Kelly', and 'Molly McAlpine', the latter air was adopted by Moore as 'Remember the Glories of Brian the Brave'.

in music, no instrument was unknown to them.

There was at one time a meeting in his house of forty-six musicians, who played in the following order:

The three Miss Irvines at the piano	3
Myself at the harp	1
Gentlemen flutes	6
Gent. Violoncellos	2
Common pipers	10
Gent. fiddlers	20
Gent. clarionets	4
	46

At the hour this gentleman's customary meetings were finished some guests contiguous to their own places went home, but those who lived some miles off remained, and in order to accommodate them Mr and Mrs Irvine lay on chairs that night in the parlour, for my own part I never spent a more agreeable night, either in bed or out of bed.

I next went to the town of Sligo, where I slept that night, and next morning went to a Parson Phibbs (a credit to the cloth) of Ardlaharly, near Ballymote. He loved music, and encouraged it, and he played well on that wired instrument called the dulcimer. If it was not that I wanted to see my friends, I could have lived with him for ever.

I went from thence to Captain Irvine's of Tondrago, County Sligo, a finished gentleman. He was a Captain of Volunteers for sixteen years, and in the Queen of Hungary's service he distinguished himself as an Irishman, not inferior to the celebrated Count Lacy.[5]

From Mr Irvine's I came to Mrs Crofton's of Longford (the name of her seat) in the County Sligo. She was the mother of Sir Malby Crofton, and the lady for whom Carolan composed the fine tune of *Mrs Crofton*. Lady Morgan mentions her frequently in her *Memoirs*, and the Crofton's were relatives of Lady Morgan's father.

---

5. See O'Callaghan's *History of the Irish Brigade*, for account of several officers called Lacy.

I remained there only a few days, and then came to Parson Hawks, of Screen, in the County Sligo. He was very like Parson Phibbs in gentility, and every other respect. He detained me a week.

From thence I came to Mr Jones of Arneyglass, next to Arthur Cooper's of Tanzy hill, next to Mr White's of Ballintogher, all in the County Sligo, where I generally stopped a few days, and was uncommonly well treated, without anything particular happening to me.

I next came into the County Leitrim to a Cornelius O'Donnell's of Larkfield, where I again met my dear Hugh O'Neill, who was there on a visit being contiguous to his own farm, in the County Roscommon, and near the boundaries of the Counties of Roscommon and Leitrim.

He brought me back with him to his farm of Lis Connor, or Fort Connor (Lis signifies a Fort). He walked me through it, and described the beauties, and could point out the best part of it as well as a man that had the gift of eyesight, and when done he says to me: "Arthur you are my relation and favourite, and if you should survive me, this farm shall be yours (accidents excepted, in case I should not make a Will) see this field, see that field, look at all, Arthur, which shall be yours."

"I see them very plainly, Hugh," says I, "and thank you, my friend."

He then brought me to his own house, where we spent that night very happy. He then brought me to Mr Jameson, his Landlord, that good landlord who would not accept of Hugh's annual rent of twenty pounds, but also gave him the receipt, of twenty pounds a year more, on the same concern.

From thence I went to Tom McGovern's of Port-na-laddin, of County Leitrim. No end to his good-nature. He was a genteel, substantial farmer, and lived in a style beyond the common. I next came into the County Fermanagh, and spent a few nights with Sir James Colville, very happily.

I next came into the County Tyrone, and stopped at Ned Conway's, near Newton-Stewart. He had a daughter that played the harp uncommon well. Miss Conway and I were closeted together for three weeks, exchanging tunes.

She gave me the tune of 'Dr Hart', and I gave her the tune of 'Madge Malone' and several other tunes mutually, that I cannot remember at present, but left the house on the best of terms.

I proceeded now to another Ned Conway's of Montreloney, in the County Tyrone who received me as well as his name-sake, and indeed my intention was to spend my Christmas with Mr Blackall of Ballinascreen in the County Derry, but was prevented in consequence of the snow, that fell at that period so much so that the deepest quarries were level with the high road, in consequence of which many travellers fell victims to their ignorance of the roads.

I next went to Mr Blackall's, who excused me in consequence of the fatality of the snow, and rejoiced that I escaped it. This was in the year of 1785 or 1786.

From that I came to Ballymenagh, County Tyrone, and from thence I went to see my brother Ferdinand, of Glenarb, County Tyrone, near Caledon, when resting my bones between riding and walking, I spent near six months, going to and visiting Mr Strong of Fairview, Captain Neville of Mount Irvine, the Rev. Dr Clarke, Rector of Clonfeacle, Captain Houston of Tillydowy, Sir W. Richardson of Augher, Dean Keating of Clogher, who would not let me touch a harp in his house, but indulged me in playing the enticing game of backgammon, whom I always excelled, blind as I was.

Thence I went to Mr Stack's of Stacks Grove, County Monaghan, where I remained eight or ten days, and again returned to my brother Ferdinand, and continued in and about that neighbourhood until the time for the third Granard Ball was announced, and I heard that James Dungan of ever respected memory, the author and instigator of the three Balls, would attend there. He came particularly from Copenhagen (amongst other business) to superintend the last and greatest Irish National Ball, respecting harpers, that ever was held in this country.

I met Mr Dungan there, and will speak of him in course, on the conclusion of the third Ball in Granard. Moreover, I will endeavour to show in these *Memoirs*, how folly and fashion will neglect the real merits of those who take pains, and prefer to encourage the works of a Sir John Plagiarist, or a Sir John Selector, or a Sir John Innovator, or a Sir John

Stevenson.[6] If my friend hereinafter named should seek for the empty title of a Knight Bachelor, he might be sure of being appointed to it if a Townsend or Rutland were to visit this country, but this Barren Knight should in my opinion confine himself to his business in Dublin, and not interfere with Mr Bunting, and I shall also endeavour to draw a contrast between the reviver and the restorer of ancient Irish music and a titled upstart that attempts to plaster his works upon those who will not take pains to look for the works of Mr B————— .

After remaining with my friends in and about the County Tyrone, in the usual manner for about nine months, I then began to prepare myself for the third Granard Ball, and set out accordingly, and trucked or stopped at almost every house mentioned in my going to the first and second ball until I got to Mr James O'Reilly's of Higginstown, County Longford, with whom I remained till the ball commenced, when the following harpers and a few more that I cannot recollect attended, viz:

Charles Fanning	Charles Berreen
Arthur O'Neill	Ned MacDermott Rowe
Hugh Higgins	Rose Mooney
Lawrence Keane	Kate Martin

James Duncan

The premiums were the same as at the second ball, that is, eight guineas the first, six guineas the second, and four guineas the third. Fanning always deservedly got the first, I got the second, and poor Rose Mooney, as usual, got the third.

A gentleman named Miles Keane railed uncommonly about the distribution of the premiums, and swore a great oath, that it was the most nefarious decision he ever witnessed. I don't know what he meant,

---

6. Sir John Stevenson, a fashionable teacher and organist of St Patrick's Cathedral, Dublin. A friend of Thomas Moore and arranger of Moore's Irish Melodies. Knighted in 1803.

but heard the expression. Lord and Lady Longford attended this ball, and the meeting was vastly more numerous than the two former ones. Quality from forty miles attended, and there was not a house in the town but was filled with ladies and gentlemen, and the town was like a horse fair, as there was not stabling for the twentieth part that came. There were at least a thousand people at the ball.

In consequence of the harpers who received no premiums being formerly neglected, I hinted a subscription, which was well received and performed, and indeed, on distributing the collection, their proportion exceeded our premiums.

This ball was nearly being spoiled, by means of a Bernard Reilly of Ballymorris, who entertained some antipathy to Mr Dungan, and took every pains to destroy the harmony of the ball. Mr Dungan, the father of the three Balls, came over from Copenhagen, as before mentioned, to see how the third and last Ball was conducted, and he got so much disgusted with the indecorous manners of the Stewards and others who superintended the management of it, that he did not attend during the performance, but only at supper. There was a very handsome ode composed for Mr Dungan on his arrival at Granard, but through jealousy or some other motive he never saw either the ode or the composer. I dined with Mr Dungan the day after the Ball at the Widow Reilly's in Granard. I do not know how I deserved his attention, but I should sit next to him, and dined with him in different places. He acquired admiration and respect everywhere he visited in consequence of his polished manners and gentlemanly accomplishments. He remained some time in and about Granard, and I understand he is now alive and well in Copenhagen.

If there was a Dungan and a Bunting in each province in this kingdom it is more easily imagined than my poor abilities can describe, to what a degree of grandeur the Irish harp, and the music incident to it would arrive.

CHAPTER XVII

MEMOIRS OF ARTHUR O'NEILL
CONCLUSION

WHEN THE THIRD BALL WAS OVER I TOOK MY LEAVE OF DUNCAN AND Keane, two of the harpers, but I forgot to mention that before the Ball opened Rose Mooney pledged her harp, petticoat, and cloak. When I make this remark of poor Rose, it is with no ludicrous intention of exposing her faults, which should chiefly be attributed to her maid, Mary, whose uncommon desire for drinking was unlimited, and taking advantage of her mistress's blindness, she always when drink was wanting, pawned any article on which she could raise half a pint, therefore poor Rose I acquit you of any meanness on your own part, as your guides and mine have often lead us into hobbles, which are inseparable from poor blind harpers, and afterwards laughed at us; but we in general think it is better for people in every station in life to have about them the rogue they know, rather than the rogue they don't know.

I made it a point to remain in and about Granard till I understood that Mr Dungan was for returning to Copenhagen, and it may be imagined that I say too much of myself, but he took me aside when parting, exchanged mutual friendship, and when done shaking hands, I discovered the weight of six guineas in mine. He added, at the same time, that I deserved the first premium as he was informed, he not attending, and he hoped I would not be offended at his making my reward superior to Fanning's. I never experienced the same feelings on parting with any friend before, except Hugh O'Neill.

In coming home I differed from the route taken after the second Ball. I went through a skirt of the County of Westmeath, into the County Cavan, to see my dear friend Captain Summerville, where frequent repetition of his promise to support me to the last was our chief conversation, and from his seat of Lough Sheelan Lodge, I pushed into the County of

Meath, and stopped at the seats of Peter Cruise (nephew to Carolan's favourite Bridget Cruise)[1] Mr James Carolan's of Carrickmacross, County Monaghan. I was much disappointed in speaking to this gentleman, as well as to a great number of the Carolans in that county, where the celebrated Terence Carolan, the composer, was born, that not one of them would claim kindred to him, which in my opinion would be no disgrace to Orpheus Apollo, or King David; from thence to Mr Plunkett's of Rock-Savage, County Monaghan, thence to Dundalk, County Louth, to see my relation Owen O'Neill, Captain Byrne of Castletown, and George and Harry Byrne. Although these gentlemen had each separate houses, they never would dine asunder, for if the Captain was invited anywhere George and Harry were sure to be there, and if George and Harry were asked to dine, the three brothers were sure to be together. They were all married, and their brotherly affection was the theme of the discourse of the surrounding country.

From Dundalk I crossed the Fews Mountains. I had a young man, a guide, named Paddy Ward, who threatened to quit me in consequence of the uncommon shower of snow, that fell after we left Newtownhamilton. Poor fellow, he was nearly famished (though a youngster) with cold, and I would not part him till we came to a public-house, that was kept by a Mrs McArdell. We scarcely entered when all our apparent wants were enquired into, and by the uncommon exertions of that good woman we were in a short time relieved from the fatigues of our long and cold journey, I in my turn to gratify her played till all was blue, and the next morning when preparing for depart, I, of course, called for the reckoning. "Mr O'Neill," says Mrs McArdell, "do you want a walloping?" (meaning a beating), and she gave me a gentle blow on the

---

1. A lady with whom O'Carolan the harper fell in love in his youth, and in whose honour he composed a well-known song. It is related that not having met her for twenty years O'Carolan was making a pilgrimage to the famous St Patrick's Purgatory of Lough Derg, Donegal. Whilst giving his hand to some pilgrims who were alighting from the ferry boat, he chanced to take a lady's hand, and holding it exclaimed, "By the word of my gossip this is the hand of Bridget Cruise."

shoulder, saying, "There's a receipt for you."

I next went to a priest O'Neill's of Ballymanab, near Armagh, who was a relation of mine, and a real O'Neill. It may be imagined that I mean to be partial to his character when I say that in all my travels I never met his superior in point of unprejudiced and unbigoted hospitality of manners. He was a respected gentleman of his order in the altar and pulpit, and out of the pulpit, but them that knew him could distinguish whether he was a priest, parson, or country squire. I had some difficulty in getting away from him, and when I did I went into Armagh, and alternately visited Mrs Alford, Mr Jenning, Dr Hamilton, and others, whom I now forget.

I went from Armagh to Caledon, and then again to my brother Ferdinand's, where, after polishing off the rust of mind and care and fatigue, my next concern was to do something for my guide, Ward. I bound him to a linen-weaver, but, in consequence of the impression of rambling he got under me for the space of four years, he quit the treadles and heavy stays, and enlisted in a regiment then recruiting in Caledon. Shortly after I went to the County Cavan, and rambled as usual, and paid my first respects to my dear, now deceased, friend, Captain Summerville, who received and treated me as formerly. It was almost what is termed a house-warming. I spent about three weeks with him in the usual manner. From the Captain's I went to Granard, where I parted my guide, who was well known to the two Dr MacDonnells of Belfast. He in some manner acquired the nickname of Grog. The Captain asked me the reason of his being called Grog, my answer was: "Grog is insipid, and so is Paddy Fitzgerald" (the boy's name). The Captain then procured me a guide, to lead me as far as Granard, and there I went to a Mr James O'Reilly's, where I spent about two months very happily. He got me another guide named Tom Hannen. He was about thirty-six years of age. He was nine years in the service of the East India Company, and, notwithstanding the vice and bad habits incident to soldiering, he was the most divested of little dishonest tricks of any other guide I ever had, not excepting Michael Hackett, my present guide.

When I was not employed poor Hannen would amuse me with an account of his adventures, and he told me some stories that were read to me since, amongst which he told me the story of his being present at the burning of a Hindu woman, a custom or law practised in that part of the East; that is when the husband dies the wife is to prepare herself to be burned on a funeral pile of wood, and that all her relations and friends attend on this solemn occasion to see the wife accomplish the burnings without cowardice, and she is to be dressed in her best attire, walks round the pile, and then takes leave of all her relations and friends; she then eats something that has the same effect as laudanum, and when the effect arises she plunges herself into the pile, and her nearest friends have bamboo poles in their hands, and when the torch is set to the pile they rush forward to assist in strangling or suffocating her before the flames can make her screech or moan. This story poor Hannen told me. I only mention it in a loose manner, well knowing that it is much better described by modern historians.

Hannen then next led me into the County Leitrim to Andrew O'Rourke's of Creevy in that county. He was a gentleman of learning, wit, and humour, which three great qualifications he never abused in any manner. As for the first, he was capable of composing, and actually did compose, several songs in Latin, English, and Irish, and played very handsomely on the harp. His wit and humour were never in my presence, nor ever to the best of my information and belief, immodestly or indelicately exercised.

From his house I went to Toby Peyton's, for whom Carolan composed 'Planxty Peyton'. This gentleman had a fine unencumbered estate, and, exclusive of the expenses of groceries and spices, he spent the remainder of his income in encouraging national diversions, particularly the harp and other wired instruments.

He lived to the age of one hundred and four years, and at the time he was one hundred he would mount his horse as dexterous as a man of twenty, and be in the first at the death of a fox or hare. This gentleman's age I mention to account for my visiting him, he belonging to Carolan's time, which was long before mine.

Thence I crossed the Shannon, and went into the County Roscommon again to Charles O'Connor's, the celebrated Irish antiquarian, already mentioned. This celebrated character always took the blind side of me in point of good-nature, as, for example, when I would order my horse, and when I was imagining myself mounting there was no horse, and, of course, I had to return into his house, where laughing and hospitality was the apology he pleaded for my disappointment. At length I stole away from him to the house of Patrick Brown of Croghan[2] of County Roscommon, about seven miles asunder, and got the most uncommon wetting I ever experienced. Hannen, my guide, was crying with the wet and cold he suffered in that journey; but my pride in not availing myself of shelter was sufficiently punished, for I was shortly afterwards afflicted by such a severe rheumatism that I lost the power of two of my left-hand fingers, notwithstanding which I went through all my old acquaintances in that county, until I came into Granard again, and there tumbled into Jemmy Reilly's, my old and before-mentioned acquaintance. In consequence of the affliction of the rheumatism, I felt myself uncommonly unhappy in not being able to exercise my usual abilities on the harp, and resolved to get home to Glenarb as soon as possible. Notwithstanding the resolution I formed, I could not resist the temptation of making a short cut to Lough Sheelan Lodge to see my dear (now deceased) friend, Captain Somerville, the almost counterpart of Captain Westenra, of Bumper Hall, in the County Meath.

Somerville was in this year, 1792, about fifty years of age, and he, perceiving my misfortune of the fingers, amused me with reading; and on reading the *Belfast Newsletter*[3] to me we found an advertisement inviting all

2. In Gaelic Cruachan was the place where stood the residence of Meave, the warrior queen who invaded Ulster and was opposed by the hero Cuchulain. The story of her invasion is related in the Epic Tale of the *Tain bo Cuailgne*, or *Cattle Raid of Cooley*. Versions in English, founded on this tale, have been written by Standish O'Grady, Lady Gregory, Miss Eleanour Hull, and in verse by Mrs A. W. Hutton.

3. Founded in 1737 by Francis Joy, is still in vigorous existence, and said to be the oldest provincial paper in Ireland. For everything relating to the history of Belfast and the North of Ireland, the old files of the *Newsletter* afford an invaluable source of reference. The most nearly complete set is in possession of the Linen Hall Library, Belfast, beginning with No. 152, Friday, 16th February 1738. Mr Joy continued to own the paper till 1795. He was father of Henry and Robert Joy, and a daughter marrying Captain John McCracken, ship owner and merchant, was the mother of Henry Joy McCracken (hanged in 1798), and of Mary and John McCracken, who were so intimately associated with Bunting.

the harpers in the kingdom to come to Belfast, bringing their instruments with them to show their love of Ireland.

When I left Captain Somerville's I next went to Philip Reilly's of Mullough, the eighteen years' constant and unchangeable friend before named. For fear I should be hurried, I will now make free to describe him and his character. He was about five feet seven inches in height, stout and well made, and left no stone unturned to show himself a real O'Reilly. "Damn the expense," says Philip O'Reilly, "give us a cooper of claret." Mrs O'Reilly was a woman of such a good-humoured turn of mind, that though well aware of his frailty, yet, without contradiction or any expression that might be the cause of an argument, while encouraging the duty of the importation of wine, she indulged him in his loose conduct and expressions, and gently reprimanded him the ensuing morning.

At this time I received a letter from Dr James MacDonnell of this town, and how he discovered where I was I never could learn; but the subject of the letter was to invite me to Belfast on the 9th of July 1792, to assist with other harpers on the national instrument.

In consequence of my rheumatism, I felt my own incapacity, and expressed it to my friend Phil O'Reilly, as I had not the use of the two principal fingers of my left hand, by which hand the treble on the Irish harp is generally performed. Mr. O'Reilly would take no excuse, and swore vehemently that if I did not go freely, he would tie me on a car, and have me conducted to assist in performing what was required by the advertisement before mentioned. I abided by his advice, and on the Fews Mountains, on my way to Armagh, I met Patrick Lyndon[4] at a public house. He knew me, and called out, asking

---

4. It was most unfortunate that this really interesting harper and poet should have gone on the spree and failed to turn up in Belfast. Arthur O'Neill was wise in trying to secure his presence, and furnish him for the occasion. He had met O'Carolan in his time, and was himself something of a Poet, and had been harp-tutor to P. Quinn of Armagh, who played in Belfast and at the Carolan Commemoration Concert in Dublin. That Bunting met Linden we know from his index, where it is noted that he got from him the following airs: 'Miss Hamilton', by Lyons, harper to the Earl of Antrim in 1702; 'Saebh Kelly', by Thomas Connallon, 1660, taken from P. Linden, harper, Newtoun Hamilton, Co. Armagh, 1802.

where I was going. I informed him, and he told me he would like to accompany me if he was better dressed. At this time I had plenty of old clothes, and I knew him to be an excellent scholar, who could read and write Irish very well, and wished to have him with me to Belfast, imagining he would be a great acquisition to this celebrated harpers' meeting.

He got my old clothes in order to cut them down, and he was so proud when he got them, that he went rambling through the neighbourhood of Ballynagleragh, Co. Armagh, in so volatile a manner, that when I expected him, according to our terms on parting, he did not appear. Indeed, what with his breach of promise and my having the rheumatism still, I found myself uncommonly awkward when I came to Belfast to endeavour to show myself worthy of Dr James MacDonnell's good opinion of me. He, perceiving my bad state of health, thought it necessary to electrify[5] me every day previous to the Belfast Ball.

Dr James MacDonnell explained to me the nature and purport of this ball, which was to show a specimen of patriotism and national ardour to the rest of the kingdom. It was held on the 14th July 1792, at which time the following harpers attended, with others that I do not now remember.

Charles Fanning	William Carr
Hugh Higgins	Rose Mooney
Patrick Quinn	James Duncan
(Welsh) Williams	Donald Black
Arthur O'Neill	Charles Berreen

Denis Hempson, Etc., etc.

On this occasion the different premiums were to be kept a profound

---

5. *See* Sir W. Whitla's account of Dr MacDonnell's fame as a pioneer in the medical world, Chapter XXIV.

secret, so much so that one harper was by no means to let the others know what he received, in order to prevent any jealousy amongst them, and to emulate them to exert their utmost skill in playing Irish airs. This meeting continued four days in the Exchange Rooms in Belfast without the smallest interruption whatsoever, and each harper exerted himself to the utmost of his ability playing Irish music. The judges on this occasion were sufficiently competent to leave no degree of jealousy amongst the harpers respecting the distribution of the premiums.

When the ball was over, Dr J. MacDonnell invited all the harpers to dine with him, which they accepted. We accordingly met and dined with him, and if we had all been peers of the realm we could not have been better treated, as the assiduity of the doctor and his family was more than I can describe. I remained four days with him after the other harpers were gone away, and then set out for home.

I went to Broughshane, from that to Cushendall, where I remained two months for the benefit of the water at John Rowe MacDonnell's, the doctor's brother. I was treated with uncommon care and attention during that time, and saw my friend Randal MacDonnell very often. I found myself much better by the benefit of the water, and then went to Ballycastle to Archibald MacDonnell's, another half-brother of the doctor's, where I remained about three weeks. Thence I went to New Ferry to Henry O'Neill's, the doctor's uncle, where I was well received and used. From thence I went to Castledawson, and stopped a week there with Dr Shields; from that to Moneymore, which I might then have justly called Moneyless, as I was uncommonly bare of money. From that I went to Hugh Stewart's of Ballymena; thence to Dungannon to my brother Ferdinand's at Glenarb, where I remained in my usual manner as after my different peregrinations. After remaining some time at Glenarb with my friends, I left my brothers, and came to Mr Stewart's of Acton, County Armagh. On leaving that gentleman's house, I met Mr Edward Bunting as I was going toward Newry, where he brought me, with whom I spent as agreeable a fortnight as ever I spent in my life. He took some tunes from me, and one evening at his lodgings he played on the piano the tune of

'Speak Oyeough', and I sung with him.

There was at that time a gentleman in Newry in disguise, who called himself Mr Gardiner, and lodged near Mr Bunting. His lady was looking out of the window, and heard us. She spoke to my landlord to induce me to spend the evening with her and her husband, which I did, and was uncommonly well used; and on coming away this Mr Gardiner, who was no other than the Scotch Earl of Galloway in disguise, slipped me a guinea, and what his notions were for disguising himself I never could learn. I left Mr Bunting in Newry, and went to Dundalk, where a gentleman, a Mr McCann, accosted me on the street, and asked me where I was going. I told him "to any place, being invited to no place." He then took me to his own house in that town, where I remained a fortnight very agreeably, and then went into the County Meath, and stopped at the house of Mr Taffe, of Smarmur Castle; thence down to Drogheda, where I stopped one night. Then I went to Dublin, where I visited a number of gentlemen for a few days, and then went to Lord Powerscourt, in the County Wicklow, to whom I had a letter. There I remained some days, and then returned to Dublin again, where I met a Miss Ryan, who played the harp very decently. She lived in Beresford Street.

When I left Dublin I returned to the County Cavan but stopped at the following places:– Lord Dunsany's, Mr Barnwall's, Lord Ludlow's of Ardsallagh, near Navan, James O'Neill's of Meathstown, John O'Neill of Kells, a respectable brewer, all in the County Meath; then to Philip Reilly's of Mullagh, in the County Cavan, the gentleman, with which the eighteen successive Christmas days were passed already mentioned. I then perambulated the Counties of Cavan and Tyrone pretty much in the same manner as formerly, finishing the journey without anything particular happening to me.

In June 1803 I took it into my head to visit Dublin once more, and passed through the Counties of Cavan, Monaghan, Louth, Meath, and Dublin, stopping at the gentlemen's houses before named in each county without meeting any matter or thing worthy of notice. I determined at this time to see all my friends in Dublin, and spent about three weeks in the house of Mr John Farrell of Eccles Street, and notwithstanding the hospitality and good-nature I experienced there, my mind was miserable in consequence of the city being like one universal barrack, with the clashing of arms, beating of drums to arms, sounding of bugle horns, and the like, in consequence of an unexpected insurrection amongst a parcel of country peasants under the influence of a Mr Robert Emmet, and a few other leaders of less capacity and education. When the executions commenced after the disturbance was suppressed, I was much surprised to hear of Mr Emmet's execution.

Previous to his sentence he informed Lord Norberry, "That were Frenchmen to assume any authority inconsistent with the purest independence, that would be the signal for their destruction, and that he would fight them with the sword in one hand and the torch in the other he would root up and burn every blade of grass in the land sooner than let a foreigner tyrannise."

I was so impatient to leave that scene of terror and alarm, that I left Dublin as soon as the first emotion of dismay was subsiding. I made off for the County Tyrone again, and notwithstanding my being blind, and of course incapacitated from being useful either in loyalty or treason, I had to get a pass; and indeed, without considering my incapacity, the wiseacres on my way home demanded my pass almost every five minutes. I would sometimes say, "Here it is," pointing to my harp; and because there was no crown on it, I was often in danger of being ill-used by the illiterate loyalists, who took pride in displaying their cautious conduct. I must say that when I was examined by superior officers, they generally assisted me in facilitating my journey until I got to my brother Ferdinand's.

My headquarters for the last ten years of my life was principally at a Colonel Southwell's of Castle Hamilton, in the County Cavan, brother to Lord Southwell of Rokeby Hall, near Drogheda. He was Colonel of the 14th Light Dragoons, I never knew a more accomplished character. I do not know how I gave him cause to fancy my company so much as he did during that period, but we were almost inseparable, and our usual salutation would be, "How are you, O'Neill?" I would answer, "Very well, Colonel." I visited a great number of other gentlemen in that neighbourhood and county, but could not be long out of the Colonel's house.

I am now about sixty-eight years of age, and have exerted my utmost ability to remember as much of my peregrinations as I thought worthy of mentioning. I cannot avoid expressing my gratitude to my best friend, Mr. Bunting, to whom I am principally indebted, for ease and comfort in my declining years, by whose means I came to Belfast in consequence of an advertisement I heard read to me. It stated the gradual decline of the Irish harp, and how meritorious it would be to preserve the music of it. The cap fitted me, and I accordingly wore it, and came to Belfast and met Mr. Bunting. By his uncommon exertions, he solicited sufficient co-operation to establish an annuity for me.

Let censure, malice, or surmise rage in what shape they may it may be imagined that I am saying too much of that gentleman; but I am sorry that I am inadequate, to record or describe his real merit, which, I am proud to say, has placed him far beyond any mercenary view of his own interest. I, on my part, would be far from acting the part of a sycophant, as, thank God, I am independent of being such a character. Finally, Mr Bunting's plan is that I shall reside in Belfast the remainder of my days to instruct such twelve poor boys as have a capacity to learn and retain the national music of the harp.

Arthur O'Neill remained instructor of the Belfast Harp Society from 1803 until 1813, and was paid an annuity of thirty pounds for life by his friends. He returned to his native county, and died 1816.

CHAPTER XVIII

FAMOUS HARPS

KEEN AS WAS BUNTING'S INTEREST IN SURVIVING HARPERS AND HARP melodies, he was necessarily also very thorough in his investigations as to any notable harps still in existence.

His 1809 volume has as frontispiece a fine reproduction of a very accurate drawing of the most beautiful of instruments, known as the Dalway Harp because it was long in the possession of a gentleman of that name in Carrickfergus. It was in a shattered condition, but is restored in appearance in this drawing, and a fairly accurate account of the inscriptions on it were given in an introductory essay by Mr Joy. They are in Latin and Irish. In Latin is carved on it: "Ego sum Regina Cithararum," the name of the maker "Donatus Filius Thadei," the date 1621, and the fact that it was made for one of the Desmond Fitzgeralds, John MacEdmond Fitzgerald of Cloyne, whose arms are on the fore pillar surmounted by the arms of England. O'Curry translated the Irish inscriptions which give an interesting memorial of domestic life in a noble family in Ireland as follows:

These are they who were servitors to John Edmond at Cluain when I was made. The Steward was James Fitz John, and Maurice Walsh was our superintendent, Dermod Fitz John, wine butler, and John Raudham, beer butler, Philip Fitz Donnel was cook there, Anno Domini 1621. Teige O'Ruairc was Chamberlain there, and James Russell was House Marshal; these were all discreet attendants upon him. Philip Fitz Teige Magrath was tailor there. Donncadh Fitz Teige was his Carpenter. It was he that made me. Giollapatrick MacCrudan was my musician and harmonist, and if I could have found a better, him should I have: Dermot MacCredan along with him, two highly accomplished men whom I had to nurse me, and may God have mercy on them all.

In Bunting's 1840 volume, an even more famous and far more ancient harp was described and depicted by the noted artist and antiquary, George Petrie.

Mr Joy, writing in 1809, had cast doubt on the tradition that it belonged to the famous King Brian Borou.

> This, the most ancient Harp now remaining, is said to have belonged to Brian Borou. His son Donogh, having murdered his brother, retired to Rome, bringing his Crown, Harp, and other regalia. The Pope is said to have sent the Harp to Henry VIII. (many centuries after) but kept the Crown. Henry VIII. gave the Harp to the first Earl of Clanrickarde, in whose family it remained till early in the eighteenth century, it came by a lady of De Burgh family into that of McMahon of Cleenagh in the county of Clare, after whose death it passed into the possession of Commissioner McNamara at Limerick. In 1782 it was presented to the Rt. Hon. William Conyngham, who deposited it in Trinity College, Dublin.
>
> This Harp had only one row of strings, is thirty-two inches high, and of extraordinary good workmanship. The sound board is of oak, the pillar and comb of red sallow, the extremity of the uppermost bar or comb in part is capped with silver, extremely well wrought and chiselled. It contains a large chrystal, set in silver, and under it was another stone, now lost. The buttons, or ornamental knobs at the sides of the bar are of silver. On the front of the pillar are the arms chased in silver of the O'Brien family, the bloody hand supported by lions; on the side of the pillar, within two circles are Irish Wolf dogs carved in the wood. The string notes of the sound board are neatly ornamented with escutcheons of brass, carved and gilt.
>
> The sounding holes have been ornamented, probably of silver, as they have been the objects of theft. This harp has twenty-eight string screws and the same number of string holes to answer them, consequently there are twenty-eight strings. The bottom which it rests upon is a little broken, and the wood very rotten; the whole bears evidence of an expert artist.

In a footnote the writer calls in question the largely traditional account of the harp, which had been communicated by a Chevalier O'Gorman to General Vallancey, who wrote and published it in 1788, and he concludes that the evidence of its connection with Brian Borou was too weak, and that the condition of the instrument did not warrant the assumption of such a great age.

In the 1840 volume of Bunting, the investigation as to this harp was pursued by the celebrated artist antiquary, George Petrie, who supplied three beautifully and minutely executed sketches of the harp, showing it from every point of view. He examined and rejected the tradition, partly on account of the escutcheon attached to the harp, as coats of arms did not come into use till the reign of Henry III. The emblem of the hand, he took to be the designation of the O'Neill clan, and drew attention to the letters I.H.S., carved in Gothic or black letter character, which had not been observed in Joy's 1809 article.

He concluded that the harp from its small size, was likely one of the class used by Irish ecclesiastics to chant hymns to, and pointed out that an O'Neill was Bishop of Clogher in the fourteenth century, and that another reigned over the See of Derry about the same period. The harp might have belonged to either of these Churchmen.

This authoritative statement by Petrie did not conclude the controversy with regard to the so-called Brian Borou harp. In fact it was yet to enter on its most interesting stage, when the great Gaelic scholar, Eugene O'Curry, came to deal with the subject of music and musical instruments, in the course of a series of lectures on the customs of ancient Ireland, given at the Catholic University, Dublin.

Matthew Arnold in his essays on Celtic literature, has paid a high tribute to O'Curry's process of reasoning on antiquarian subjects. Never was it exercised in a more extraordinarily interesting manner than when he turned to the pages of old Irish manuscript literature, to seek for evidence with regard to this harp. He did not reject the tradition with regard to its ownership by a Donogh O'Brien, but sought for facts, which, however distorted, might have given rise to such a tradition. A wonderful sequence of literary and romantic events was discovered, and I cannot do better than give, in a condensed form, his reasoning and conclusions.

O'Curry seized at once on the traditions which Petrie had rejected, for lack of evidence; firstly that the harp had been given by Henry VIII. to a Lord Clanrickarde; secondly that it had belonged in former days to a Donogh O'Brien, said to be the son of Brian Borou.

With regard to it coming to Ireland as a gift to Clanrickarde, he says this was most unlikely to be a fabrication, for any one inventing a story on the subject would have made Henry VIII. give it to Murrogh O'Brien, who deserted to the English and was created Earl of Thomond on the 1st of July, 1545, on the same day that the Norman Irish Chief, MacWilliam Burke, exchanged his Chieftain title for that of Earl of Clanrickarde.

The harp had indisputably belonged to the Clanrickardes and had most likely as stated come to them as a gift from England.

Chevalier O'Gorman had turned to *The Annals of History* to seek for a Donogh O'Brien, who might have owned it, and found that King Brian's son, who went to Rome was said to have laid his crown at the feet of the Pope, in contrition for a fratricide. If the crown, why not the harp argued the Chevalier, and without further evidence, he romanced.

O'Curry turned to the manuscript remains of Irish poetry, and with which he had such an extraordinary acquaintance, and recollected a later Donogh O'Brien, a descendant of King Brian, living in the twelfth and thirteenth centuries who owned an extraordinarily beautiful gem-set harp, which was the subject of poetry. This harp had been lost to its princely owner, and last heard of in Scotland, whence he had in vain tried to recover it by ransom.

O'Curry's mind fastened on the fact that the regalia of Scotland and the crowning stone of Scone had been taken away to Westminster. With them, perhaps, went this splendid harp, which was among the royal treasures of Scotland.

The surmise was a likely one, as Donogh Carbery's lost harp was lost sight of in Scotland, though Irish bards and minstrels going there would surely have kept track of it.

As to Petrie's objection to the escutcheon, O'Curry thought this was apparently of much later date than the main body of the harp, as were also the letters I.H.S.

Let us now turn to the documents on which he founded his line of argument. He writes:

> There is in the possession of the O'Conor Don, a Manuscript Volume of family and historical poems in the Irish language at various dates, say from the tenth to the seventeenth century. The volume had been compiled at Ostend in Belgium for a Captain Alexander MacDonnell (*possibly Alastair, son of Colkitto, ancestor of Bunting's friend, the Doctor*).

From this volume, the diligent O'Curry copied one thousand quarto pages, including one hundred and fifty-eight rare family poems of which he had never seen copies in Ireland.

Much tragic history would have to be repeated to explain how these manuscripts were thus in exile, but we must proceed.

Amongst them, O'Curry recollected two concerning Donogh Carbery O'Brien (descendant of the great Brian Borou), who attained to the Chieftainship of his clan in the year 1204, and died in 1242.

The poems in question are by a northern poet, Gilla Brighde MacConmee. The first poem is in the form of a vision in which, carried to Limerick on the deck of a ship, the poet sees a young man seated on a chieftain's chair or throne. He describes his manly beauty and splendour of attire, and praises his skill as a harpist.

> *Strings sweet as his conversation*
> *On a willow harp fingers have played,*
> *Nor have the youth's white fingers touched*
> *An instrument sweeter than his own mouth.*

The second poem reveals the fact that Donogh had in some way lost a treasured harp, and that the bard, Gilbride Mac Conmee, had been sent on a mission into Scotland to recover it by pleading or purchase.

The poem was doubtless composed by the bard for the occasion, and recited by him; the latter verses, however, read to me (O'Curry has not pointed to this) as if a Scotch poet, in response, was arguing against the release of the harp. This would bring the poem into the class of dramatic dialogues. However, Mac Conmee begins asking for the harp that he may play upon it, thus showing that he was a minstrel as well as a poet.

> Bring unto me the harp of my King
> > Until upon it I forget my grief,
> A man's grief is soon banished
> > By the notes of that sweet-sounding tree.
>
> He to whom the Music tree belonged
> > Was a noble youth of sweetest performance
> Many an inspired song has he sweetly sung
> > To that elegant sweet voiced instrument.
>
> Whenever his hand touched
> > That home of music in perfection
> Its prolonged, soft, deep sigh
> > Took away from all of us our grief.
>
> When into the hall would come
> > The race of Gas of the yellow hair
> A harp with pathetic strings within
> > Welcomed the comely men of Cashel.
>
> The maiden became known to all men
> > Throughout the soft-bordered lands of Banba,
> "It is the Harp of Donogh," cried everyone,
> > " The slender, thin, fragrant tree."

O'Brien's harp! Sweet its melody
 At the head of the banquet of fair Gabhraii
Oh how the pillar of bright Gabhran called forth
 The melting tones of the thrilling chords.

No son of a bright Gael shall get
 The Harp of O'Brien of the flowing hair,
No son of a foreigner shall obtain
 The graceful, gem-set fairy instrument.

(Here I surmise the poet of Scotland may begin.)

Woe to have thought of sending to beg thee
 Thou harp of the Chieftain of fair Limerick,
Woe to have thought of sending to purchase thee
 For a rich flock of Erin's sheep.

Sweet to me is thy melodious soft voice,
 Maid who wast once the arch-King's,
Thy sprightly voice to me is sweet
 That maiden, from the island of Erin.

If to me were permitted in this eastern land,
 The life of the evergreen yew tree
The noble chief of Brendon's hill (i.e. O'Brien).
 His hand harp I would keep in repair.

Beloved to me it is natural for me
 Are the beautiful woods of Scotland
Though strange, I love dearer still
 This tree, from the woods of Erin.

O'Curry proceeds to state that this poem gives no clue to the circumstances under which this harp went to Scotland, that the harp remained there and may have been brought to Westminster along with the stone of Scone with the tradition as to Donogh O'Brien clinging to it.

Tradition in this case would have unusual weight for Donogh, as a musician and patron of the bards, would be endeared to the whole bardic order, dispensers of popular fame. By following the career of Donogh as patron and protector of poets O'Curry comes on the track of a series of remarkable incidents which may account for the exile of his treasured harp.

The Annals of the Four Masters, compiled in the seventeenth century from ancient books then existing, record for the date 1213, a homicide, which reminds us of the doings of Benevuto Cellini. But in this case the artistic temperament was not judged an excuse for the delinquent.

> Finn O'Brolachain, Steward to the O'Donnell, went into Connacht to collect O'Donnell's rent. The first place he went was to Carpre of Drumcliffe. He then went with his attendants to the house of the poet Muireadach O'Daly of Lissadilli, where he fell to offering great abuse of the poet . . . . The poet was incensed by him and he took up a keen-edged hatchet in his hand, and gave him a blow that left him dead for life.

O'Daly fled to the Clanrickardes in Connaught pursued by O'Donnell, and then into Thomond, where Donogh Carbery O'Brien sheltered him till O'Donnell and his army appeared at the gates of Limerick. Donogh sent the bard by ship to Dublin, and O'Donnell returned to the north, but without rest set out for Dublin and demanded his person. O'Daly was sent over sea to Scotland, where he remained, according to the annalists, for some time, sending three conciliatory poems to O'Donnell, till at length peace was made. In one of these poems addressed to O'Donnell's young son, and preserved in the Bodleian Library, he describes his wanderings on the Continent and up to the Mediterranean Sea.

During the period of his exile he also addressed a pathetic poem to the cousin and heir of Donogh, in which he says:

Guess what my profession is,
  Guess what my name is,
Guess what country I come from.

He then says he has been going about the world, that Muireadach of Scotland is his name, that he knows the O'Briens would protect him, and in the last verse he appeals directly to Donogh Carbery.

Donogh Carbery of the smooth skin
  Out of Scotland of the feasts and of the fields,
Of Steeds, of spears, of Islands,
  My run to Erin on my return
How soon shall I make! and guess.

This poem was likely sent as a message by O'Daly when he had been forgiven by O'Donnell and could return to Ireland, only that the Scotch King or Chieftain now detained him for love of his art.

O'Donnell, who had granted a surly forgiveness, could not be expected to pay a ransom, hence the appeal to Donogh Carbery, lover and friend of the bards.

What ransom did O'Brien send? There is no record, nor talk of a ransom either in this poem. But O'Curry found another clue. In a compilation known as the *Book of Fermoy*, made up in the year 1463, there is a poem by a Connaught poet, Brian O'Higgins, who wished to ingratiate himself with David Roche of Fermoy. Praising the hospitality he had received at his house, he broadly hints that he would have no objection to desert Connaught and live in Munster permanently, and he quotes the case of Muireadach O'Daly, who, after his return from exile, lived with Donogh Carbery in Munster.

The jewel of Donogh Carbery having been sent
  To release the Chief Poet of Scotland.
This it was that brought him over the sea.

O'Curry points out that the jewel here alluded to was almost without doubt Donogh Carbery's harp. O'Daly had become chief poet in Scotland, and could not depart without a kingly ransom.

So the harp, he assumes, was sent, and afterwards when O'Daly was safe in Ireland, Gilbride Mac Conmee went on his mission to beg for its release, perhaps indeed, I would add to O'Curry's argument, to offer himself as part of the ransom, for this Gilbride became known also as *an Albanach*, or the Scotchman.

Such is the scope of this most interesting enquiry, prompted by the Petrie article in Bunting's volume.

Whatever may be the final judgment on the O'Brien harp, O'Curry in the course of his disquisition threw a flood of light upon the life of the bards of ancient Ireland, and opened up the hidden chronicles of early Gaelic literature with extraordinary effect.

The personality of the last of the harpers who mustered in Belfast, will have added interest from what has here been told of their predecessors, Donogh Carbery, the princely musician, MacConmee, the Ambassador Bard, O'Daly, the exile. Later on you will read how Hempson the oldest of Bunting's harpers, went also wandering through Scotland, and how Arthur O'Neill re-strung and played on the O'Brien harp through the streets of Limerick, where long ago Donogh had harped on his royal chair.

We conclude by quoting the following letter to Mary M'Cracken, in which you will discover Bunting with this remarkable instrument in his hands.

DUBLIN,

Wednesday, Sept. 14th *1808.*

I had commenced a letter to you yesterday, but was called away by Mr O'Flanaghan, Professor of Irish to the College, whom I intend employing to translate the songs. He is preparing for the press translations of several old Irish MSS., under the direction of the Gaelic Society. I searched the College Library for "Galileo Galelie" but it is not there; and will you tell Mr Joy there are no drawings of harps in Norden. Dr Burney was right certainly, in refusing me any information respecting musical rhythm, as he is engaged already in writing on that subject for another. As to Mr Ledwich, he has published all he knew on the subject. My business lately has been looking after Irish and Welsh scholars. I have been examining Brian Borhoim's harp, and find Vallancey's description to have been inaccurate. I purpose measuring it to-morrow, I have got some addition to my stock of airs.

CHAPTER XIX

BUNTING AND THE COUNTRY SINGERS

IN ADDITION TO PRESERVING THE RECORDS OF THE MUSIC OF THE HARPERS, Edward Bunting and his Belfast associates recognised the importance of collecting the melodies and song words from the lips of the country singers, who had received the traditional method of rendering them from preceding generations.

The harpers, as we have seen from O'Neill's *Memoir*, frequented the homes of the landed proprietors, but Irish song echoed by the firesides of lowly cottages, in the milking shed, in the harvest field, and in such places through the four provinces of Ireland, Edward Bunting became acquainted with the sorrows and joys of the people. His note-books and letters make us acquainted with the frequency and distance of his wanderings, and as the years passed the airs noted as taken from harpers became fewer, those taken from rural singers are in the majority. In his 1840 index, the earliest date given us when a song was noted, or likely in this case, we should say, heard, is 1780, the air 'White Maive', singer "Kitty Doo at Armagh." This was likely a nurse, or some country woman in his childhood's home, for in 1780 he was no more than seven or eight years of age.

It is sometimes stated, that Bunting put a higher value on the music of the harpers than on traditional song. This is not true with regard to the ordinary harpers, intense interest was only shown in the performance of those who, like Hempson, were regarded by him as the last repositories of ancient art. In the following passage which I quote from his 1840 volume, it will be seen what a degree of reliance he placed on the traditional singer.

Poems and histories, when orally delivered will from time to time be corrupted and interpolated. Thus of all the poems attributed to Ossian, it is now impossible to say whether any, or any part even, be undoubtedly genuine. So also, but in a higher degree with regard to songs. The words of the popular songs of every country vary according to the several provinces and districts in which they are sung: as, for example, to the popular air of 'Aileen-a-Roon' we here find as many sets of words as there are counties in one of our provinces. But the case is totally different with music. A strain of music, once impressed on the popular ear, never varies. It may be made the vehicle of many different sets of words, but they are adapted to it, not it to them, and it will no more alter its character on their account than a ship will change the number of its masts on account of an alteration in the nature of its lading. For taste in music is so universal, especially among country people, and in a pastoral age, and airs are so easily, indeed in many instances, so intuitively acquired, that when a melody has once been divulged in any district a criterion is immediately established in almost every ear. And this criterion being the more infallible in proportion as it requires less effort in judging, we have thus in all directions, and at all times, a tribunal of the utmost accuracy and of unequalled impartiality (for it is unconscious of the exercise of its own authority), governing the musical traditions of the people, and preserving the native airs and melodies of every country in their integrity from the earliest periods.

It is thus that changes in the actual frame and structure of our melodies have never been attempted, unless on the introduction of the altered tunes for the first time amongst those who never heard them in their original state; as in the instance of Sir John Stevenson's supposed emendations of the Irish Melodies on their first introduction to that extended auditory procured for them by the excellence of Mr Moore's accompanying poetry; and thus it is that so long as the musical collector or antiquary confines his search to the native districts of the tunes he seeks for, he always may be certain of the absolute and unimpeachable authenticity of every note he procures.

Were it not for this provision for the transmission of tunes in a perfect state from the earliest times, there would be no such thing (at least in our age of the world) as musical antiquity or the means of judging from musical remains of the genius and sentiment, and through them of the mental refinement and social progress of our remote ancestors for musical notation is of comparatively recent origin, and without it we have nothing but this tradition to depend on.

This testimony, to the worth of tradition in relation to music, may be questioned when we recollect the change that can easily be wrought in an air by a change of accent and time. We find from time to time, moreover, among country singers that several airs may be variants of one original. In coming to this decided conclusion Bunting, however, was guided by the fact that he had collected Irish melodies from boyhood through a long lifetime, and in the four provinces of Ireland from singers who had no common model, such as a printed version to study from. They had received from their ancestors, had carefully preserved the form and handed it on to posterity. The peasant poet moulded his words to the music of antiquity, which he delighted in and reverenced, and from which he received his inspiration.

It was left for Thomas Moore and other poets who got their music out of books, to experiment in making the melody accord with the metres of their verses.

As a test of Bunting's estimate as to the value of tradition, it is open to us to go into Connaught or the hill country of Derry and Tyrone and seek for the songs which he set down a hundred years ago. We will hear them from the lips of the descendants and successors of the men and women who sang to him, and in all cases I think our conclusion will be that his judgment was correct. I myself made a journey of investigation quite recently (May 1910). In a country parochial house[1] in County

---

1. The residence of the Rev. Matthew Maguire, P.P. He is one of the leading Gaelic language and Irish industrial pioneers. The Connaught teacher referred to, Mr Waldron, is making a collection of songs of Tyrone.

Tyrone, I had the pleasure of meeting a native Connaught teacher, and put in his hands a volume of the songs words taken down in Connaught in 1802. His exclamations of pleasure and familiarity were pleasant to hear. "My mother had that very song." "I know a man that has that one." "They sing that still about Castlebar, and I can tell you a story about the man that wrote it."

The value of the manuscript collection of Gaelic songs is enhanced by the fact that it affords a key as to the airs to which songs were sung. Several important collections of Gaelic poems have appeared, without any guide being given as to the melody belonging to each. I need only point to Hardiman's *Minstrelsy* published in 1831, and Dr Douglas Hyde's *Love Songs of Connaught*, which appeared in 1893. These are veritable collections of words without songs; and vice versa we have songs without words in the great Petrie collection and in Bunting's own published volumes, inasmuch as only the first lines or names in Irish of each song is given. To the present day musical collectors are at work, who never trouble about the Irish words; and industrious Gaelic scholars go about taking down lyrics without any attempt to preserve the melodies. Bunting and his friends were wise in their generation, and as proof of the trouble and expense which they went to, we have amongst the manuscripts, and now published for the first time, the journal and letters of Patrick Lynch, who was sent to tour Connaught in 1802, to find out songs for Bunting, and take down the Irish words of them, while the musician following later on in his track secured the melodies.

Before coming to this detailed account of a song-collecting journey, it will be well to insert a brief account of the remarkable man who was Bunting's guide and entertainer on the occasion of his earliest visit to Connaught. Shortly after the Harper's Festival when preparing for the publication of his first volume, you have seen that he spent much of his time with old Hempson at Magilligan.

But in 1792, the very year of the Festival he went to Connaught, under the guidance of Richard Kirwan. I can scarcely doubt, but that Whitley Stokes who was acquainted with this eccentric genius, was the medium of introduction.

In the 1840 index we find an air, 'The Rejected Lover', set down as being taken down from Mr W. Stokes, Dublin, in 1792. Bunting was then likely en route to Connaught. (This air, by the way, is one which has been admirably set by Sir C.V. Stanford with words by Mr A. P. Graves, beginning 'In Innisfallen's Fairy Isle'.)

A number of songs are given as being taken down in Connaught at this date, including 'Health from The Cup' from Richard Kirwan, Esq., 1792. 'Clara Burke' from Mrs Burke, Carrakeel, County Mayo, in 1792; 'I am a Fisherman of Lough Carra', also from Mrs Burke, and the following were taken down at Deel Castle, Ballina singer not named: 'Mary with the Fair Locks', 'In this Valley there lives a Fair Maid', 'The White Blanket', 'Young Brigid', 'The Pretty Brown Maid'. At Ballinrobe he noted 'Is it the Priest you want?' 'The Blackbird and theThrush', 'The Blackbird and the Hen', 'Preparing to Sail Away', 'The White Calves'.

Richard Kirwan of Creggs,[2] who pioneered Bunting on this tour, was the younger son of Martin Kirwan, a Catholic gentleman of one of the old Galway tribes, and was given a liberal education partly in France. On the death of his mother in 1751, he fell into a melancholy and religious frame of mind and went to St Omer, the famous Jesuit Novitiate. His elder brother being killed in a duel, he succeeded to the family estate, and, giving up his idea of a religious profession, married a Miss Blake of Menlo. He had the unpleasant experience of being arrested and imprisoned for her debts the day after his marriage. Later on in life he became a Protestant, and qualified for the Bar; but amid a variety of tastes and occupations his ruling passion was for scientific research. Living for a while in London, he pursued this study of chemistry, and was in communication with all the learned societies of the Continent. The Empress Catherine of Russia sent him her portrait in recognition

---

2. Richard Kirwan, F.R.S., was born in Cloughballyinore, County Galway, in 1733, died in 1812. Famous chemist and mineralogist. In 1799 (on the death of Lord Charlemont) he was elected President of the Royal Irish Academy.

of his merits. Returning to Dublin he helped to found the Royal Irish Academy, and was president of that Institution from 1800 to 1810.

He was a man of many eccentric habits. Even at Courts of Justice and at Vice-regal levees he wore a large slouched hat, and summer or winter received his friends at a roaring fire. He had a special abhorrence of flies, and according to the latest theories about the part they take in spreading disease, was not far wrong in this. He always dined alone and took no other diet than ham and milk. His death occurred in 1812 as the result of starving a cold.

In an old book the *Worthies of Ireland* published in 1810, we find the following reference to his musical tastes:

> His leisure hours were amused by the national music of his country. On one occasion he made a tour with Mr Bunting into the most unfrequented parts of Ireland for the purpose of collecting old Irish airs, particularly those of Caladon and Carador (? Carolan and Connelan). He procured very few of them in Donegal; but was more successful in Galway, where a lady who had invited the travellers to her house, on discovering the motive of their journey, sent a message thirty miles across country in search of a harper, whose extensive acquaintance with national music amply compensated them for much of the trouble they had undergone. The latter years of his life were devoted almost exclusively to theology, and his opinions in many subjects were as varied and fanciful as can be imagined. His conversation, however, was still much diversified and highly amusing from the variety and extent of his knowledge. Miss Owenson (later known to fame as Lady Morgan) visited him very frequently, and even in the midst of his theological pursuits he was always ready to canvass the merits of a romance or to discuss the chemical composition of a new cosmetic, which latter is said to have very frequently formed the subject of their conversation.

We must picture to ourselves the youthful Bunting among the wilds of the West in company with this extraordinary but talented man, who, doubtless, did his part like Dr MacDonnell in giving the musician a taste for antiquarian research in connection with his art.

The following extracts from letters written by Bunting to Miss Mary M{c}Cracken, when at a later date he went forth on a similar mission, give us a vivid glimpse of his manner of travelling, of his method of work, and of the company he frequented. The allusion to the 'collar' shows us that he did not ride, but drove some sort of vehicle. The 'old mare' was likely owned by the M{c}Cracken family, and accustomed to go on regular journeys in connection with their business.

BELFAST, 30th *Aug.,* 1808.

The old mare performed her part, to my great satisfaction never refused except at Lurgan, where in passing the old inn which is not kept at present she wanted of all things to turn into the gateway; however, she behaved herself as well, if not better, than almost any beast. I intend setting off for Sligo to-morrow, and would have gone to-day, but the mare's neck was a little rubbed, and I wished to make some alteration in the collar, etc., that she may not suffer pain. I found the old lady in Dungannon.

She appears to be a very fine specimen of the ancient gentle-woman. She has the poem descriptive of a battle, and the song. The battle is Aughrim, and the tune is something like what I have heard the women sing after the dead bodies in the County of Armagh; the poem, I think, is the composition of some of up-country bards, as they were called, that is the Kerry gentry, of whom we have some specimens. I rather think this poem and tune will not be worth the trouble of sending a person to write it down, but when I come home we must have a consultation on the subject. The old lady was much gratified at the idea of being of so much consequence, and her daughters were indeed very civil; they asked me to drink tea with them, which I thought was kind of them as I had no introduction.

I had a letter from Mr Joy to Mr M{c}Dowel, of Augher; but I passed through that place so early that I could not deliver it myself; but another letter of his to Mr Irwin, of Enniskillen, I gave in person, and he expressed many kind wishes for my success. It will depend on what I hear from Thady Conlan, whether I shall go to Limerick, as I think it likely he will be found fully competent to do all we shall require from an Irish scholar. I have made every inquiry relative to Irish manuscripts, and saw one in the possession of an old woman, who, when asked whether she would dispose of it, answered, "I'll never part with it till I die," and with some difficulty was persuaded to allow it to be copied, provided the person appointed to do so "were well recommended."

Of the "Up-Country Gentry" or Munster school of poets mentioned in this letter, memoirs and relics have been preserved in Hardiman's *Minstrelsy*, and in a publication called *Poets and Poetry of Munster*, published in the forties. Clarence Mangan did many translations for the latter work, and in the introduction of one of the editions the following passage is quoted:

A queer set of fellows were those bards! One hour rollicking in the Shebeen-house, and the next seated in some tradition-haunted rath, bewailing the woes of Inisfail and the persecution of the old religion. . . . Moore's songs were made for the ballroom and for gentle maidens, who sit down to a piano, manufactured by some London house. They are beyond a doubt matchless in their caste, but before Moore sang, our grandmothers at the spinning wheel and our great-grandfathers whether delving in the fields or shouldering a musket in the brigades, sang these time consecrated verses to keep alive the memory of Ireland, her lost glories and cherished aspirations. Before Moore was, these bards were, and it is but fair to give their memory that honour which some would exclusively bestow on the author of the Irish Melodies.

The names of Donogh Mac Con Mara, Shawn O'Tuomy, Andrew Magrath, Egan O'Rahilly, Teig Gaedlach O'Sullivan, John Clarach MacDonnell, Owen Ruadh O'Sullivan, and William Heffernan, may be set down here as eminent in the eighteenth century as "Up Country"

or Munster poets. There were many others. The name of Piers Ferriter
deserves to stand out starlike in the turbulent era of the Cromwellian
wars. The poems of the Munster men have been collected and edited by
the Rev. Patrick Dineen of Dublin in our own day. Peadar O'Duirnin
was a Southern eighteenth century poet, who became a schoolmaster in
Ulster, and lived not far from Edward Bunting's native district of Armagh.
We find amongst the Bunting MSS. some poems in an exceedingly ornate
hand, signed by one Thomas O'Duirnin.

The southern poets were accustomed to hold bardic sessions or
competitions, at certain centres, among which we may mention Croome,
County Limerick; and Charleville, County Cork. From these assemblies
noted poems wedded to melody were dispersed through the length and
breadth of the song-loving land.

Here are other extracts from his correspondence with Miss
McCracken at that period.

SLIGO, *September 1st, '08.*

I am to dine to-day with Mr Everard, Jun., who has kindly promised to
call on the celebrated Dr O'Conor, who is now preparing for publication
the *Annals of the Four Masters* and the *Book of Ballymote* two old Irish MSS. He
should be written to. Perhaps it might be found that he had met with
something relative to my work. He had been collecting for some time
poems, and Irish MSS. for the Marquis of Buckingham. It is probable
he could assist me. Please let Mr Joy know this, to whom I would write
but that I hope you will let him read this, which will answer the same
purpose. I find that your friend (to whom I am indebted for many
favours), Mr Alfred Blest, has put all the "irons in the fire" for me.
When I inquire whether in this part of the country, any one has any
knowledge of a collection of Irish tunes, the answer is, "Oh, Mr Blest
is making a collection—he's the man." I feel much indebted to him for
his kindness. Mr Everard, the elder, is an excellent judge of the Irish

language, and he has asked Mr Thady Conlan to dine with him on Sunday next, when he will question him, and will, from his knowledge of the Irish language, be enabled to inform me whether he will answer my purpose. I fear, from what Mr E——— says, that I shall be obliged to go to Limerick to see Mr Elligott.[3] I shall see Mr Blest to-morrow, and shall tell you of any information I may obtain from him.

DUBLIN, *Sept.* 10, 1808.

I am glad to find that Sir J. Sinclair has sent the tunes. I am to dine with Stokes[4] on Monday, and he will introduce me to all whom I wish to be acquainted with here. I leave this for Limerick on Tuesday. I find that Dr Beaufort is now on the tour for the purpose of collecting information respecting the parishes in the South of Ireland for the placing of Irish masters in. I shall meet with him if possible, and I have no doubt but that he will give me all the assistance in his power. I got some curious airs from the people in the neighbourhood of Sligo during my visit to Mr Blest; but I met with very few tunes indeed, that I had not before. Those you mention as taken down by Mr Broadwood,[5] I have already, but am nevertheless much obliged to him.

DUBLIN, *Sept.* 16, 1808.

I shall not forget Harry Joy's message to Mr Ledwich, but do not like putting that gentleman to any trouble, particularly as there is a copy of

---

3. This is probably one MacElligott, a scholar whom Lynch and Bunting met in Limerick, in 1802. A letter from him couched in very stilted English is among our manuscripts.

4. Whitley Stokes, who was present with Wolfe Tone at the meeting of harpers in Belfast 1792.

5. Miss Lucy Broadwood states it was her great-uncle, Robert, who was Bunting's friend, and also Anthony Bunting was representative in Dublin for the Broadwood pianofortes.

Cambrensis in the College, to which we can refer. Will you tell Mr Joy that I am sitting with O'Flanagan who is making out, *much to my satisfaction*, the twenty-four measures of music, which are pure *Irish*. O'Flanagan is also to make out the roots of the different technical terms, etc. I have got another march, called 'The Cavalcade of the O'Neils' (a curious air), with the words; so you may perceive I am not idle.

DROGHEDA, *Sept.* 18, 1808.

I have written to Counsellor Fenton, in Pembrokeshire for a translation of the twenty-four measures of music, which I mentioned in a former letter, not being quite satisfied with Mr O'Flanagan's assertion that they were pure Irish. If they are Irish, or should prove to be *Cornish*, which is a dialect of the Celtic, it will be a great matter for me. I came down here to see my brother, but purpose going back to-morrow, to meet O'Flanagan, *Cody*, a piper, and a woman from the County Mayo, whom I accidently heard singing in the streets.

DUBLIN, *Sept.* 21, 1808.

I am employed in watching O'Flanagan, while he translates some of the songs. I have got three tunes, one of which *Cody*, the piper, calls 'O'More, King of Leix's March', and two others, viz.: 'The Cavalcade of the O'Neils', and 'The March of Owen Roe O'Neil'. I am anxious to have everything done in the best manner. I have gone too far to recede, otherwise I should, from the difficulty of the undertaking, give it up altogether. I think Miss Balfour's 'Fairy Queen' very good. The 'Fairy Queen' of Carolan, however, was not intended by him for words, but as a piece of music for the harp; therefore, it would not answer to have it now set with words. These some days past I have been running after an old woman named Betty Walsh, whom I have seen once before, and heard her play. It is possible I may pick up some airs from her. I have been making every exertion to find out her residence. I intend setting off for Limerick to-morrow eve, and shall leave my *Irish affairs* in such a train, that I can depend on the business being executed as well as if I were on the spot; at any rate, I have got one material part finished, that of the technical terms, etc., with their roots and translations, which we could not do without for the memoir.

DROGHEDA, *Sept. 29*, 1808.

I am so far on my way home. I have got in Limerick what I think will turn out well; and from Walker, the Highland airs, and also a book from him on the bagpipe principally.

In this connection I give here extracts from letters written to Miss McCracken in 1809 when he went to London about his publication work. He was assisted in the business arrangements by Mr J. Sidebotham, a solicitor and intimate friend of musical tastes. The letters particularly refer to the difficulty he experienced in trying to urge the poet Campbell to attempt rivalry with Moore, by translating some of the Gaelic lyrics.

LONDON, *March 8*, 1809.

I received your letter, and shall take care to have the paper enclosed relative to the brass trumpets, etc., inserted in its proper place. I have been these two days with Mr Campbell. He approves very much of the treatise, which he says is very ingenious, but wishes to make some alteration in the language, which he considers in some places not sufficiently explicit. There are also some notes, which, he thinks, may be left out; but, before any change is made, I shall inform our friend Harry Joy. This evening, Mr Campbell and I intend beginning our selection of songs. I cannot help observing, that I cannot be expected to entertain very friendly feelings towards Power (Stevenson's publisher), connected as he is in the success of a work decidedly stolen from what I have been labouring for so many years to produce, and which I look on as my undoubted property. He endeavours to persuade every one that Moore's work and mine do not clash. Certainly they do clash, unfortunately for me. I shall let you know by to-morrow what Campbell thinks of Miss Balfour's songs.

LONDON, *March* 15, 1809.

I have so far discharged *Cody*, that I mentioned I had nothing farther for him to do, unless he could procure me some tunes, words, etc., in the southern parts of the counties Derry, Antrim, and Donegal. I have already amply remunerated him for his visit to the North on my business. All my friends here approve highly of my intention respecting the literary part of the work. I expect to have an interview with Dr Burney in a few days. I am at present hard at work, studying the obsolete notation in the Welsh Archaeology, and expect to make something out of it for Mr Joy. I purpose calling on Mr Jones (who published the Welsh music) in a few days.

LONDON, *April* 12, 1809.

I have not got the words from Campbell yet. I am vexed when I think of all the time and money which I have expended in the prosecution of my work, with so little prospect of remuneration, as I have computed the cost of getting out the *first* volume alone at not less than from seven-hundred to eight-hundred pounds for one-thousand copies. I do not expect to reap from the publication what will pay me expenses . . . . I send you an engraving of the harp.

LONDON, *May* 5, 1809.

I have altered my determination with respect to the Treatise, etc., and shall now have the letterpress the full size of the music, viz.: *folio.* I hope to have the work out in the course of three months. I have now as many tunes as will compose a *third* volume. Let Mr Joy know this resolution of mine. I have received the poetry, and shall make use of some of the songs.

LONDON, *May* 24, 1809.

Campbell begins to take an interest in the business now; and I expect shortly to have his part quite ready. I am certain I shall not make anything by all my trouble and expense. I would be obliged by your sending Miss Balfour's 'Pretty Girl milking her Cow'. I received 'The Dawning of the Day'. I wish much to get the drawing from John,[6] its not being sent keeps me back.

LONDON, *Sept.* 1, 1809.

I received your letter and am obliged for the song. I have got a very pretty song from a Mr Smythe, of Cambridge, a professor. I shall adapt it to the 'Girl I left behind me'. Campbell also has written a song, which he calls 'The March of the Men of Erin', and it will answer the only specimen I have of the war-song of the Irish, which is, 'At the Foot of a Rath'. I expect soon to be able to inform you of an end to my labours, at least for a time, as I am determined to have the second volume out if possible in Spring. Give my respects to Mrs Connor. I have set her little air, 'McFarlane's Lamentation', to the original words, which are well adapted to it.

LONDON, *Oct* 2, 1809.

I have finished with Campbell, at least for the present; and he has promised to exert himself to the utmost for my next volume. I have

---

6. Most probably a sketch portrait of Arthur O'Neill, the harper. An engraving of it appears in the second volume, and the original is among our manuscripts.

copied out from my papers nearly 100 pages of poetry; so you may perceive how much my songs have accumulated. I am far from being well at present, and this proceeds perhaps from my great anxiety about this work. For, as I must have during my long absence lost my business in Belfast, I have nothing to depend on but the sale of this work, for some time at least.

LONDON, *Oct.* 7, 1809.

I am sorry to hear of Cody's intended departure from Belfast, as he may have some airs which I have not heard. Will you try and keep him in Belfast till my return? I begin to print the music next week. I think my book will have something to recommend it, as all the airs contained in it, with the exception of fifteen, have never appeared in any previous publication. I see by the papers that Paddy Quin is at present in Dublin. This is in my favour. I have been exceedingly vexed by Stevenson's having taken my tunes.

MANCHESTER, *Nov.* 24, 1809.

I arrived here last night, and have brought with me one hundred copies of my book. I will make all possible dispatch in getting home, as I require a little rest, but cannot afford to indulge long, as it is my intention to publish my second volume directly.

The most detailed account that remains to us of the process of song-collecting as carried out by Bunting is to be found in the diary, hitherto unpublished, of Patrick Lynch, who was his envoy to Connaught in 1802. This diary with numerous letters is among the manuscripts, and will be found in the following chapters. It is proper to state here that the MSS. of Buntings own letters to Miss McCracken are not in our possession, but that the extracts which we have quoted from them were made for publication from the originals.

CHAPTER XX

DIARY AND LETTERS OF PATRICK LYNCH

W E NOW COME TO THE MOST IMPORTANT PERIOD IN CONNECTION WITH Bunting's preparations for his second volume of *Ancient Melodies*. As we have seen, he had followed up the work done at the Harpers' Festival, by going out himself on the track of these itinerant musicians into Ulster, Munster, and Connaught. His visit to Richard Kirwan had resulted in a plentiful gleaning, and now again he turned his face to the west. Owing to the ties which hound him as an organist and music teacher, his time was necessarily limited. He had besides to make an important business journey to London at the beginning of this summer, of 1802 for he was now acting as agent for the sale of Messrs Broadwood's pianos. So in order to make the most of the holiday which was in prospect, he sent a pioneer forward into Connaught ahead of him in the person of Patrick Lynch, a native speaker of Irish, who was able to take down both the words and music of the songs.

W. H. Grattan Flood, Mus. Doc., the well-known authority on the subject of Irish Musical biography, has supplied us with information as to the origin and varied acquirements of this man. We have besides at our disposal many of his letters, and the diary kept during this tour. For certain incidents in his career, we have but to turn to the pages of the history of a tragic era as recorded by Doctor Madden, in his *Lives and Times of the United Irishmen*, and the Belfast newspapers of that day give an even fuller account of the painful part which he was forced into taking.

As regards his birth and career outside the scope of our history we may here give Dr Grattan Flood's account in full. The other incidents will be related in order as they occur.

Patrick Lynch[1] was born near Quin, County Clare, in 1757 or 1758. For many years he acted as a private tutor. And in 1790 settled in Carrick-on-Suir. Many writers incorrectly state that he was a native of Carrick. In 1791 he finished a work, entitled 'Chronoscope' or a chronological tale of events, but finding no publisher he constructed a rude printing-press, and printed it himself. Two years later, John Stacy, a regular printer, set up in Carrick, and from his press there was issued in 1796 a book by Lynch called *The Pentaglot Preceptor* with instructions for the study of English, Latin, Greek, Hebrew, and Irish. In 1800 he issued an Almanack, but though these books were printed in Carrick he was at the time of their publication already living in Belfast. He had, doubtless, been invited there by the group of eager students of Irish, who had been connected with the Harp Festival. There were many schools in Belfast, and doubtless the author of *The Pentaglot Preceptor* found occupation as an instructor of youth. Amongst those who studied Irish with him was Thomas Russell, one of the leaders of the United Irishmen, who had retired from the army, and had taken the position of librarian in the newly started Belfast Library. Russell, however, was arrested and taken out of Ireland as a state prisoner in 1796, and he and Lynch were fated not to meet for many years. After nine years in Belfast he went to live at Loughin Island, in County Down, bringing with him his children, but from one of his letters we would conclude that he was then a widower.

This was his home when, in May 1802, he started out on the Connaught tour. In 1803 we shall see he fell into disfavour with his Belfast employers. Dr Grattan Flood tells us that he returned to Carrick, and published in 1805 his *Plain, Easy, and Comprehensive Grammar*. In 1806 he settled in Dublin and opened a private school. In December of the same year he became secretary of the newly founded Gaelic Society, which numbered among its members Father Denis Taaffe, Father Paul

---

[1.] See Preface. The identity of the Southern Lynch, with Bunting's man has been disputed. I have not found it possible by any method of investigation to decide whether Dr Grattan Flood amalgamated the lives of two men into one.

O'Brien, Edward O'Reilly (compiler of the well-known Irish Dictionary), Theophilus O'Flannigan, and W. A. Halliday. All these names will be familar to those interested in the history of the Gaelic revival. In 1808 he helped the Rev. W. Neilson with his Irish grammar, which, by the way, after a hundred years, has been largely drawn on by the Gaelic League compilers of phrase-books. It contains a fine version of the famous poem 'Deirdre's Lament'.

In 1808 and in 1810 Lynch edited *Wogan's Gents, and Ladies Almanacks*. He also got employment as a copyist of Gaelic MSS. in Trinity College, and the Royal Irish Academy. His death took place in 1829.

From all this you will gather that Lynch was a typical pedagogue, but of more than average capacity, even if we assume that there was a certain amount of pretension shown by the author of *The Pentaglot Preceptor*. What he had of Hebrew we know not, the proofs of his diligence as a collector of Irish Songs lies before us in his numerous note-books, and in the two large volumes in which he has made fair copies of the song words.

We shall now quote from his diary and letters. As Bunting was leaving Belfast for London only the first letter is addressed to him. It tells how Lynch arrived at the house of Mr Anthony Bunting at Drogheda, and received directions and introductions.

DROGHEDA, *April 25, 1802.*

DEAR SIR, — I came here on Friday evening, and I set off for Connaught to-morrow morning. Your brother has just now given me three letters; one from Mr O'Connor, to the Rev. James French, West Galway; one from Miss Bellew, to the Right Rev. Dr Bellew, Ballina ; and one from Mr Edward Bellew, to the Rev. James Magee, Lackan, Killala. Your brother has advised me to take the northerly course, and has drawn from the map the route I am to take from Drogheda to Cullen, Kingscourt, Cavan, Swadlingbar, Manorhamilton, Coloony, Ballina, and to Killala, and round the County Mayo to Newport and Castlebar. I expect you will meet me there when you return. I shall write to Mr McCracken from

Manorhamilton, and I promise to you that I shall be as diligent and zealous for your interest as I can, and shall observe your instructions; and am. — Sir, your humble Servant,

PATRICK LYNCH.

P.S. — I have also a letter from Mr Connor of Belfast, to Wm. Bartley, Esq., near Manorhamilton. I suppose I shall stay a week thereabout.

To Mr EDWARD BUNTING, Belfast.

Then follows a long letter to Mr John McCracken describing his progress:

BALLINA, *May 7ᵗʰ* 1802.

DEAR SIR, — I left Drogheda on Monday, 26ᵗʰ April. The rain came on. I stopped in Slane two hours. Came to Navan, fourteen miles. I slept there, having suffered greatly by the rain. On Monday, waited awhile in Navan in order to see Dr Plunkett, Bishop of Meath, as I was advised in Drogheda. I did not get speaking to him; he was about some business. On Tuesday, from Navan, by Kells to Virginia, eighteen miles; on Wednesday, by Cavan to Belturbet, twenty-one miles; on Thursday, through part of Cavan and Fermanagh to the Black Lion, twenty miles; on Friday, to Manorhamilton, eighty-two miles from Drogheda; and six miles more that evening, to a place called Killargy, near where Mr Bartley lives. I had a letter to him from Mr Pat Connor. I stayed there, at a public-house, till Monday evening. I got but six songs from Mr Bartley; indeed, they are some of the best of Carolan's. I got about sixteen more at the public-house. I came three miles to Dromahare on Monday evening; took breakfast at Coolooney, eight miles off, on Tuesday; came to a place called Skreen, in the Barony of Tyreragh, County Sligo, where I got five good songs from James Dowd, a farmer; that night I treated him and his family to some whiskey, where I got the five songs, some good potatoes and eggs, and a bed in the barn. I came to a public-house on Wednesday night, within eight miles of Ballina. Yesterday, 6th May, I came to this town. I found Dr Bellew very civil; I dined with him and his clergy. I wait here to-day to get a few songs from a Mrs Burke. I am advised to proceed directly to Irris, across the country; and to the Mullet, in the most westerly part of the County Mayo. I do not know how long this may take, but I am resolved to be always either writing or travelling, and to make the best I can for my employer. I am sure I shall be in want of money by the time I am at Castlebar. On my return from the mountains of Mayo, I know that every week will cost me a guinea, whether I travel or stop. Mr Bunting allowed me to keep account of every expense I should be at on account of the songs; but I find this cannot be well done, because my own travelling expense is so connected with the expense of procuring songs that I could not well keep a separate account. You will please to let Mr B——— know that I expect he will allow me a guinea-and-a-half per week for altogether, and let me bear the expense for songs which may be to little purpose; at other times I will get a parcel of songs at less cost, and I would not wish to have any complaint at my return for extravagance. I am now convinced that the best way is to go to the shebeen-houses, and find out some little blasting schoolmaster, and warm his mouth with whiskey; and he will find out the singers for me. For my own part, you may depend on it, I shall drink no whiskey nor spirits until I return to Belfast. I shall live as the case requires in this wild country. I hope I shall be able to show twenty-one songs for every week that I am on this tour, and more if I can. I have no place as yet that you could write to me; I suppose that I shall appoint Castlebar for my address.

P. Lynch.

P.S. — I have just now procured a correspondent in Castlebar by means of Dr Bellew. You will direct a letter to me, on the receipt of this, to the care of the Rev. Dr Egan, Castlebar. Dr Bellew will write to this gentleman to release and keep the letter for me until I come. Should it be there before me, you will please to send me three guineas by this conveyance. And oblige yours,

P. LYNCH.

Mr JOHN MᶜCRACKEN, Jun., Belfast.

A copy of this was sent on by Mr McCracken with the following letter from himself. It refers mainly to business transactions, but begins with a pet name, possibly bestowed on Bunting by the child referred to in the postscript. Eddy pronounced with the broad Belfast accent, and imitated by an infant learning to speak, would easily turn into "Atty."

To Mr EDWARD BUNTING, c/o Messrs Broadwood & Son,
Great Pulteney St., London.

May 15ᵗʰ 1802.

DEAR ATTY, — I received your letter from Liverpool, and was glad to hear you had a good crossing, and I hope your journey up to London was equally pleasant. I annex copy of Lynch's letter to me. I posted the money as he desired me. A letter from Wa——— (*name here torn out*) to hand which mentioned his intention of coming to this town immediately as a musician under your auspices, and for fear of a disappointment, I have informed him of your absence, and the probability of your not returning for about six weeks.

Nothing new has occurred except that we have got the great Mr Ireland at work, and Mrs Shock on the slack wire. I have Master H. Graham lodged in Carrick, and yesterday one Geo. Hadskis, T. Erskine, a publican, and Mrs Walker, whose husband made his escape out of the Prevot, were also committed for forging bank-notes, and she is said to be giving information, therefore I expect this town will be free from forgers and swindlers for a while. Mr McTear promises to claim the year's rent, and when paid to let me have the amount of the I.O.U., which there is little doubt of his doing. I have just received ten pounds from Mosey Moreland's Note, but Knox would not pay the four-and-ninepence without his orders to do so. I likewise called on Dr McGee this day, and he says that he will pay me seven guineas to make up ten with what you got from him. When I get it I will no doubt inform you thereof. Eliza Templeton wonders where he got money to purchase the organized piano from you. She has been with us these some days. I hope you will not forget to call on Mrs Green and pay her. I enclose you the bill you got from Mr Potter, which was forgotten, and also a bank note for five pounds, thitrteen shillings and nine pence., and when you write mention what money you want. Please to give my compliments to your brother, and believe me so as ever, — Your friend,

JOHN M^{c}CRACKEN, Jr.

P.S. — Loughy thinks great long for you, he wakens the whole house at four o'clock, and won't let us sleep till I get up. I hope when Frank comes home he will keep him in better order.

Lynch in due time reached Castlebar and reported progress to Mr McCracken.

CASTLEBAR, *May* 24th, 1802.

SIR, — I received your favour of the 13th, this morning, with the notes three pounds, eight shillings and three pence enclosed. I came here last night from Newport.

I left Ballina ou Friday, May 7th; went about five miles to Priest Conway of Ardagh. He was hospitable, directed me to a Schoolmaster, Anthony Carrin near Killala; picked up two songs on the way cost a little whiskey, and tobacco. On Saturday evening treated the Schoolmaster in a Shebeen-house, stayed there all night, got but little rest, came to the Schoolmaster's house on Sunday morning early; took down two songs from him, went to Mass, from thence to another Shebeen-house, where I got four good songs from the man and the woman of the house; the

Schoolmaster left me there; presently some people came in who began to whisper to the man and woman of the house, that I was come on some other device than looking for songs, and that I had written down their names, and would have them ruined for selling without License; the man of the house told me that he did not believe that I intended him any harm, but I found his wife growing very shy, and also a neighbour of theirs, who was to meet me and give me songs. I had to set off. I did not know where I should lodge that night; by good fortune I met the Priest, who brought me to his own house where I stayed all night, and came to the Schoolmaster on Monday morning.

I got but one song more from him three in all, and four in the Shebeen-house, and two on the way on Saturday before nine since I left Ballina. Having travelled many miles through the Barony of Tirawlay, I set off in every direction to Crossinoligna, where I bought paper, and tobacco, and set on Monday evening towards Erris, a dreary, bleak mountainous country. I came to a place called Duliag, where there was but one house, I stayed there all night, and gave the people some tobacco for their hospitality. I got up early and made a journey of upwards of four miles that day. I had to cross a great moor, such as I had never seen before, which fatigued me very much, until I crossed a great river, called Avonmore, where abundance of salmon are caught. When I found myself growing very feeble, on the side of a mountain, I espied a sorry looking cabin, where I rested near an hour, got one song, gave them tobacco, they gave me potatoes, and milk, and I found myself quite refreshed. I had now divided my tobacco. I enquired and found a place where they sold some, at three and threepence a pound [weight]. I bought half a pound [weight] of it, and came late in the evening to Daniel Kelly's near the entrance of the Mullet, where I was well entertained with potatoes, and eggs, and fresh oysters, with plenty of milk and butter. But they make no use of bread in this country. I came into the Mullet on Wednesday to Mr Richard Barrett's of Corn; I stopped at a Shebeen-house hard by. I had been advised by Dr Bellew, Mr Conway, and others at Ballina, to go to Mr Barrett, he being a man of good information of a happy retentive memory, a good singer, a born poet in short, that he was equal to any of the Bards if not superior.

Mr Barrett is certainly a very agreeable companion, and I found him exceedingly civil; yet I found myself greatly disappointed with respect to what I chiefly wanted. I got after waiting some days six songs from him, pretty good ones. He was short of tin. He keeps a little Academy, for the gentlemen's children of the Island. There are a great many genteel people, men of landed property in the Mullet. I suppose the young men of them had most of their education from Mr Barrett; they pay him great respect, and are very fond to see him in the evening in the whiskey house. I must tell you, Sir, that one evening, as Mr Barrett and I had been in company with three or four of these young bucks, a Mr O'Donnell called him aside, and after returning says, "I think Mr Barrett has no right to give away his own compositions, the fruit of his own brain, too cheap. If he is willing to give me the copy and copyright of all his own songs I shall be willing to give him five Guineas for them." "Sir," said I, "I think Mr Barrett has a right to the profit of his own works, and I doubt not but they are worth more, meanwhile I have no orders to take the works of any Poet now living." "How so, why so," cries all the company, "what have you come here for? Was there ever any poet in Connaught, ancient or modern, superior to Mr Barrett?" "Gentlemen," said I, "I make no doubt of the excellence of Mr Barrett's compositions, but my orders are to collect the songs of the old Bards, and I was told that Mr Barrett could give more old songs than any man in Connaught." Thus it ended.

Whilst I stayed on the Island I made three or four excursions, to different little villages, for their cabins are all in clusters on the sides of the hills, and they seem to live very comfortably. There are a good many neat slated houses interspersed through this Peninsula where the owners have some free lands, having income, some two hundred pounds, some three hundred pounds, and some five hundred pounds a year, they live cheaply here and seem to be very happy. I was not invited to any of these gentlemen's houses, though I had seen and conversed with some of them; but I understand it is not their custom to invite anyone below their own rank; but if they come of their own accord they are welcome and treat them very hospitably. I had to call for whiskey wherever I applied for songs, and they sold whiskey everywhere. I left the Mullet on Thursday and came to Daniel Kelly's outside the Peninsula where I got four songs; cost me two shillings, eight and a half pence for whiskey. Friday came to Avonmore; the flood was so high I stayed all night in Patrick Deane's by the riverside; he sent his horse with me over the river. Saturday morning I crossed the Craggy Mountain, and the roughest road that ever was travelled; saw no house for sixteen miles, but one cabin at a distance, having waded to the knees through or across seven rivers, till I came to Strathfern. where I thought to stay, but the few huts dispersed about the place were hard to come at. I crossed a watery marsh to come at one of them, where I found one old woman, and a dozen of kids, and two young calves. I asked a drink, I got good milk, I returned tobacco, but I could see nothing like a bed in the house. I asked how far to Newport, they said four miles. I set off and crawled along very tired, came to Newport about ten at night.

I met a Dr Mack, who told me he had songs. I treated him, and found he wanted to be very costly to me, and that he was but a poor sconce.

I left Newport on Sunday at three o'clock, and came here last night, and am, Sir, with respect and gratitude, Your humble servant,

Patrick Lynch.

P.S. — I have just fifty songs in all, I shall use my utmost endeavours. You shall hear from me again. I do not know how long I shall stay here. I suppose I shall go next to Westport, but I must look out for some place for your next remittance, which will be wanting in three weeks from this date. I wish I could hear from Mr Bunting. If you have any to send immediately, you may direct here as before.

We now turn to the traveller's diary, in which he recorded a parallel account of his adventures.

CHAPTER XXI

DIARY AND LETTERS OF PATRICK LYNCH (continued)

THE FIRST ENTRY IN THE DIARY IS DATED MAY THE 12th, AND SIMPLY NOTES his arrival at Mr Barrett's of Corn on Bellmullet. Then follows a list of nineteen songs taken down there. Next comes the brief significant statement, "May 29th, at Kelly's four songs, four half-pints." Some additional details are given regarding the difficulties of his journey, already related in the letter. It will be seen that quite unwillingly he laid himself open to a charge of cattle-driving, and had considerable difficulty in obtaining a lodging in Newport. In short, it is apparent that our "Pentaglot Preceptor" was not the sort of man to inspire confidence. Recollect that only a few years before the very ground on which he had walked at Killala and Castlebar had been marched over by the invading army of Humbert. There had been the "Castlebar races." There had been later arrests and executions. The first letter which he posted to Mr M°Cracken, drew down a storm of suspicion. The diary proceeds:

21st May.— Came to Amhan Mor, six miles. Can't get over the river. I am now waiting for the flood to fall at evening. I suppose I must stay all night in this house by the river side.

Sat., 22nd.— I stayed at Amhan Mor last night in Pat Dean's. I got his horse this morning over the river, about nine o'clock. They told me that Newport was twenty miles off, a bad road, no houses on the road, all moors and mountains, it's a shocking road to Tarsnach five miles, I lost my way at the river, I wandered along the river, stripped and crossed twice. I discovered a few huts, and men setting potatoes. They invited me to come in. I declined, as I found I should have twelve miles more of a mountain, and no house, but one, and that I should be late before I reached the next cluster of huts, which they called Strath-Fairne. I sit now at a river side, between two high mountains, it is about three o'clock. A little heifer has followed me these three miles.[1] I can't get it beaten back, she is lying chewing her cud hard by me where I sit.

STRATH-FAIRNE.— It is seven o'clock. The heifer has followed me over five branches of this river. There are but few huts here. I cross a moor to a cabin of stone. It is the best looking of them. I got a drink, gave tobacco, and took a smoke. I am very tired but I see no way to stay here all night. The house is full of young kids. Oh, what goats. I wish I had straw I would stay here. The woman tells me there is a house two miles on, where I may lodge. I leave the heifer in her charge.

The sun is down, I sat down on a stone before the door. I asked for a drink, I get it, but no invitation. I got into Newport about nine. I asked where James Connor lived. A young man came to show me, he leans over the half door, I asked for the Landlord. He is over the way sends for him he still holds the half door Landlord comes I want to speak to the young man. "Sir," says I, "can I have a bed here ?" "I am not sure," says he. Dr Mack comes out. "How do you do, Sir, I hope you are well?" "I thank you, Sir" said I. "Come in, Sir" said the Dr. I got in with some difficulty and sat down. The Dr sits down by me. "You must have lodgings here, Sir, I insist on it." He asked me questions, I declined.

After a council was held the Landlady comes and says, "Sir, I have no lodging for you, here." "Good night," said I. The Dr follows me. I strive to shake him off, he pursues and calls. I stop. "Sir," said he, "I'll find you a lodging." "Sir" said I, "do not trouble yourself, I shall make out one myself."

"Do, Sir, come with me. I'll find you a good bed shall cost you nothing." I go with him to the house of one Cannon. He invites me to coffee. He orders bread, butter, sugar, and beer to be sent for. He said they are

---

[1.] Query was Lynch singing as he went along? Cows are said to be attracted by music.

already paid for, but I had to pay for all but the coffee. He invites the whole family. They seem not pleased with the Dr for imposing on me, but I saw at first sight that he was a old sponge. However I pressed them all to take share and we had plenty. I got a good bed. The breakfast was ditto. I got a song from the Dr, Got Mass at one o'clock — promised to stay with the Dr, if he would give half a dozen songs before dinner.

NEWPORT, *Tuesday, 2 o'clock, May the 23rd, 1802.*— I went out to the top of the high hill east of the bridge to view the town, it looks very pleasant, Sir Neal O'Donnell's mansion at the south-west end, the shell of a good new chapel on the north of the town. At a distance I see an agreeable prospect of the Rick or Cruach Patrick on the south, and the lofty Mount Nefin on the north. Achill on the west, and the awful promontory. Clare Island with many other islands on the south-west.

3 o'clock.— I found the doctor's songs would be dear bought. Set off for Castlebar arrived at eight took a private lodging waited on Doctor Egan on Monday at nine o'clock. He was just going out on business had the good luck to get Mr McCracken's letter from Belfast with the three guineas — it's past ten, I have taken breakfast in a private house — Doctor Eagan did not invite me but said I might call again in the course of the day. He made an apology that his house was crowded with billeted soldiers.

I went to the house of John McDermud, a shoemaker, where as I had been told, I might have a room and bed he had none to let — I told my business — he promised to assist me. I dined at my lodging, having written a long letter to Mr John McCracken giving an account of my travels and progress. I went to the Post Office — and having the letter unsealed, I went into the hall or shop of the Office where I saw a civil-like young man behind a counter, as one who attended the Office. I asked for a wafer which he gave me cheerfully. I asked him to put his own seal on it, he did so. While he was sealing the letter, I asked him some questions about the despatch of letters, about the time of the post coming in and going out. This gave occasion to a curious circumstance incident, blunder or balderdash which came about next day. Monday evening about nine o'clock, I treated M{c}Dermod to beer in John MacVeily's. This landlord sung a good song and told me the names of some who could sing for me, particularly Joe Rush, a shoemaker, and Pat Lynch, a hairdresser. Tuesday morning I went to this Lynch to be shaved. Let him know my name — treated him and his wife in MacVeily's. The barber asked me to come back to his shop to get my shoes and coat brushed, and whilst he was brushing my back — in came Doctor Egan and two or three more along with him. I understood he had been in search of me — I was a little surprised, and after a short salute, he asked me if I had examined the silver he gave me yesterday. I told him I did not. "I expected you back in the course of the day," said he. I answered that I had gone twice in the evening, but that he had gone out. He said there was one shilling and eight pence due for the postage of the letter. "Sir," said I, "I did not recollect at the time, but I assure you that I was at this instant going to wait upon you." I found myself growing a little warm and confused. I did not know what to think. A gentleman whose patronage I had sought and expected whilst I had stayed in town, I had been warmly recommended to him by the Bishop of Killala. How could he think that I would run away immediately without paying the expense of the letter? But that was not all, I pulled out my purse and paid him. He gave a nod, a wink, and a side grin, to some man who stood by, and then asked me if I had been at the Post Office yesterday evening. I told him I was. "Well sir," said he, "I am informed by good authority that you demanded a certificate of that letter having been in the Office and given to me." "No sir, I asked no certificate, my business was to post a letter, I asked nothing but a wafer from a young man who attended in the office. He sealed it for me, and returned it to me again and told me to drop it in on the outside."

"Sir," said he, "the lady who keeps the Post Office says that you stood in the hall while another person went upstairs and asked the certificate for you which the lady refused to give. Now, sir, I would not for a thousand pounds that it should be said that I would deny the letter or the money contained in it when the proper person appeared to demand it."

"Sir," said I, "it must be a mistake, I know nothing of it." "Will you come," said he, "and face the lady." "I shall," said I. We went in a crowd to the Office. The lady was called down. "Well, madam," said the Dean, "is this the gentleman who wanted the certificate?" "Yes," said she, "I heard his voice. He did not come upstairs but Mr Gallagher came up and asked it for him, and I said I would give no such certificate without letting Dean Egan know of it. My little boy saw him whilst he waited in the hall for Mr Gallagher. The boy was called, and testified that I came in with Mr Gallagher, that I stayed in the hall while Mr Gallagher came downstairs, and that we both left the house at the same time. "Now," said the Dean, "this lady would say nothing but the truth, and this innocent child would not tell a lie." "Sir," said I, "it is all a mistake, I spoke of no certificate, I spoke to no person here but to the young man who attended the Office. Let him be called he can testify. I know no Mr Gallagher." The lady gave a stern look and says, "Lord, how can you be telling such barefaced lies?" We left the shop. The Dean looked sour. The street was crowded with decent-looking people, looking and listening to the trial. I was condemned. All the people staring at me, I was still calling for the young man who had attended the office on the evening before, but he never appeared. I had called for Gallagher — the Dean had sent for him. He would not appear, I called out in the street for Gallagher. I begged of someone to show me where he lived. The lady then gave tongue out of the window and said I knew well enough where he lived. The crowd still continued. I had to make a public speech in the open street of Castlebar in my own defence.

The Dean then asked me if I would give him a receipt for the money. I told him I would with pleasure. After I had given him the receipt he told me that I need not give myself any further trouble for that he was now satisfied. I told him that I was glad to hear it, but that I was not satisfied myself to be accused of any design of fraud, and to be publicly called liar by that lady, and that I would not quit the town until I should prove the falsity of the accusation. I set off to the barber's and begged of him to show me where this Gallagher lived. He came with me. I showed the letter to Gallagher, and asked him if he knew me, or if I had ever applied to him to get a certificate for me, or if he had asked for one in my name at the Post Office yesterday evening. He said no. "Well sir," said I, it behoves you to step forward and testify the truth." Gallagher then looked at Lynch the Barber and said, "Damn your soul, sir. Why, but you told the Dean immediately. Was not it you that went with me to the Post Office? Wasn't it for you that I asked the certificate? What did I know about this gentleman? Did not you tell me the letter was for you, and that the Dean would not show it to you? Go directly and tell all about it, or by heavens I'll kick you."

I requested Gallagher would come himself. He gave a note to the Dean which explained the mystery and cleared me. The Dean seemed now to be convinced. I told him I would be thankful to him if he would take a walk with me along the street, and let the people know it was a mistake. He did so. We came to the Post Office, but the lady would not appear. The Dean stopped to tell every one that he met how I was wronged. He came with me to the fields, for there was no other way.

So much for a cheap lodging. I paid but one shilling and seven pence a day for diet and lodging, and I think it was dear enough. I resolved to leave the Town on Wednesday, June the second, and called on Dean Egan, and told him that I was about leaving the Town, and that I wished always to have the sanction and approbation of the clergy as I travelled, and that I hoped he would give me a few lines as Doctor Bellew had written to him in my favour. He did not deny me, but he looked very queer as if he was afraid, and after a short pause he suddenly started off and bade me good morning. "Good morning, sir," said I.

I set off to Belcarra, four miles east from Castlebar. I stopped at Tom Walsh's, a pretty good kind of Inn, and very civil people. I stayed there two nights, got ten songs.

From Belcarra he wrote the following letter to Mr McCracken, omitting any reference to his difficulties with the post-office; but it is evident that Dr Egan, who looked so queerly at him in parting, must have suspected that he was really on a political mission from the McCracken family and the Belfast United Irishmen.

Belcarra, near Castlebarr,

June 3rd, 1802.

Sir,— I made good progress in Castlebar. I got forty-seven songs in it, having stayed ten days, it cost me just two guineas, notwithstanding that I had taken lodgings in a private house, where I paid but eightpence for dinner, eightpence for breakfast, and threepence for the bed; so that I lived as low as possible, in order to spare the more for procuring plenty of songs in a short time. Here is the method I took. Finding that Dr Egan was not going to give himself much trouble about me or my business, I resolved to apply myself to the lower classes. Thus, on Monday evening the 24th, having posted the letter to you, which gave account of my travels and progress, together with the receipt of yours of the 13th and the notes enclosed, I walked about the town, not knowing whom to apply to, and passing by a brogue-maker's shop, I heard him singing a good Irish song. I stepped in and asked him if he would take a pot of beer. He came with me to the house of a John McAvilly, a jolly publican, who sang well, and was acquainted with all the good singers in town. Under Tuesday I found out a hairdresser, a shoemaker, a mason, and a fiddler all good singers. I attended the mechanics in their own houses and workshops. They would take no money. I had to treat them their wives and children. I stuck close to the business both early and late, till I drained them of all the songs they had in a short time. It is rare to get past four songs from one person, unless such songs as I have already. I got these forty-seven songs in Castlebar from nine different persons, and as soon as I found myself unemployed, I set off out of town, and stopped here in the house of one Walshe, in this village called Belcarra, four miles from Castlebar. I have got six songs last night in this place. I mean to go through some of the villages in this neighbourhood, and in about a week I shall be in Westport, and shall be in need of money. You will please to remit me four or five guineas, and direct your letter thus — "Mr P. Lynch, Irish Professor, now on a tour through Connaught, to the care of the Rev. Dr Lynagh, Westport, County Mayo." I have just gotten in all a hundred and three songs. I would wish to have instructions from Mr Bunting, otherwise I would be glad you would give me your own opinion and say whether I am going to too much expense or not. I hope Mr Bunting will come and meet me, if not in Westport, at least at Galway. You shall have another letter immediately, after I receive yours in Westport, and I am, Dear Sir, your humble servant,

PATRICK LYNCH.

P.S.— Dear Sir, you will please to write a line or two to the Rev. P. McCarten of Loghin Island, and let him know that I am alive. Or send some word to my children, and it will oblige me much.

Again we turn to the diary:

Came to Westport on Friday evening June the fourth. Posted a letter to John McCracken, Belfast. Took lodging in a Public House, Tom McMyler's, good bed, good diet, but it is too dear for me, two shillings and eight pence a day. I spoke to the Rev. Doctor Lynagh, on Saturday, he seemed to be clever and willing to encourage me, but he was thronged with confessions and an ordination which he has to attend. He is gone to Tuam. They told me of a great many good singers in this Town, but I find myself often disappointed. They offer me the same songs I got before. I have got six from Redmond Stanton, two from Pat Gibbons, two from John Moran, and one from old Mr McMyler, my landlord's father-in-law. Some of them I had before, but I think I have got a proper copy of 'Tigherna Muigho' from old Redmond Stanton, the blind man.

On Wednesday, June the ninth, I bought half a pound of tobacco, and made an excursion eight miles from Westport south in a mountainous country called Drummin to the house of a John Gaven, he is gone to Ball Fair.

Thursday, June the tenth.— In John Gaven's I got eight songs from Norah Denny, Nancy McLoughlin, and Mrs Gaven.

Friday, eleventh.— From Mrs Gaven, one, from Mrs McLoughlin, four, from Sally Hanretty, three.

Mr Gaven came home on Saturday morning. On Saturday I went to Coill Mor, one from John Gaven's to Pat McDonall's. I gave his daughter some toys. I got four or five songs, and dined there on fresh trout.

A friar came from Westport and said Mass in John Gaven's on Sunday. He stayed till Monday.

Monday, June the fourteenth.— I spent this day writing a list of my songs. I drew one for myself and another to send to Belfast. Next Tuesday fifteenth and Wednesday sixteenth, I spent this time in Mr Gaven's, got a few songs and went to Westport in the evening. I enquired for the letter in the Post Office. I found it was not come nor was Doctor Lynagh at home from Tuam.

Thursday the seventeenth.— I expected the letter, I went to the Post Office, I enquired if there was a letter for Patrick Lynch to the care of Doctor Lynagh. The Postmaster said no, and I said it was a wonder for I had posted my letter on Friday was eight days. While I was speaking the sulky Postmaster shut the door against me. I went to my lodging, met with John Gaven and his wife, I sat with them some time to treat them for their civility, when I found that Kelly the Postmaster, had told several persons that I was a suspicious person that would soon be taken up. Now I found myself in an unpleasant situation. My money gone to a few shillings. No remittance coming, and told by several people that I would be reported to the Marquis of Sligo by this Kelly, the Postmaster, and that he was an ill-disposed orangeman.

Friday morning, June 18th. — I waited on Doctor Lynagh. I found him very civil and seemed willing to oblige me. I showed him what papers I had from R. I. Academy from Mr Forde and from Mr McCarten. He told me they were sufficient to keep me from much trouble, but that I ought also to have some credentials from Belfast from whence I had my mission something to show when I came into any town explaining the nature and design of my business, certified by some gentleman well known. He told me he would go to Kelly and convince him that I had no design but merely what I professed, and that he write with me to a priest in Murrisk on Sunday and not to write to Belfast till Saturday expecting better news.

Friday evening, June 18th I left Westport and came to John Gaven's where I found myself made welcome.

Saturday, June 19th. In John Gaven's of Drummin, south of the Rick three miles from Westport.

Sunday, June 20th. — Came from Drummin to Westport eleven o'clock. Doctor Lynagh is gone to Newport. No letter. I have but a crown, my dinner is to pay out of it. I do not know what to resolve on. No answer to the letter I posted on the fourth instant. I suspect my letter has been detained by Kelly.

"*Monday, 21st.*— I went to Lewisburgh ten miles south-west from Westport, had a letter from Dr Lynagh to Mr Ward the Parish priest. He was in Westport behind me. I thought to have stayed at Murrisk four miles from Westport, but could get no lodging. I proceeded to Lewisburgh and slept in a public-house. Hugh O'Donnell's cost one shilling and seven pence.

Wednesday, 23rd.— I went three miles further west to Duach McKeon in quest of an Owen O'Maily, a school-master, who I was told was an Irish scholar, and had manuscripts. I saw none with him. He repeated a long song which I wrote concerning an image which had been cast ashore in the West, or rather of two images, the first of a fine woman, and the second of a Turk or Saracen. This was the third time I had written some parts of that song. In the evening the schoolmaster brought me to a farmer's house, Patrick Gibbon's, where I stayed at night and got two songs, but I lost my knife.

(The loss of the knife, carried for the purpose of mending his pen, accounts for the brevity of further entries in the diary.)

CHAPTER XXII

DIARY AND LETTERS OF PATRICK LYNCH (continued)

AN URGENT LETTER WAS NOW WRITTEN TO MR JOHN M^cCRACKEN, enclosing a list of 150 songs as evidence of his diligence.

WESTPORT, 21st *June* 1802.

DEAR SIR, I posted a letter to you on friday the 4th of June inst. that you should remit me 4 or 5 guineas and direct to the care of the Revd. Doctor Lynagh in Westport. I have gotten no answer. I am uneasy. I suspect that my letter was suppressed or detained so that it has not come to your hand. I hope the money is not lost. I know not what to think of it or how to proceed. The Revd. Doctor Lynagh is a worthy gentleman. I have agreed with him that you shall write immediately to him and send the notes enclosed for me without having my name on the outside and they shall be safe. But if you have received my letter and have sent the notes and that your letter is detained from me, in that case I must leave it to your judgment how I shall be relieved out of this place. There is a Mr Patten a merchant in this town perhaps you could find means to draw on him for a supply to me. Dr Lynagh advises me to procure as soon as possible some credentials in form, declaring the design of my Mission and this formula to be approved and signed by some well-known military gentleman such as General Drommend, etc. I am sorry I had not such with me from the beginning for though the times are peaceable the people here are still suspicious of strangers and it is with difficulty I can convince them that I have no design in travelling but merely to procure Irish songs to be set to music.

I have had good success till now but the want of money impedes my progress. I send you here a list of 150 songs with the names of the persons and places, where I got them, for Mr Bunting's use. I would be glad he was here now. I wish you could let me know whether I may expect him or not. — I am, Sir, with respect Yrs.

PATRICK LYNCH.

Mr JOHN McCRACKEN.

This letter, with an accurate list of the songs and singers, is among our MSS. It was evidently handed by Mr John McCracken to Bunting, so that when, at a later date, he set out to follow Lynch, he was able to call at the different singers on the way and hear the songs himself. That he brought the document with him, had it available for ready use in his pocket, is proved by the fact, that on one of the folds of it is noted a list of the places visited on the return journey and their distances. This will be quoted in its proper place.

> *Thursday, mid-summer day.* — I came back to Lewisborough, inquired for Mass, was told it was to be had a mile and a half south towards the mountains. I met the priest, gave him Dr Lynagh's note.
>
> He had Mass in a gentleman's house, a Mr Garvay's. This gentleman kept me for breakfast, it was one o'clock. I heard of a blind piper, a Billy O'Maily, who had the greatest variety of Irish songs. I came to him he had a house full of young people dancing. I found he had many songs which I had not got before. I agreed to meet him next day.
>
> I returned to O'Donnell's, got some dinner, had some beer with a Tom Byrne, a weaver, a quack, and farrier, a conversable man, who offered to introduce, and direct me to all the best singers, and also to get me free passage into all the islands.
>
> *Friday 25*th. — Paid my bill two shillings and two pence, and went to the house where I had seen Blind Billy yesterday, sent for him gave him a shilling, and grog, took down six good songs, cost me two shillings and eight and a half pence, my money is near gone. I came to Westport.

Saturday, June 26th — In Mr McMyler's I visited Dr Lynagh twice — no letter come — I called with a Mr Watt O'Malley, a shop-keeper, he gave me two songs, and two epigraphs. I have but one shilling and am due in five shillings and five pence to the Dr.

Sunday, June 27th — Due to Mr McMyler since last Sunday, to wit.

Dinner and lodging

Dinner on Monday

Lodging   do.

The entries from 27th June record only a dismal list of dinners, breakfasts, and nights' lodgings for which he is in debt to the landlord, McMyler. There is a due admixture of pints, quarts, and naggins, which may or may not have been consumed by singing visitors. No names of any are given, however. It is evident his credit was good, owing to the kindly recognition of the Rev. Dr Lynagh, but he was in a miserably anxious condition, imagining that some catastrophe had overwhelmed all his Belfast friends. It is quite possible that they had recognised that correspondence with them had brought the unfortunate man under suspicion, and forebore writing on that account. Bunting had by this time set out too meet him, but unaware of approaching relief, he continues his dismal notes of beds, breakfasts, and dinners. On the margin of the book is written a Gaelic phrase which translates, "A pity of a lonely man, without friends."

McMyler, the landlord, had only one poem to sing or recite for him. It was a lengthy one, on the subject of the Day of Judgment. This only served to deepen the gloom.

Tuesday, 29th June, he records as the Feast of St Peter, leaving St Paul out of the question, though half the honour of the day is his by right. Evidently Lynch celebrated, as there is a note of "three quarts, and a naggin raw." On 2nd July he wrote in despair to Miss Mary McCracken, and to Dr MacDonnell, sending the letters to Castlebar.

WESTPORT, *July 2nd, 1802.*

MADAM, I am too long detained in this place, expecting the return of letters I wrote to your brother John; one on the 4th of June, and the other on the 21st. Finding no answer coming to either of them, I have taken this liberty to write to you, and to let you know that it was agreed before I left Belfast, that I should correspond with your brother, in the absence of Mr Bunting, and that he would remit me such sums as would be necessary on this journey. Consequently, I wrote to him from Ballina, on the 7th of May, and received his answer according to appointment, in Castlebar, with three guineas in notes enclosed. I wrote immediately, on receipt of this giving account of my progress through the mountains of Erris. I stayed in Castlebar some nine or ten days; had good success; got near fifty songs and chiefly from the mechanics. I found it expensive. It cost me two guineas. I went to Bellcarra, and stayed there two days. I came to Westport on the 4th of June, and posted a letter to Mr John McCracken, giving a further account of my progress, and requesting another remittance of five guineas, to the care of the Rev. Dr Lynagh in Westport. I must now tell you, Madam, something about a bitter orange. When I went to the post-office I had no wafer. I asked the postmaster to seal it for me; I said it was for Belfast. He looked very sour; he gave me the wafer, but refused to take the letter in his hand. He told me very roughly to put it in outside; and immediately he closed the door against me. I found before I was three days in Westport, that this postmaster, whom they call Sergeant Kelly, had told several persons, that I should and would be apprehended as one on some secret mission from Belfast. I could not get many songs in Westport on account of this report; for the persons from whom I expected them were afraid to be seen in my company. On the 10th of June I left the town and went eight or nine miles into the mountains, south of the Rick, where I got about thirty songs at a cheap rate. On the 16th I returned to Westport. On the 17th I inquired at the post-office if there was a letter for Patrick Lynch, to the care of Dr Lynagh. Kelly said no. Said I, "it's a wonder. You mind, Sir, I posted a letter here on Friday, the 4th?" He made no answer, but looked sulky, and closed the door against me. Whilst I was speaking, I began to suspect that Kelly had suppressed my letter. I was told by several persons that Kelly would have me confined, unless I had good credentials to show. On Friday, the 18th I waited on Dr Lynagh. He was very civil. He told me to have patience for two or three days; and hoped that my letter had not miscarried; and that he would go to the post office and convince him that I had no design, but merely to look for Irish music. I went back to the mountains in the evening and stayed till Monday, when I returned to Westport. On, Monday, June 21st, I wrote a letter to Mr J. McCracken, and enclosed a list of 150 songs, with the names of the persons and places, from whom I got them. I waited on Dr Lynagh. He was very kind. He wrote the superscription of the letter, and went with it himself to the post office. I agreed with the Dr that I should order the direction of the answer of my letter to be in his name, and that my name should not appear on the outside; and that whatever remittance should come would be safe for me. The Dr then lent me some silver, and gave me a letter to a priest in Louisborough, ten miles to the west. I went to Louisborough on Tuesday the 22$^{nd.}$ I stayed at a public house. On the 23rd, I went three miles further west in quest of a schoolmaster. Got three songs from him. On the 24th I returned to Louisborough, and heard of a blind piper. I went to a dancing where I found him, and appointed to meet him next day at Hugh O'Donnell's in Louisborough. Friday 26th I took down six good songs from the blind man; and I never found any one who had so great a variety of good old songs, and tunes, nor any one who could repeat so correctly. He sings well, and has a great memory. In short, he would be more useful to Mr Bunting than any man in Connaught. However, I could not stay by him for I was out of money, and had to return to Westport, where I am running in debt, and getting no songs. Lord, how long must I be confined this way? My credit will not last long here. No answer coming. Have all the posts conspired to stop my letters? I'll post this in Castlebar to-morrow morning. Or, is it possible that Mr J. McCracken is not at home, and that there is no one allowed to open or answer his letters. My dear Miss Mary, I hope you will see me relieved out of this hobble; and direct to the Rev. Dr Lynagh, Westport, and it will ever oblige, your humble servant,

PATRICK LYNCH.

To MISS MARY McCRACKEN, Belfast.

WESTPORT, *July 1st, 1802.*

DEAR SIR, I request you will call upon Mr John McCracken, and let him know that I am uneasy about an answer to the last two letters I wrote to him, the one on the 4th of June, and the other on the 21st. In the first I gave account of my progress, and desired him to remit me five guineas to the care of the Rev. Dr Lynagh, in Westport. I made some excursions into the country from Westport, until the 21st; and finding no answer, I doubted there was some miscarriage. I wrote a letter, and enclosed a list of one hundred and fifty songs, with the names of the persons from whom and the places where I got them; and by the advice of Dr Lynagh (whom I found to be a worthy gentleman) I ordered that the answer with the remittance should come with his name alone on the superscription. The motive for this precaution was that Kelly, the post-master of this town, had told several persons that I was soon to be apprehended, as a suspicious character, on some private mission from Belfast. And this was whispered about, from the first week I came to this town; and in consequence I found that some people, from whom I expected to get songs were afraid to be seen in my company; and, as I found no answer coming, I was afraid that my letter had been suppressed. Dr Lynagh advised me to procure some credentials from Belfast, declaring the meaning and design of my business, approved and signed by some well-known gentleman. The Dr was so kind as to write the superscription of my letter of the 21st, and to go with it to the post-office himself, and calls daily for the answer. Dear Sir, if it be that Mr John McCracken is not in town (which I can hardly suppose), you will be so good as to go to his sister, Miss Mary, and let her know that it was agreed, before I left Belfast, that Mr John was to remit me such money as would be necessary on this journey; and that she may open my letters if they are come to hand; and I hope that she will answer the demand. This delay hinders my business very much, and renders me very uneasy. I found a blind piper near Louisborough, about ten miles from this, who had the greatest variety of songs, tunes, and genuine poems, of any I ever met. I got a few good songs from him, and he has a great many more; but I could not stay by him for want of cash; I stay here on credit, and am, Sir, your humble servant,

PATRICK LYNCH.

P.S.— I have made good progress — one hundred and seventy-seven songs.

To DR MACDONNELL, Linen Hall Street, Belfast.

A few days later he found an opportunity of sending a letter to Belfast by hand, and addressed a second one to Miss Mary McCracken as follows:

WESTPORT, *July* 9th, 1802.

The bearer, Mr Bernard O'Byrne, is a respectable shop-keeper in Westport. I find he deals in Belfast. If my letters are come to hand you may trust him with any commands to me. I wait for relief. I wrote to your brother on the 4th of June, requesting five guineas remittance. Got no answer. I am detained here wanting money. On Monday, 21st of June, I wrote to Mr John McCracken on the same subject. Got no answer. Saturday, the 3rd of July I wrote to you. I have got no answer. I fear there is something wrong. My dear Miss Mary, I have been very attentive, very zealous, and very diligent in this business; I have near two hundred songs; I have done all I could; yet I am detained for want of travelling charges. Your brother was to supply me. I hope you have got my letter. I am in a very uneasy situation. I hope you will excuse this trouble, as I suppose your brother is not at home, and that you will do something to relieve Your humble servant,

PATRICK LYNCH.

To MISS MARY M^cCRACKEN.

On Saturday, 3rd July, he was cheered up by a visitor, and records:

"One naggin of punch at night with Mrs Fitzgerald." Referring to the list of songs we find her name appended to the 'Red Salmon of the Erne', 'Murrisk of the Harbours', and 'Young Coolun', all gems of pure poetry. On 4th July he went to dinner with a Mr O'Malley. On Monday, the 5th, there was nothing to tell of but his two meals, and on Tuesday he seems to have been in the act of entering "to Break ———" the word is cut short in the middle, and there is the joyful announcement "Mr Bunting came," followed by "settled with Mrs McMyler. nineteen quarts, and twenty-one meals, and four-and-four-pence borrowed."

It will be observed that whilst Mr McMyler recited poetry about the Day of Judgment, his better half kept the accounts.

Lynch next notes that he took Mr Bunting off to "Nora's" (evidently a public-house), and Blind Billy was sent for. There they remained till Thursday night late, taking seventeen songs from Blind Billy, which cost six and sixpence. The expenditure seems to have been all for refreshments for the company, and in no case is it reported that singers expected to be paid for their trouble. Mr Barrett of Bellmullet was no exception, he seems to have parted freely with his songs and compositions till his admiring pupils opened negotiations with Lynch on the delicate question of author's rights. The diary would now seem to end ignominiously with the statement that since last settlement there was a debt for "one breakfast, one dinner, two quarts, seven naggins and a glass"; but after a few blank pages we come to another piece of narrative, and that the last. From it we see that they remained nearly a fortnight in Westport, and without doubt the time was spent in revisiting or interviewing those whose songs had been already taken down. Then he records:

Thursday, 22nd July.— Mr Bunting and I left Westport at twelve, stopped at Partry. The fields covered with strata of limestone in form of ridges, some horizontal, and some with a little slope like the waves of the sea. Here and there some green level walks between them, some sheep feeding in these fields, but the rocky or stony parts, I think, can never be reclaimed. I dined and lodged in the inn in Ballinrobe with Mr B ———, sixteen miles from Westport.

Friday, 23rd — Set off at seven, by the Neale, the seat of the Browns
and Cross, and by the Abbey of Ross to Headford, twelve miles from
Ballinrobe, where I took breakfast between twelve and one, and to
Cahirmorris, where I found Mr B ——— .

It would seem that Bunting was driving a light vehicle of some
sort. In a letter, quoted previously, describing his start on a song-
collecting tour, he refers to the rubbing of the old mare's collar. We
may presume that Lynch had not to trudge along wearily any longer,
but had a seat in the gig, except when, as in the expedition to the seat
of Browns of the Neale, he made some detour in special quest of a
song. On this last date noted in his diary, he probably took down the
song relating to the trial of one of the Browns for duelling, which
will be quoted in the next chapter.

Turning to Bunting's music MS. books, we find a long narrow
one which could have been slipped into a pocket. On the first page
is scribbled the word—"Castlebar," and a note, "Left Belfast 1802,
2nd" it must be though it reads like 20th July for Connaught. The
first song taken down is 'Bradan ruad na heirne', 'The Red Salmon
of Loch Erne', one of the songs sung by Mrs Fitzgerald for Lynch
on 3rd July. On another page in faint pencilling is written, "Paid Mr
Lynch four guineas and five shillings and five pence out of my own
pocket." And also the following: "Revd. William Burke, Parish Priest
of Ballinrobe, mention his name to Mr Anty O'Flaherty, Benville
in Connemara, Mr Nics. Bodkin of Omay in Connemara, Martin
O'Mailey recommended to him by Dr Lynagh." And beneath the air
of a beautiful song 'Young Cusack' is written "Father John Joice in
Galloway." Some items of a washing list are noted. We thus get a
guide as to how the return journey was made. The travellers came to
Galway, thence to Limerick.

On the back of Patrick Lynch's letter to McCracken which

Bunting carried all the time, is noted the following:

> 257, Limerick slept 2 evenings. 12, Kilbraustullagh dined fed H. (evidently the horse). 9, Nenagh slept. 6, Toomvara breakfasted H. 10, Roscrea dined. 6, Burris in Ossary slept. 7, Mountrath Breakfasted and fed H. 7, Maryborough fed H. 10, Monasterevan slept. 11, Robertstown fed Horse. 6, Sallins. 8 (illegible ending in ck? Kilcock). 4 Cloondalkin. 4, Dublin arrived at 8 o'clock.

And beneath is written "81 Belfast."

There is no word as to Lynch, but it may have been that he lingered in County Clare to visit his kindred there. Nor do we find any note of songs taken down after Limerick. Bunting, however, had musical and learned friends in that city, others in Dublin, and his brother Anthony in Drogheda, and taking this circuitous route could visit them all. So ended the great Tour in Connaught.

CHAPTER XXIII

SONG WORDS IN THE BUNTING COLLECTION

Bunting's first collection published in 1796, and his last (1840), consist of arranged melodies without words. It was only in connection with his 1812 volume that he attempted to supply words, and this effort, as already mentioned, was prompted by the immense success of Thomas Moore, in wedding the old melodies to national songs. The Lynch tour to Connaught was undertaken so that the original Irish should be available for publication and for translators. The manuscripts include a volume in which is copied, in one fair handwriting, the efforts of the translators. The scribe was doubtless Tom Hughes, who was also employed to take down Russell's speech from the dock, and O'Neill's *Autobiography*. Bunting seems to have had considerable literary taste and acumen, and he recognised that the English translations did not adequately represent the spirit of the original Gaelic.

The volume of literal translations of Gaelic lyrics is throughout marked critically, and initialled by him, as regards what he thinks fine, and we have evidence here that he appreciated what was best and most characteristic. This discernment was, without doubt, inherited from his O'Quinn ancestors.

To give an idea of the character of the large mass of lyrical poetry in the collection, I shall quote from these literal translations.

Turlogh O'Carolan, harper, composer, and poet, fills a large place in public estimation. We have it from his contemporaries, and even from those who were his friends, that he was not by any means a first-class player on his instrument. His poems do not strike us either as above the average, and his fame probably rested on his talent and originality as a composer. He is credited with a large number of airs.

He was, moreover, a poet of polite society, most of his verse being made in honour of patrons, or of fair ladies of good family in different parts of Ireland. Here is a typical eulogy:

FANNY POER

> I incline to speak of a sprightly young maid
>> Most noble in mind and lovely in features,
> Who lives in a town on the banks of Loughrea
>> I would be happy to live hard by her.
>
> May I not leave the world till I find myself heartily
>> Dancing and sporting and I at her wedding,
> I would challenge the man that would ask any cows (i.e., dowry)
>> With the young pearl of the fair white hand.
>
> A stately gay maid of pleasing accomplishments,
>> A pretty bright gem, heart's delight of all Erin,
> Drink a good health and make no delay
>> To Fanny the Daughter of David.

And here is how he praises one Dennis O'Connor:

> His house is full of cheerfulness
>> Commodious and respectable,
> A free welcome for all men
>> At all times in his Castle.
>
> Where there is music sweetly played
>> By the bards it is regulated,
> Conversing and dancing with wit and diversion, and drinking good ale:
>> In a word, there is enough to serve a whole province.

The lightness and brightness of Irish verse carries it off to the swing of the music, but the subject matter is not interesting.

Carolan, of course, could do better than this, but he wrote a great deal of this sort of thing.

Here is another complimentary poem that has a story connected with it.[1] It is attributed to David Murphy, a seventeenth century harper, who composed both poem and air to conciliate a patron, Lord Mayo, whom he had offended by being too long absent. Arriving on Christmas eve the harper concealed himself till he had an opportunity to surprise the lord and his company by playing the superb air and singing the plea for forgiveness from which I quote the following:

Never more impeach me, oh, blossom of the noblest blood,
And I swear by all that is to be found on holy cold stones in Rome,
That I shall not be so long away from you, oh, branch of conquering
heroes,
Till I go to my grave and the clay is lain on my old blind body under sod.

Standard for Irish and English round which rally clergy and laity,
May the clay not cover your head until it is grey exceedingly,
Receive once more your blind man in friendship and favour,
And I shall be running in your train with the loudest cheer.

By all the peace offerings that were laid of old in the temple,
By the race of Abraham and by all the tribes,
Not a drop shall I drink of beer, wine or brandy,
Till I get the benediction of my Lord Mayo.

I shall give bail, both clergy and laity,
And if you do not believe me I will take the Bible in my hand,
That I shall not stay so long away without paying a monthly visit,
If you will receive me this time with my song and my music.

[1.] Gaelic traditional singers often attribute the song 'Lord Mayo', to Carolan, but are in error in so doing. The reference to blindness sets them astray. The names of the children of the family give a clue to the date.

Having quoted St Paul concerning pardon being assured by true repentance, he invokes the lady of the house to plead for him, and her children too, "young Tiobod Burke, young Susan and the three little ones, John, Betty, and Miss Biddy, the pearl of the golden hair."

> *I am your blind man returning with love and gratitude,*
> *Though I have been neglectful this past year or two,*
> *For sake of this great festival of the only Son of God*
> *This is the Eve of Christmas, let strife be stayed, my Lord Mayo.*

This song shows us how the attendance of the poets and harpers was valued by noble families in Ireland, and the custom of affording free hospitality at Christmastide, and bestowing gifts on literary men and musicians was kept up among the old Gaelic families and by the old Irish-English like the Burkes of Mayo. Harper O'Neill's *Memoir* shows us that the custom continued. He went to the house of an O'Reilly for eighteen successive Christmases.

Here is an extraordinarily interesting poem which illustrates the fact that the medicinal art was hereditary in certain families:

> *The house of Fergus, that harbour of hospitality,*
> *May the branches of that family increase and wear the laurels,*
> *This is the tribe that extirpate every kind of distemper*
> *These are the champions of the quickest dexterity,*
> *In knocking down pains and stitches of every kind,*
> *And have dived down to the bottom to the very bed-rock*
> *In the wisdom of those sciences.*

> *A hundred welcomes home to you and may you enjoy life and health*
> *My friend John, my brave rock of destruction,*
> *Who would not give time to Death to be staring,*
> *To be standing, waiting or turning,*
> *But he would dash himself through the very body*
> *Of that old havoc-maker.*

There is the princely Patrick, that lofty, clever man,

His table is spread for strangers, and he feeds the weak and hungry,

His hand is not slow in attending, all distressed with sickness,

And he is a powerful enemy to desperate disorders.

I am certain my friend Hugh, the son of Owen, is no slacker,

He is the man who crossed the sea to obtain the arts,

He is the sovereign balm and remedy to raise the dead to life

Provided the Soul did not leave the body entirely.

The goodly youth Randal, we have now in high esteem,

He is the fine graceful flower, the choice of the orchard, and pure heart of corn,

It is he that is at home with us in practice through Erin,

This country would suffer if the noble lion left it.

I am certain, my friends, that these gentlemen are not

The weaker to have the advice of their old Uncle Matthew,

His prayers are good, both morning and evening,

And he has excellent memory, as a gift from heaven.

The house of Fergus here alluded to would appear to have been a regular hospital with various members of the medical family fulfilling varied offices.

John, who would not give Death time, may have been the surgeon who took prompt desperate measures. The princely Patrick looked after the diet and nursing of resident patients. Hugh, the sovereign balm, had been to a college and taken his degrees. The goodly youth Randal, like many a doctor's assistant, seems to have gone out to the patients in their homes, and old Uncle Matthew, who had stored the wisdom of preceding generations, could give the benefit of his experience in consultation.

Here is a rural song, the complaint of a girl who loves a youth of higher station than her own:

There is a quicken tree out in the garden,

   That still drops honey when I lay my hand on it,

Only Son of Mary and King of Graces,
> *Who can blame me that my heart is grieved.*

Was it not great patience I had this quarter
> *To remain alive behind you, oh, my thousand loves,*
And your last promise which you did not fulfil,
> *Leaves me in grief every Sunday evening.*

You are handsome as you stand and your smiles are enticing,
> *Your two cheeks are as red as a rose in the garden,*
With your fine flowing hair under a laced hat,
> *Alas, I am afraid that you are not decreed for me.*

My love remains on the side of the mountain
> *Writing on paper and reading Gaelic,*
And when I thought to go to see him
> *Death struck me on the forehead.*

My love is like the blackberry blossom,
> *Or like the moss-berry blossoms on a bright day of sun,*
And as the blossoms of the blue-berry on the mountain-side,
> *And there has often been a fair body under a black head.*

Treasure of my breast you would not ask anything with me
> *(i.e. no dowry)*
> *But for the false people, who were always putting between us,*
And my blessing attend your fine flowing locks
> *And we shall be married yet, and no thanks to them.*

Here is a poem that tells the story of a forcible abduction. The event would seem to have occurred near a sea bordering country, probably in the O'Brien country of Clare.

Mairsil [2] ni Brian, maid of the lovely hair,
    Who has distressed one half of Ireland,
Don't suffer me to be punished by any one because of you
    As God has given you a virtuous mind.

It would delight me more to see you approaching
    Than a light on the height to guide the mariners,
I protest to the Lord that with grief after you
    The heart in my left side is failing.

We brought her along without hurting or harming her,
    Across the moors and the mountains,
Until sleep overcame us and we sat down to rest
    And she was taken from us by superior force.

I lie here confined on a narrow bed in pain,
    Nor can I sleep any part of the night,
But tossing in torments like stormy winds
    Which sickens and confuses my senses.

My pure delicate bright babe of the heavy curling locks,
    If I don't get my desire fulfilled of you soon
I shall stand up in the fair and I swear I shall cut
    And mangle their flesh with edge of the sword.

Now she is far from me in the Island of Saints
    I think every week as long as a month or a quarter.
Ye winds convey the blessing of my heart
    To the damsel of the beautiful tresses.

O you Sea of the King that separates her and me,
    Tell my love how I am,

---

2. Marcella

That these pangs have undone me and wounded my heart,

And that the wind has cast my boat away.

The abductor does not seem to be in prison, but lying in hiding from pursuit and unable to follow the fair one across the seas. He hopes he has made some impression on her, and wooes her in impassioned verse while still threatening violence. She has been taken away for safety to an island, possibly to Aran of the Saints.

Elopements of this forcible character suggest duelling. Here is how a poet of Connaught mourned in exaggerated diction for the absence of a gentleman, John Brown of the Neale, who had killed his man in a duel, and was forced to stand a trial in Dublin. It reminds us of the nursery rhyme in which "all the birds of the air fell a sighing and sobbing."

The eagle declared that he would not visit the place

And that he would remain in the lonely glens,

The swan on the coast was as black as a coal

And her feathers hanging down drooping.

The cuckoo cries, "Uch! Uch!" and she shivering with cold,

And says, "I know not what time I shall sing.

Alas, to my grief! I cannot see John Brown

Till I would play for him the summer trumpet."

The stag and the doe are in grief on the mountain,

Gazing from on high toward Dublin;

Young children become grave like gray old men,

And both birds and fishes have changed their form.

The fruits are declined, nor is there any dew on the plain;

There's neither corn, grass, nor flower as usual.

The bees have ceased to look for honey with grief,

And if John Brown is lost they will die.

It was worth while to be a Connaught landlord in those days. The firmament above and creatures of the great deep were concerned about the trial at the High Courts:

> *The moon and the sun are slow in their courses,*
>> *And they have lost the two-thirds of their brightness ;*
> *The porpoise, the sail, the sea-hog, and the whale*
>> *Have lost their quick motion on sea.*

But good news comes of the acquittal, and the lugubrious poem ends merrily:

> *It is often that mists and dark cloudy skies*
>> *Pass away without any storm.*
> *We shall have sport in the Neal from this till Doomsday,*
>> *The like has not been seen nor shall be hereafter.*

> *Liquor and wine in the middle of the road,*
>> *Powder aburning and shooting like thunder.*
> *The health of John Brown is drunk by everyone,*
>> *Here he is home alive,* Deo gratias.

All's well that ends well. John Brown might have been hanged like that famous fire-eater, George Robert FitzGerald, nephew of the volunteer Bishop of Derry. This mourning of nature is in the style of the old bards. We have the same affectation in another Connaught Elegy for one Barbara Routledge:

> *The cuckoo who sang so sweetly is under a cloud in the glen,*
> *Since the protectress of strangers is dead who gave shelter and*
>> *support to poor wanderers.*

Another verse, following still the old fashion, weaves the date of Barbara's death into its rhymes, so that we know she died at the time of the great war of Ireland, when there would be many poor wanderers in the wilds of Connaught:

> Sixteen hundred years, as we read in black and white,
>
> Forty more comes after and nine exactly added
>
> From the birth of our Lord, who paid for the sins of Adam,
>
> Until Barbara Routledge was taken from us and stretched in a wooden coffin.

A pathetic touch relieves the dry formality of the verse, when her orphan children are counted:

> May the protection of the Heavenly King defend the three children she
>
> > left behind,
>
> Thomas, Frank, and the fair flower, the sweet, gentle Barbara!
>
> May they flourish and increase in estates and free lands,
>
> And the nurse and those that guard them, may their charge prosper.

With the Cromwellian Settlement coming on Connaught in a few short years, it is to be feared prosperity was not for these orphans, who were evidently without a father.

There is a great deal of talk about courting and hiding in woods and mountains, where the priests will not know of it, and also mockery of marriage in some of the songs. If these were sung widely, and represented the thoughts of any class of people except dissipated vagrants, a great change has come over Ireland since then. I expect a lot of these songs have gone out of use because of the nature of the words. One wooer in a well-known song says:—

> I think it is a very foolish thing to use a finger ring for binding love,
>
> Or to go to a fair to be settling the match, and wanting cows with a fine young
>
> > girl.
>
> I have a wife in Cashel, in Killala, and in Tuani, and a wife beyond in
>
> > Ballynahinch,

> *I have a wife in every town I go to, and the wife that does not please me*
> *I let her go.*

I find among Lynch's gathering a song called 'Plearaca Chuan-na Mara', the complaint of a man who married and repented. It commences thus:

> *He is to blame who would choose or desire to have any wife in the world.*
> *At All Saints last year I had a good coat, and my hat was the best in the*
>   *country;*
> *My under coat was neither worn nor scuffed; A handkerchief I had on*
>   *my neck which I bought in Cork,*
> *I suppose it cost me a crown;*
> *My shirt was quite fine, and the dearest stuff*
> *That has been woven in Sligo in my time*
> *Not to mention my gloves that were made*
> *Of very good Spanish leather ;*
> *I had a store of tobacco of the best flavour*
> *That ever grew in the land of Ireland;[3]*
> *If you would see my gaiters, it was they that were gaudy,*
> *Baboru, but marriage is pretty!*

Since he married he goes undarned and unpatched, and every penny is needed for rent, priests' dues, or house-furnishing. Amongst the necessaries he mentions the following spinning requisites:

> *A clove, a hackle, wool shears and cards,*
> *A woollen wheel, with a shrew at the end*
> *With ears of straw and broaches.*

Lynch collected versions of a great many of the songs that are in Douglas Hyde's *Love Songs of Connacht*.

Brief reference must now be made to others who aided Bunting in

---

3. Note that at this era tobacco was home-grown.

his work of collecting.

After all that I have quoted from Eugene O'Curry on the subject of the Irish harp, and in criticism of the articles prefacing the 1840 volume, it is interesting to come on a sheet of paper pinned into one of the MS. books bearing the signature of that famous scholar. He gives a verse, of a song in Irish, with a translation. The Irish is in Roman character, and may be reproduced:

Eider bhad an challadh is faithche Ohill Diomo

Maidin bhog aoibhinn tamall roimh la,

Do dhearcas an aindir, sas cuma ca mbion si

Acht gur chrioth naigh ma chroidhe le vaith neamh da

      pairt,

Do bhi guma breac, uirthe, falaing is *Roundskirt*

Don fhaision bhreagh ghallda, ta anois aige mnaibh

Bhi Hood, agus Hata, uirthe, *Box* i's *Pendowdle*

Is cnota na ceann go burraiceach ard.

which, being interpreted, is:

Between the Ferry-boat and the green of Kildimo,

A soft happy morning awhile before day,

I espied the fair damsel, no matter where she lives,

But that my heart for her friendship did tremble and ache.

She had on a speckled gown, a mantle and round skirt

Of the fine English fashion, which women now have;

A hood and a hat, with a box and pendowdle,

And a knot in her forehead high pending in air.

Added are notes to the effect that he is uncertain of the words "round skirt" and "box" having been in the song, and that the ferry-boat and Kildimo are both on the bank of the Shannon below Adare, Limerick side.

The signature is "E. Curry," but we feel certain that the handwriting is that of the famous Eugene by comparison with a MS. copied for Sir Samuel Ferguson,[4] in which he signs also without the O. O'Curry spent his boyhood on the Clare side of the Shannon, and this song of the Ferry would be easily borne over to him.

It may here be mentioned that O'Curry had experience of taking down the Irish words of Folk Songs, and that his MSS. made for Petrie were, like those of the Lynch-Bunting collection, laid aside and never used, whilst the melodies alone were given to the world.

Lord Adare, afterwards first Lord Dunraven, and a distinguished antiquary, was amongst those who congratulated Bunting on the appearance of his 1840 volume in the following letter:

> SIR,— Tho' personally unknown to you, as I am a lover of Irish music, will you allow me to say how grateful I was at the appearance of your volume of Ancient Irish Music, and how I hope you will give to the world the remaining part of your collection. I take the liberty of enclosing four airs, copied for me by Miss Mansell of Dunboe. If you have not got them already, perhaps you would like to insert them, for which purpose I send them; if they form part of your present collection, or that they are not serviceable to your purpose, please to return them. In case you make use of any of them, they had better be inserted as given by Miss Mansell.
>
> You have, of course, got 'Shule Agrah'. — Allow me to remain, yours faithfully,
>
> ADARE.

I do not find any trace of these songs, so they were possibly returned, but a copy of the Jacobite air, 'The Blackbird', is fastened to the following letter:

> SIR, — I take the liberty of enclosing another air from Miss Mansell,

---

4. This MS. was sent by Sir S. Ferguson's brother-in-law to an exhibition in Belfast on the occasion of the poet's centenary, March 1810.

in addition to three I forwarded before through Dr Todd, and which I
hope you received; it may not be in your collection. — I remain, your
obedient servant,

ADARE.

Dr Todd here referred to was the translator of *The Wars of the Gaedhil
and the Gall*, relating the authentic narrative of the death of King Brian
Borou at Clontarf.

Miss Mansell was a member of a well-known County Limerick
family noted for musical taste. In fact a Miss Mansell of an earlier
generation eloped in 1766 with an Italian singer, Signor Tendacci.

A faded slip of MS. music has two lines of a melody with these words:

Och! the thoughts of my mother do cause me to weep,
Oh, where shall I wander when she is asleep;
She tenderly nourished me, clothed and fed:
All joy is over since she is dead.

On the reverse is written:

From Mary Brett to her dear Master, Mr Bunting, as a small token of
her sincere gratitude for all his kindness to her.

CHARLEVILLE, *Sept.* 11th, 1819.

Charleville here is not the well-known town in County Cork, but was
the name of the family residence in Brett's Glen, near Belfast.[5]

The song of 'Ballinderry' has been made familiar in the version of
words by Mr Alfred Perceval Graves. The air was published by Bunting
in his 1812 volume as 'Cronan na n'Bann'.

On a loose sheet of paper among the MSS. we find the original country

---

5. Sir Charles Brett, Vice-President of the Belfast Philharmonic Society, informs me that
harpers were accustomed to frequent Charleville in the old days, and were received *en fête*.

version of English words known in the district around Loch Neagh:

> *It's pretty to be in Ballinderry,*
>> *It's pretty to be in Aghalee;*
> *But it's prettier to be in little Ram's Island*
>> *Sitting under an ivy tree.*

> *Oh, that I was in little Ram's Island,*
>> *Oh, that I was with Phelimy Diamond;*
> *He would whistle and I would sing*
>> *Till we would make the whole island ring.*

>> *Och One ! Ochone !*
>> *Och One ! Ochone !*

Additional stanzas are given as sung by Mr Mitchell.

The following is evidently by some one who liked the tune, but not the sentiment of the original:

> *It's pretty to be in Ballinderry,*
>> *It's pretty to be at the Cash of Toome;*
> *But it's prettier to be in sweet Portglenone,*
>> *Drinking whiskey-punch in the Lodge-room.*

Next two specimen verses are given of the style of words that were adapted to this popular air by parties of country people, who were accustomed to come down to the banks of the River Bann, and from opposite sides of the water taunted and hailed each other in song:

> *Make my respects to that young man*
>> *That has got on the coat of green.*

> *Ask him, does he remember the day*
>> *When the wind did blow my hat in the Bann?*
>>> *Um-m-m-m.*

(A humming chorus followed here, instead of the too mournful "Ochone," then another verse.)

> *Make my respects to that young man*
>   *That has got on the coat of brown;*
> *It was not the coat I valued a farthing,*
>   *But for the ribband my true love put on.*
>   *Um-m-m-m,*

and so on, no doubt in salutation to young men with every colour of coat. A MS. note says, "Ask Mrs Hill Wilson to show how the humming was done."

I cannot say whether this custom of singing across the river still prevails along the Bann shore. The song would have to be different in these days, when nearly all young men wear coats of the same colour. The fact that it is called a Cronan is of interest, as the humming of a bass to a melody is one of the lost arts of Irish music.

CHAPTER XXIV

LETTERS FROM DR JAMES MACDONNELL 1836-1840

So much has been said of Dr MacDonnell in connection with the preservation of Irish music and the revival of the harp, that it might be supposed he was a man of leisure who had ceased to practise medicine and devoted himself to the pursuit of private hobbies.

In justice to the Doctor we will preface his letters by the following testimony from a high authority: Sir William Whitla, M.D., in delivering his presidential address to the British Medical Association, meeting at Belfast in the summer of 1909, paid the following tribute to the memory of Dr James MacDonnell. Having sketched the rise of the Belfast Medical School up to the year 1826, when a course of clinical lectures was instituted, he goes on to say:

The first theatre lecture of the systematic course was delivered by Dr James MacDonnell, a very remarkable man an intellectual giant in his day whose name is associated with every movement for the advancement of medical education and for the relief of suffering. If any one name is to be singled out from amongst the founders of the Belfast Medical School, as we look backwards at the present momentous stage of our progress, it must be that of MacDonnell. To him we owe the origin of the first hospital established in Ireland for the treatment of fevers, and to him is due the honour of founding the Belfast Dispensary. Malcolm relates how that in times of the greatest apathy towards this his favourite project, when almost unassisted by an encouraging hand he continued to tend and watch over it with fostering care and unabated interest until it had reached a vigorous maturity. He was the leading spirit in the campaign that called into existence the Belfast General Hospital. He was also founder of the Natural History Museum still standing in College Square, and still doing duty as our only scientific museum for the education in natural history of the people of the city. In the midst of his arduous labours in the interest of humanity MacDonnell found time for the pursuit of original research, and contributed valuable additions to our knowledge upon the mechanism of the circulation. His work upon the variations in the pulse under diverse physical conditions and alterations in the body posture shows the remarkable originality of a mind, capable at the same time of patiently accumulating enormous numbers of observations and rightly interpreting their physiological and clinical importance. Born in the Glens of Antrim in 1762, MacDonnell graduated in Edinburgh in 1784 and lived till 1845.

We may add that a fine marble bust of the Doctor is in the collection of the Natural History and Philosophical Society's Museum, of which he was one of the originators. The bust is by Christopher Moore, the sculptor, responsible for the unsatisfactory statue of Thomas Moore, which stands at the Brunswick Street side of Trinity College, Dublin.

The letters from Dr MacDonnell to Bunting, so far as they have been preserved for us, commence with the following, written at a time when Bunting long resident in Dublin was supposed to have abandoned the idea of further publication:

BELFAST Oct. 26th, '36.

DEAR BUNTING,— You will not recollect my hand-writing, but I wish to bring to your recollection a subject we were speaking of when you were last here. It was about some songs or dirges, composed for Sir Alexander MacDonnell who was assassinated in the south of Ireland when a prisoner by a partisan of Cromwell's. He was my Great-great-grandfather, and the son of Coll Kittagh.[1] I mention these things to induce you to find those tunes, and to send them to me if you can get them. I heard that some of them were printed, and

1. Coll Kittagh means "left-handed Coll."

I think you told me that you had gotten some of them, which you had arranged and harmonised.

When you publish your music, which I now never expect to see, as I am so old and you so indolent, be sure to print some commentary upon the tunes, stating all the conjectures that you can form about them, and this desire which I feel of preserving some record of what I call the "Literary History of Music," which seems never to have been done with any care in any country, reminds me that I once lent you a volume of Hawken's *History of Music* — if it be lost don't mind it, but if you can find it, give it to my son John, or to my son Alexander, whom you know best, or your obliged friend,

JAS. MACDONNELL.

Alastair MacColl MacDonnell (*English, Alexander*), referred to above, was leader of the Irish contingent in Montrose's rising. After the fall of Montrose, he returned to Ireland and got a command in Munster on the royalist side under Lord Taafe. The latter was opposed by Lord Inchiquin on behalf of the Parliament. The armies met at Cnocnanoss between Mallow and Kanturk. Alexander commanded three thousand foot and two regiments of horse. The battle began by MacDonnell ordering a charge of cavalry, which shook Inchiquin's left wing and succeeded by advance of MacDonnell's foot regiments. Inchiquin's army retired to the gates of Mallow, Inchiquin's right wing was more successful in opposing Taafe's left. MacDonnell is said to have retired to a hill to reconnoitre, and was surrounded and captured on the promise of quarter from a Cornet O'Grady. An officer in Sir John Clotworthy's regiment, who preserved a contemporary account of the war, writes, after describing MacDonnell's capture on the promise of quarter:

At which time comes up one Major Pardon after baronetted and demanded the Cornet who it was he gave quarters to. On which he told him; on which Pardon was in a fury and shot MacDonnell in the head being the other's prisoner, and so MacDonnell was lost. In revenge of which the Cornet for seven years fought Pardon every year but most commonly got the worse which the more was the pity . . . . The loss of this field was much attributed to the want of ready conduct, and those on the right hand did not fight so vigorously as MacDonnell did on the left hand; but it was his Destiny to be so lost after these many fights and dangers he was in, in the wars of Scotland, being as stout and strong a man as ever carried a broad sword and targett of late days, and so vigorous in fight that had his conduct been equivalent to his valour, he had been one of the best generals in Europe. Cnocnanos was fought 13th November, 1647.

The following letter accompanied the one regarding the the character of Arthur O'Neill, which we gave as an introduction to the *Memoir*. Alexander, the doctor's son, held a position under the National Education Board, and wrote from a government office:

CASTLE, *Nov.* 15th '38.

MY DEAR MR BUNTING,— I have great pleasure in sending you the accompanying letter from my dear Father. On the day when it was written he was suffering under one of the worst attacks he has had, so much so that my Mother was much alarmed. His mind, however, was you will see as full of serenity, kindness, and intelligence, as if he was enjoying perfect health. Believe me, sincerely yours,

ALEXANDER MACDONNELL.

P.S.— I should have called with this letter, but must leave town to-morrow for Belfast.

The next letter from the Doctor shows with what interest and enthusiasm he hailed the news of Bunting's progress with his last volume, and heard of his continued interest in the attempts to preserve the harp.

BELFAST, *Sept.* 10th 1839.

DEAR BUNTING, — You will scarcely believe how much the receipt of
your letter has raised my spirits, 'tis the best cordial I got since I saw you,
and I now think the publication of this volume may be the means of
yet reviving this Society,[2] for as Rainey[3] was better than O'Neill, and as
there was yet two persons nearly as good as Rainey, besides the Master,
why need one despair that others might not succeed?

Mr Price is the gentleman, at present, fondest of the instrument. He gave
my little harper, Pat Murney, a guinea the other day, and has sent for him
again, where I have consigned him to Captain King and the ladies, who are all
taken with him, and although you took so little notice of him, I predict that
he will do. Don't omit mentioning Rainey in your Preface, as having been a
nephew of Robert Burns, the Scotch poet. I have a long letter yet to write to
you about the music, and then I have done with that subject. I hope Ferguson[4]
is recovering. Do not be huffed with Donovan or Petrie,[5] they could both be
useful to you, and both must be naturally fond of the object.

I enclose two stripes of paper written in your hand, which I found since
you left here. They relate to the Highland blind woman's song of 'Dardrae'[6]
which she sung so often to my dear friend, the old Marchioness of Londonderry.
You took it down, and I beg the favour of you to write it over again, and return
it to me as a keepsake explaining the matter, as a curiosity, and proving it to be
the same with what you got at Murlogh.[7] I don't think you lay sufficient stress
upon this curious co-incidence I wish you to compare ' Col Kittagh's March,'

[2.] Refers to the Belfast Harp Society.

[3.] Rainey taught harp after O'Neill's retirement.

[4.] Samuel Ferguson who revised the *Memoirs of the Harpers.*

[5.] [John O'Donnovan and George Petrie — SCL] Both learned antiquarians, and
collectors of folk-songs.

[6.] [Deirdre 'of the Sorrows', heroine of the Fate of the Children of Uisneach – SCL].

[7.] Murlogh, near Fair-head, County Antrim, where the Doctor had a country house.

not the one called after 'Oilestrum ' in Croker's book, but the ' Father's March' which has been printed in Scotland.

J. MacDonnell.

In the year 1839, when his book was on the verge of publication, Bunting visited Belfast, several little notes from the doctor were sent to him by hand, showing us that he was reading the manuscript before publication. The first refers to Arthur O'Neill's *Memoir.*

> Dear Bunting,— Ferguson said he would drink tea with us to-night at eight o'clock if he could, but he was not sure of coming, he had not got the second proof I think it essential to cultivate this man I have read fifty-nine pages of the *Memoir,* which has greatly the air of truth come to us if you can, and bring the ladies with you, if they have nothing else in view, to your obliged
>
> J. MacDonnell.
>
> *Thursday.*

> Dear Bunting.— Send me more to read and come soon. I talked with Finerty last night, and showed him most of the Greek terms, one of which only has any affinity with the Irish, so that there is little chance of finding any genealogy for ours unless in the Hebrew, Chaldaic, Syriac, Arabic, or Sanscrit languages, all of which particularly the last should be searched for their affinities, do not fail to do this in Dublin. Come to me when idle. Believe me, yours sincerely,
>
> J. MacDonnell.

Finerty was the Belfast Gaelic teacher at that period, who was evidently consulted concerning Irish spelling.

> Dear Bunting, — When you quote from Moore or any one else retain their orthography of Irish words, names, people or tunes; but in writing the names yourself be very careful in spelling the words, so as not to leave them

to be guessed at. Thus at the end of page thirty-five "Ul a Cando wo" I heard always sounded "Ooligan dooh oh." I know not the meaning of the word "Ooligan," it seems an expression of endearment. The word sounded "Dooh" is written "Dubh". I have had great pleasure in reading this manuscript.

The following has no commencement or address:

I am very much obliged and pleased with your account of the audible sounds per second. Be sure to explain fully your own ideas as a musician and a philosphical reasoning man about the whole subject, and endeavour to show how it happens that other musicians, although expert and learned in their art never are able to play a Scotch or Irish air with any effect by any mode yet discovered of committing them to writing. Just as we see that no person can speak any living language merely by book knowledge, I never heard an Irish air played properly by a person who did not hear it played or sung by an Irish person, or by one like you taught in that manner.[8]

J. MacDonnell.

To Edward Bunting, Esq.,
Mr M'Cracken's, Donegall Street

Dear Bunting,— I return both the letter and this print. It is a great matter to have enlisted such a person[9] as this in your favour, for although she be so perfectly heterodox in politics that I can conceive nothing more perverted and dangerous, yet the warmth of her heart and her love for some things in Ireland might be turned to advantage if she could be prevented from her vile orange railing. Send me word how your daughter is, and send me more to read. And believe me, ever yours,

J. MacD.

---

8. The Doctor would have favoured the "Direct Method" of teaching languages, and the study of traditional singing now advocated by the Gael League.

9. The print referred to was a portrait of the lady known as Charlotte Elizabeth, author of a popular novel *The Siege of Derry*, and of various Orange ballads. She had, however, a taste for Irish music.

Sunday night.

DEAR BUNTING,— I wrote yesterday to my son about the Dedication. You should do nothing until you have completed the explanation be sure to amplify it, so that every one could understand it. I see from the Greek names of the notes and their positions upon a monochord that any lady can understand their canon of an "immutable and mutable system."

Mrs Garner is to be at Mr Pratt's to-morrow, where I hope you will sit beside her at dinner and direct your conversation to her favourite subjects.

The English word "Base" and the Italian "Basso" are evidently of Greek origin. The lowest note or sound on any string would be "Proslambano-menos," let the monochord be long or short and the octaves to this whole string, counting from above downwards, or from below upwards, is always called "Mese" from which our word medium or middle is derived, and this is the note which the harpers speaking English called "Sisters," but their word "Havlai" is not in vulgar language convertible literally into the word "Sister," which the Scotch express by "Derfur."

Make Finerty examine all the Greek and Latin words upon the monochord, and get some one to find out the Hebrew, Arabic, Persian, and German, but above all the Sanscrit words to discover whether the Irish terms which you have got can be turned into any Oriental language. Dublin the place finally for this, and yours will be the first attempt to explore it. One thing appears plain that the further back we could go in any country the nearer will the scope of the tune, the number of notes come to the scope of the notes which the natural voice can express, viz., if any tune has a greater compass than this it must be instrumental, no doubt the first instruments were fifes, flutes and pipes, then comes the lyre and the Jewish instruments. If there are any old Irish tunes that have a greater range than the pipes, flute, and human voice they probably belong to the harp, and this will be almost certain if they want the semi-tones that you have always mentioned. I do not think the Irish had a violin, because their word for that instrument is "Fiol" or "Phial," which is nothing but a corruption of the English "Fiddle."

You mentioned often the word "glass." I thought it meant to tune or to put in tune, but I recollect since that it also means a lock, or to lock.

Spend a good deal of time with Finerty, and make notes of anything that is dubious, in order to have a final correction in Dublin, where there is a Professor of Sanscrit with whom you should certainly converse.

As languages become more numerous, and the intercourse between nations increase, then the peculiarities of each language diminish and almost disappear, as was in the "Lingua franca," so as musical instruments increase in number, the peculiarities of national airs will certainly decrease until at length they will all be confounded, so that no human being can trace each to its native seat, and the same is true of religions as they increase they will be apt to blend with each other.

Fanning's harp had thirty-five strings, fourteen below and nineteen above the "Sisters" — the eleven upper strings of iron wire. Mr Shannon, an Organist, I believe at Randalstown (when there was no Organ at Belfast) constructed a gamut for Fanning's harp.

Black's had eleven below and twenty-one above "Sisters" it had three circular, divided openings in the belly, resembling a guitar — the pinboard was warped, which did not impair its tone.

Rose Mooney's had thirteen strings below and eighteen above the "Sisters." A piece of timber of triangular shape (the angle truncated) was placed within the belly of the harp, through which the strings passed, being fixed by transverse pegs of wood, like quills of the Welsh harp differed in this respect, and there was of consequence a greater facility in replacing a string. The belly of Mooney's harp was split and cracked upon one side where it was covered with canvas, or pasteboard beneath yet it was light, sonorous, and much superior to Quin's harp. Its body was composed of three pieces of timber. There were four strips of copper placed transversely, and one strip longitudinally, to strengthen the timber. The transverse strips were closer as you ascended to the treble, where the tension of the strings or purchase is greatest. The obliquity of the short strings is greatest, and the management of this is a principal difficulty in the mechanical construction of the instrument.

With a view to discover the theory of the curve in the pinboard, I had all the harps measured carefully, preparatory to engraving them upon a scale, but these notes are lost by Mr John Mulholland, who took them to London, I had no duplicate.

This letter is unsigned, and addressed simply "Edward Bunting, Esq.," as if sent by hand, so he was evidently still in Belfast, and the doctor, either ill or too busy to call on him, sent notes with every book or manuscript he returned.

Here is a letter from the Mrs Garner referred to:

MY DEAR DOCTOR, — I have scribbled out three little airs, which I would be very glad if you could procure Mr Bunting's opinion of I mean as to what the country they belong to, or if they bear any distinct national character. I am on my way to Purdysburn, to remain for a couple of days, but hope to see you on my return on Thursday, as I have procured a more manageable horse. I am deeply interested on the subject of Music as connected with Sound, for I never heard anything that gave me the least philosophical satisfaction on the subject yet; the nearest to it was that you threw out the other night, about the measure of lines of Poetry being regulated by the human respiration, but that does not, as far as I see, apply to sound in general. — Ever your gratefully attached friend,

MARIAN GARNER.

Tuesday.

E. BUNTING, ESQ., Donegall St.

MY DEAR BUNTING,— If you have not packed up your movables, let me read Lynch's journal[10] but if it be packed up don't bother yourself it is possible, if I had read over all the papers along with you more

---

10. This is the diary which is published for the first time in this volume.

deliberately, that I could have made some other remarks, but at any rate, I am very glad I saw them, and that I observe your wife, so competent to assist you in a matter of such moment.[11]

I am, dear Bunting, ever yours,

J. MacD.

The next letter shows him busy in trying to secure the Queen's consent to have Bunting's volume dedicated to her. "The Tournament," was the famous one organised by Lord Eglinton.

DEAR BUNTING. — What I suspected turned out to be the case the letter I wrote to Lord Belfast did not go until my son returned from London, and as there has been since a sufficient lapse of time and no answer, I must either write again or abandon that method of trial. Perhaps it will be most prudent to wait until the Queen returns from the tournament — after which if you call on my son he will converse freely with you, and consider the best mode of proceeding. You may direct me. I do not like any delay and hope you are making a daily progress in the printing. I wish much to see every sheet before it be printed off, and my son would forward it to me — I wish now to get the remainder of the Prospectus.

If you have hit upon any distinct rules for guiding musical criticism so as to enable one to discover what constitutes identity, or individuality in an air, and then to determine of two airs known to be of a common root or origin which was the original; and finally be able to class airs according to their native countries, and I do think if you achieve these or any of them you will deserve much praise. Don't cease to endeavour after it. When you have developed the principle, I beg you may send me an extended account of it, such as a person like me can comprehend. I can scarcely think that any two persons ever fell by mere accident upon the same identical air, so that with respect to each author it might be an original — this

---

[11.] Bunting's wife prepared and copied all his music for publication. (See his allusion to her in his letters to Mary M'Cracken.)

can't be — no two persons could hit on the same stanza of poetry — they might hit on the same thought, but will never express any train of thoughts in the selfsame manner without borrowing, and yet people may imitate and borrow without recollecting from whence. Although one may acquire internal evidence from the analysis of an air, or a poem that *one* has borrowed from another, how are we to, proceed in discovering the Borrower from the Lender? I hope you will examine 'Bumper Squire Jones' rigorously with a view to this beautiful question. Supposing it to have been stolen by Carolan from an English tune called 'The Rummer' first having found nearly the date of Carolan's tune, composed for the Great-Grandfather of the present proprietor of the Money-Glass estate, nick-named "Bumper," the companion and neighbour of Charles O'Neill (mentioned in your MS. *Memoir*, and Grand-Uncle to the present Lord O'Neill) this will make the tune above a century old. Now the word "Rummer" does not look like an old word. "Roemer" in Dutch is a drinking glass, rum is not an old liquor.

None of the Irish people, musicians or not, ever heard a doubt expressed of the originality of the air, nor was a man of such high inventive power as Carolan, likely to think of borrowing; nor was a community like this at that period, in which music was more practised than at present, nor a family so patrician as Jones's likely to be imposed upon in this manner and to remain undeceived for a hundred years, during which, the tune was not merely propagated, but printed, and its words, both in Irish and English, circulated over all Ireland. Moreover Carolan was never known or suspected of any other plagiarism, he indeed, imitated something from Corelli, but he did so avowedly as an amusement. I have more doubts about 'Loughaber' because this tune while I was in Scotland was never suspected of being Irish, if it be so, it must have gone over to Scotland very early, as the poems of Ossian almost assuredly did. Whether the Highlanders and Irish have music as well as poetry, truly Ossianic, I know not. I am, Dear Bunting, sincerely yours,

J. MacDonnell.

Edward Bunting as a collector and musician was a much better judge of Carolan's genius as a composer, and he was quite justified in saying that Carolan's music was not so Irish in construction as many of the other harpers. It is now quite certain that Carolan set words to many of the old Irish airs, and in time the airs were supposed to be his, for instance 'the Hawk of Ballyshannon' was set to Carolan's words and in time was named 'O'More's Fair Daughter' from the ballad of that name set to the air by Carolan. Dr MacDonnell also mentions 'Loughaber' as being of Scottish origin. The *Memoirs of the Harpers* by O'Neill settles this point.

Lord Belfast wrote on the subject of the dedication.

Buxton, *Sept.*

My Dear Doctor, — I have not replied to your letter earlier, having been in hopes of sending Mr Bunting the Queen's sanction to dedicate his Work to Her Majesty, every post.

I finished a letter, to Her Majesty making the request, as soon as I received yours, but I presume that in the hurry of the Court moving from London to Windsor it has been overlooked.

I will write again on the subject in a day or two in the meantime I answered your letter, in order that you may not complain of my not answering your letter. — Believe me, yours obediently,

Belfast.

Dear Bunting, — I hasten to enclose this letter from Lord Belfast, to which I shall reply immediately on hearing from you. I hope you and your wife and Ferguson are all busy in improving and augmenting the book. I have examined Crofton Croker's book, and always find every new thing helps to improve the knowledge we have, and we should never despise anything that bears on the subject. I met with a Mr Thynistan who is a fine classical scholar, to whom I showed the Greek musical terms employed by Euclid; and to my great surprise, he said they were not strictly and properly Grecian, he not seeing how they could be derived or analysed in fact, they were quite new to him, particularly the words "Nete" and "Lychanos."

I had written so far when your friend Mary called on me with your letter in consequence of what I shall repeat my solicitation to Lord Belfast. I have always found in experience, that anything one undertakes which depends on co-operation from others, is apt to be protracted, and ultimately to fail. You may probably have ultimately to depend on yourself, yet still I think Ferguson the most likely person, from his habits, studies, and capacity to be of use to you. I shall explain what you mention to Finacghty. The pronunciation of all living languages must be for ever perplexing. The mourning songs, or rhapsodies, sung in a kind of recitative by old Irish women at wakes, is pronounced "Keena," and this word changes into a participle as "Ta sheed i cheenan". "They are singing the dirge." Croker finds it in Hebrew and Welsh, but does not notice its resemblance to the Latin "cano" to sing.

Never rest until you find some person, who can find the East Indian terms for music, Persian, Arabic, Hindostanny, etc., but above all Sanscrit. This can be done easily in Dublin or Oxford, as they have got Professors there of Sanscrit, who might probably engage with eagerness in the pursuit. Get also some Hebrew scholar to look at your terms, and particularly compare them with the odd words in the English Psalms, which no one can translate, and which I told you of. I shall write soon again. — I am, Dear Bunting, yours most sincerely,

J. MacDonnell.

Very soon a letter arrived from Lord Belfast announcing that he had received the Queen's consent to the Dedication. He had probably a real interest in promoting the publication, being a man of liberal and enlightened tastes. His young son, who was shortly to succeed to the title, had intense and literary taste and Irish sympathies, and some talent as a composer. He died at an early age. Lord Belfast, writer of this letter, was the grandfather of the present Earl of Shaftesbury, president of the Irish Folk-Song Society.

Buxton, *Sept.* 8*th* 1839.

My Dear Sir, — Perhaps you will be kind enough to give the enclosed to Mr Bunting, as I am not acquainted with his address.

Her Majesty has been graciously pleased to grant his request to allow him to dedicate his Work to her. — Yours truly,

Belfast.

To Dr MacDonnell.

This is the letter to Bunting:

Buxton, *Sept.* 8*th* 1839.

Sir,—, I have received the Queen's commands to inform you, that she has been graciously pleased to approve of your dedicating the forthcoming Volume of your Irish Melodies, to Her Majesty. — I have the Honour to remain, yours obediently,

Belfast.

On receiving the above Dr MacDonnell wrote:

Dear Bunting,— I think it best that you should yourself, as well as I, return thanks to Lord Belfast.

The notes I last sent were a Copy from the original, which I now send. This will tend as I believe it written in your own hand, to make the matter clearer, because I think this of great moment, there being some reasons for believing the story to which it relates as old as the Christian era, or older, for, although Ossian is represented as Co-eval with St Patrick, this appears only to be a fiction of the Poet, introducing St Patrick in a Dialogue but in the story of "Dardrae" in all its Copies,[12] of which you have got the

---

12. Dr Macdonnell was assuredly familiar with Bryson's copy of *Deirdre*, made in County Antrim, which Dr Douglas Hyde quotes in his *History of Irish Literature.*

worst, there is no mention of Patrick (in five or six that I have seen), nor is there any allusion to anything connected with Christianity, neither places nor people.

The word translated "Druid" in the MS. is written "Draoi" and there is no evidence that this is equivalent to Druid there is a supposed allusion to the game of Chess, but this I also found to be a conjectural word.

Take care to make out all the tunes called after Coll Kittaugh, because one of them which I have heard, is not a March, but a kind of wild extravagant Rhapsody, like grief and lamentation, supposed to have been played by his own Piper, then a Prisoner in the Castle of Dun prior to the massacre which took place there about 1645, in which three hundred of Alister's soldiers were immolated in cold blood the Piper played the tune to deter the Father from landing at the Castle, to which he was steering, not knowing it to be then taken by Lesly, and in the hands of the Covenanters, who, on discovering that the Piper had effected his purpose cut off his fingers and threw him into a cavern, from which he continues to play underground from that day to this.

This letter ends abruptly and is unsigned.

Coll Kittagh (*i.e.*, left-handed) MacDonnell, the Doctor's ancestor, had been a famous soldier in his youth. In his old age when his son Alastair fought under Montrose, he again took arms and was put in command of the Castle of Dunyveg in Islay in the royalist interest which he held from 1644 to 1647, when he was entrapped into surrender by General Leslie who promised him honourable protection. However the old man fell into the hands of his enemy Gillespach Gruamach, Earl of Argyle, who had him tried by a jury of Campbells and executed by being hung from the mast of his own galley fixed across a cleft of the rocks near Dunstaffnage Castle. The incident of the piper's warning may have occurred at Dunaveg. A natural son of old Coll's held another little fort in Islay, and may have been coming by sea to join with his father in the pacification till the pipers' shrill lamenting note warned him of treachery.

The following reference to Ferguson's co-operation with Bunting is of interest. The Anthony first referred to may be either brother or son to Edward. The second reference is undoubtedly to the son.

BELFAST, *March* 8th, 1840.

DEAR BUNTING, — It is now Sunday night, and yet no word about Ferguson, but I am on the look-out for him and will take advantage of the hints you give me observe, that I was not sure you were right in beginning to pay, for I never saw a poet, a publisher or writer of any kind, that ever was contented with any kind of pecuniary remuneration they all estimate their own services very highly however, my opinion now is that you can't be now dished or deserted, for I am convinced that your wife, yourself, and Anthony can do all that is requisite, supposing you to obtain no further assistance from Petrie, Donovan or even Ferguson yet I do not slight their services, they must each be very useful in his own way, if they can be induced to give their minds to it. No one can estimate them too highly. Donovan is very important. Remember the word "Gille" which you pronounced with a soft instead of a hard G, is "a servant boy," but "Gowle" is "the shoulder" as if two people were travelling or working, "shoulder for shoulder" helping each other. Tell this to Mr Donovan. I am writing the sound only.

Anthony[13] drank tea with us last night, and I am much pleased with him. You don't mention having got my long letter in a double cover, about ten days ago, it is no great matter, yet it would be odd if it were lost. — Your sincere friend,

J. MACDONNELL.

The book was published in 1840, and copies were presented to the Queen and Prince Consort by Lord Belfast, who wrote :

LONDON, *July* 17th, 1840.

DEAR SIR,— I have the honour to acknowledge the receipt of a parcel

---

13. Bunting's son.

containing three copies of your work. I yesterday had the honour of presenting those intended for Her Majesty and Prince Albert, which they were graciously pleased to receive. I also request you to accept my best thanks for the copy you were kind enough to present to me. — Allow me to remain, yours obediently,

BELFAST.

Dr MacDonnell wrote in rather critical vein:

BELFAST, *Aug.* 16th '40.

DEAR BUNTING,— I would give a great deal to know how this friend of yours Charlotte Elizabeth derived such pleasure from the harp, hearing that she is subject to such deafness.

I have a Poem written by an obscure person, in which there is a sentence, that might apply to her Picture,[14] if she be pallid, and delicate.

> *Upon a rock lerne sad reclined*
> *And gave her locks dishevelled to the wind*
> *Her cheek, which once the crimson morn displayed*
> *Was pale as Cynthia, daughter of the shade ;*
> *Her harp, unstrung, was careless laid aside,*
> *She only listened to the murmuring tide*
> *And sighing gale, which scarce was heard to blow*
> *But seemed from sympathy to breathe her woe.*

I hear of a very noble piece of Statuary having come from Italy, but the design and work of an Irish Artist, in which a figure, personifying Ireland, is supported by Dr Doyle — if you hear of any Print from this statue let me know of it. Your friend, Charlotte Elizabeth, will have no great liking for the Dr, but might admire the workmanship.

---

14. Charlotte Elizabeth, the Orange authoress, had been portrayed in the character of Erin, and apparently a statue of Dr Doyle, the celebrated Catholic controversialist, had also been executed in allegorical character. In each case the effect must have been absurd.

The only harp-maker in Belfast is the one who made Pat Murney's[15] which you heard. I think it was eight pounds it cost, and I was the Paymaster. There are some ornaments upon it. If you desire it, Miss M‹Cracken and I might superintend the work, and pay him as he proceeded for he is poor. Mr M‹Adam knows him — he worked there.

The only defects I see in your Preface are two you don't dilate and address yourself at sufficient length, for persons unacquainted with the Language of Musicians — of what use is it to me for instance to hear about the Diatonic Scale, the Diatessaron, the forth, the sharp seventh, the chord of the sixth, etc., and yet all this might have been rendered intelligible in an additional page, even to the vulgar.

Don't neglect this I entreat of you, to find out the Arabic, Persian, and above all the Sanscrit terms of art, because the roots of the words are not in Greek or Latin. In the next place, you say nothing of the spirit of patriotism, and the actual utility in a national point of view, of keeping alive all opinions, customs, and innocent prejudices, which bind mankind to their country, wherever that may be, whether it be the Deserted Village, or the mountain that leads them to the storm — these when early cherished, act like instinctive impulses, and carry with them a magic charm, they are delightful in prosperity, console us in adversity, they accompany us in the city, or in the wilderness — when old, we dote upon them. Now there are no associations or feelings of this kind so strong as those connected with music and language. I therefore argue that the Harp School should be revived, and if no other party of more moderate people take it up, I will urge M‹Adam,[16] Bell, Tenent [17] & Co., to appeal to O'Connell [18] to adopt it; but I would gladly see it resumed by such people if we had them, as Joy, Bradshaw, and Williamson, Fulton

---

15. A young harper who played at Glenarm Castle, 1839. [See ill. 10 & 11 — SCL].

16. M‹Adam was a Belfast man, and Secretary to the Irish Harp Society.

17. Tenent was a son-in-law of the M‹Cracken family.

18. Daniel O'Connell.

and McCracken, with Bunting at their head. — Your affectionate friend,

J. MacDonnell.

Dear Bunting,— I enclose you nine pounds, and have given to our friend Mary the odd money, for the six copies of your book that I had for sale it is a great pleasure to see it completed. My little harper pleased two or three great people very much, who visited this since you were here — viz. the Bishop of Derry, Lord Lansdowne, and Mr Blake of Dublin. I have a great desire that you should endeavour to keep the instrument as well as the music alive, and you are perhaps the only person who can now do it — my son Alexander was here with Lord Lansdowne.

Do not rest content with what you have done, but use the name and influence you have obtained in augmenting the volume, both in notes, words, and prefatory matter, particularly expanding that part respecting the "essential differences" between the music of different nations, with the causes of those differences; for this is the point in which the connection between this art and the history of mankind is most connected.

One can't think or hear of the history of any art or science without going back immediately to Greece, and from thence to Egypt, in which we soon lose our way then we find another route into the Scripture, and there stop again. Sir William Jones has traced something in Persia, and the thread of this ends at Benares in the Sanscrit tongue, where it should undoubtedly be followed by you into Thibet, and if nothing can be made out there, or in China, we are at the end of our tether. All further hope is almost evanescent.

The Greeks and Romans traced every old and good and great thing to Zoroaster and Pythagoras who got their sublime views of the mind in the East. I read the Institutions of "Menu" translated by Sir William Jones from Sanscrit, which is a most wonderful work, but contains nothing about music or Physick, which disappointed me. There is a great Sanscrit scholar in Dublin connected with the College. You should talk with him also — get translations of the few such books extant, one of which is by Euclid on music. In the last number of the *Phrenological Journal*, about two months ago, there is a paper you should peruse. Continue to correspond with Charlotte Elizabeth.

Your ever obliged friend,

J. MacDonnell.

September 28th, '40.

CHAPTER XXV

LETTERS *RE* PUBLICATION

A Voluminous correspondence has been preserved, with regard to the business arrangements and engraving process of the final volume. The letters are mainly from Mr J. Sidebotham, a solicitor, resident in London, who had at one time lived in Belfast. He had helped Bunting through with his 1809 volume also, and had been business director of the great Belfast Musical Festival at which the *Messiah* was produced.

A few selections from his letters will suffice.

No. 26 Hatton Garden, London.

My Dear Mr Bunting,— Your letter gave me inexpressible pleasure, its contents recalled to my remembrance those very happy days when you and I regularly met to supply the scientific composer and pewter-puncher (Skarratt) with correct copies of some of your valuable MS. for publication, to say nothing of those glorious repasts or Breakfasts, which usually preceded our delightful occupation. I need scarcely say how proud I shall be to second your views in any manner which you may require and first as to the Law.

At the time your work was published, in 1809, the only statutes relative to Copyright were one of Queen Anne and the 41st Geo. 3$^{rd.}$ cap. 107, and which alone govern the contract between you and Clementi as to the sale: by the acts referred to, C. obtained only an interest of fourteen years exclusive sale, and at the expiration of that time the work reverted to the author (if then living) for another exclusive term of 14 years (in the absence of any *special agreement or deed in writing to the contrary*) — you have therefore lost the advantage of the last fourteen years exclusive sale. In the year 1814 there was another act passed (54th Geo. 3, cap. 156) by the 4th Section, of which it was enacted that "from and after the passing of this act, the author of any Book composed and not printed and published, or which shall hereafter be composed and be printed and published, and his assigns shall have the sole liberty of printing and reprinting such Book or Books, for the full term of 28 years, to commence from the day of first publishing the same, and also if the author shall be living at the end of that period for the residue of his natural life" — by which you will perceive that the term was considerably exceeded. I should therefore advise that a written notice immediately be given to Willis to stop his further interference with the work, and if you think proper I will immediately send over the proper forms to be given that your signature may be added and witnessed thereto. A Copyright cannot be legally conveyed from its author excepting by some Deed or *Instrument in writing* therefore the alleged sale of the plates was and is worth no more than what they will weigh at the price of old metal; the time, however, has expired, and therefore no more need be said on this subject.

I would take leave to suggest the reprinting the contents of the 1st Vol. as single pieces (as well as altogether in one book) in the way in which Operas are now published, many purchasers would be found at two shillings for a single Song or Tune, who cannot spare fifteen shillings. or twenty shillings for a Book. Power latterly found his account in adopting this plan in Moore's Books of Melodies, and thousands became purchasers who otherwise would never have bought the work. Of course you will also consider whether it will be worth your while to revise or reset some of the old favourites in the *Moorish* style both as regards *Poetry and Accompaniment.*

The great Beethoven Wire-workers (I am afraid) do not purchase songs, the money is to be made from "the masses" (senza the first letter), who encouraged only such works as abound in one-fingered Basses, they abhor and detest all left-handed fly-catching passages, and Galvanic starts by which the fingers of one hand are trying to snatch the notes from under those of the other, followed by dislocating Extensions, and a continuous rumbling of most alarming-looking Chords in all Keys, moods, and tenses.

If I can be useful in superintending the Publication of the proposed works, correcting Letter-press, &c., you may command my services upon your own terms, according to the success you meet with in bringing before the public those rich stores of melody, which I know it is in your power to produce — let me entreat you to lose no more time. I am really alarmed when you bring to my recollection that it is twenty-eight years (28 years) since you and I were so agreeably associated together in bringing out the 1ˢᵗ Vol.

    With many kind regards to Mrs B. and family.—
    Believe me to remain ever sincerely yours,

J. SIDEBOTHAM.

Thursday, Aug. 16ᵗʰ, 1838.

N.B.— I was out of town yesterday when your letter arrived, otherwise I should have answered it instanter.

    You omitted to state the place of your present residence. I have directed this at random, and from an imperfect recollection of the name of the street.

26 HATTON GARDEN, *July* 19ᵗʰ, '39.

DEAR BUNTING,— Herewith you receive the whole of the corrected proofs, together with the original ones of the ninety-five plates, as well as two new plates of the Ossianic airs. There remains nothing more to be done but the unfortunate 'Cuckoo'. The whole of the ninety-seven plates, and all the MS., are in my exclusive possession, and wait your further direction. Skarratt has nothing whatever belonging to you but the said 'Cuckoo' notes. I have examined every plate myself with your corrected proofs, and I think the additional matter marked by you in red in has been faithfully attended to and transcribed to the plates. You will observe that pages forty-four, sixty-eight, seventy, seventy-one, as proved after Skarratt said he had corrected them (and delivered to me this week as such), were in some particulars erroneous, but which I detected on examination soon afterwards and sent back to him, and I have got them again in a perfect state, notwithstanding the proofs now sent which appear still faulty. I received your letter, dated Belfast, and should have answered it immediately, had not Skarratt kept pouring in the plates so fast upon me, that I found (for a certainty) that I could send the whole at one blow, and also my letter along with them. The one shilling and two pence per plate, I suspect, was easily earned, for he appears to have set aside all his excuses and Cathedral Chaunts, and attended solely to your business, and during the last fortnight he never missed a day without sending me a dozen of the plates, whether it was dinner-time or not.

I have paid him to the uttermost farthing, and he is very obsequious and anxious for more MS. Hackett's work on *Psalmody* is now finished, it is a folio work, price twenty-five shillings to subscribers. The publishers live in Preston's old house in Dean Street, Soho, now I believe "Coventry and Hollier."

I am glad that you were able to take a journey to the North. I wish it had been possible for me to have met you there. I don't know anything which would have given me greater pleasure than to visit Belfast, and contemplate those days of old, and our "merry meetings" at the Commercial Rooms, where with yourself, Moorhead, Bob Haigh, May, Gunning, Soane, Drs Thomson and Magee, we had used to meet every week to *scratch* Haydn and Beethoven; by the bye, it was on these occasions that I first heard those celebrated three Symphonies of the latter Author, or rather of two of them in C and D — the third (*Eroica*) looked so ferocious (at the basis particularly) that we postponed it by universal consent, and considered it "Holy ground" until the "Light of other days" should come upon our benighted understandings, and teach us how to pack four bunches of five semi-quavers each, in a quick movement intended by other authors to hold only sixteen, I have for many years past retired behind a tenor, and in the winter season am much engaged in various musical Societies, and of course often meet with Beethoven's Symphonies, particularly the three first, and I always think with pleasure on the company amongst whom I originally found him. I should hope that there will now be no further delay in bringing out your valuable work, and believe me, that no time shall be lost on my part to forward so interesting an object. — I am, dear B., very truly yours,

J. SIDEBOTHAM.

100 HATTON GARDEN.

DEAR BUNTING,— I was prepared for the melancholy news respecting the Ogle family, having previously heard of the hopeless state in which the late Mr and Mrs Ogle were in about four weeks ago. I have heard nothing of Pearman lately, so I suppose that he has received your directions as to the delivery of the Music when printed. Skarratt had his five shillings and cab-hire on the very day he did the job, having called upon me with his usual ready money eagerness on his way home from Pearman's house. I suppose that we shall soon see the Book. Your friend Earl Belfast (Chamberlain to the Queen) ought first to introduce you to Her Majesty with a copy of the Work, *at one of the Levees.* This would give it great *éclat.* Amongst the presentations in the Court-circular; the public would read "Mr Bunting to present a copy of his New Work on Irish Music, dedicated to Her Majesty" (obbligato for Bag-wig, embroidered coat, Sword, and Diamond Knee-buckles).

Wishing you all sorts of success, I remain, very truly yours,

J. SIDEBOTHAM.

May 2nd, '40.

100 HATTON GARDEN.

DEAR BUNTING,— It was only yesterday (the 14th inst.) that I received the box containing 3 parcels severally addressed to "Messrs Broadwood" — "The Earl of Belfast" and the "Countess of Charlemont," together with thirteen separate Books, all of which were personally delivered by Self and Cab within two hours afterwards — viz.: at the Earl's house, No. 3 Eaton St., Belgrave Square — the Countess' at 49 Grosvenor St., and Messrs B.'s parcel, and the thirteen loose copies at their old and well-known Warehouse. The work may therefore be said to be now fairly afloat in the high places here. I suppose that Willis (whose Warehouse is now in the same street with the Countess) will shortly be applied to for copies. You should loose no time in supplying the Warehouses here. I have, on the other side, sent you the finishing account of my Stewardship, and wishing you all happiness and Prosperity, I remain, dear Bunting, truly yours,

J. SIDEBOTHAM.

Wednesday 15ᵗʰ July, 1840,

(St Swithin).

100 HATTON GARDEN.

DEAR BUNTING,— The error was yours, as to the copy misdirected to the Countess of Charlemont. However, I have succeeded (after several applications) in getting it returned, and I have repapered and redirected it "To the Rt. Hon., the Countess of Charleville" after which I delivered it personally at the house, No. 8 St George's place, Knightsbridge; she never lived in "Grosvenor Street" at which latter place the parcel was particularly addressed by Messrs Hodges & Co.

I have obtained the plates referred to for correction, and Skarratt promises next week to knock them off without fail. Mr Chappell has sold some copies, but does not want any further supply at present, having received twenty-five copies yesterday from Dublin — the Duke of Leinster came to Bond Street yesterday, expressly (as he says) to purchase a copy. I have apprised Messrs Broadwood's man of business (Rose) of the wholesale and retail prices of the work — (one pound four shillings — One pound eleven shillings and six pence), which he says shall be attended to; as to the Messrs B.'s, they are quite inaccessible to commoners like me. Pearman can be getting on printing the other plates, if you like, so that Skarratt's work when delivered will not occupy him (Pearman) twenty-four hours. I congratulate you on your Son's good fortune and expectations. Oh, that my Boy had such an Uncle,[1] however the time for starting him is not arrived, and when it does, who knows what fortunes may turn up the "pleasures of hope" are a favourite study with all mankind. Yours truly,

J. Sidebotham.

Wednesday evening, 22ⁿᵈ July, 1840.

100 Hatton Garden.

Dear Bunting,— Since you will not present the work to her little Majesty *in propria persona*, there will be no difficulty in conveying it to her by other means, viz., through the Lord Chamberlain's office, with an Autograph letter from yourself to accompany same, and I will undertake the delivery of it myself, the proposed letter should be submitted to some of your literary friends, as there is a knack and style in doing these things which none but professed scribblers can accomplish. I hope that the alterations in the plate of the 'Irish Cry' which you allude to, was very material. The plate must have been worked off before you wrote to Skarratt as there certainly was no time lost *on that occasion at leas*t he came to me breathless with haste and showed me your letter, and he and the cab went about it instanter.

As you wish to know my opinion of the present English musical taste I must say that I consider it as decidedly against national or any other melodies. Nothing goes down at present but Straus's Waltzes and others of that school, worked up through a whole quire of music paper into variations (and aggravations) in all moods and tenses both major and minor. However, I do not despair of your book having a tolerable sale here, being an historical work, and the *dilettanti* if they will not play

---

1. Anthony Bunting, who helped his brother's son, young Anthony, at the outset of his promising career as engineer.

from it, would like to have it in their book case for occasional reference. If only one third of the musical people here take a copy the sale will be enormous. Hoping to see you and your son before the summer is over. Mrs S—— and myself unite in kind wishes for your welfare, and with best regard to yourself and family. I remain, dear Bunting, yours truly.

J. SIDEBOTHAM.

P.S. — Excuse scribbling in haste as my harvest is on, and will continue until the Courts of Equity close, August next.

Saturday, June 6th 1840.

The next letter is from Skarratt, whom Mr Sidebotham employed to engrave the plates for Bunting.

5 EYRE STREET HILL,
near Hatton Garden.

DEAR SIR, — In one of your letters to me you state that "the pen has hardly been out of your hand for eighteen months" on the contrary the pen has hardly been in mine for the last eighteen months, or you would have had an answer to your letters; but now having leisure am taking it up, I will not lay it down till I have endeavoured to make an ample apology for my neglect of not writing to a valuable old friend, and one who is valued by poor me, if that be of any avail. I don't know how it is but sometimes the mind will lapse even to the injury of the possessor's interest and duty. So I occasionally prove it. I have thought without action, action without thought. They are like two pigs on a string, I can't get them to go well together. Although I have neglected my duty to write to you, your kindnesses have ever been gratefully remembered by me, and *ever will be.*

In one of your letters you ask my opinion of your work, this I consider an honour conferred on myself, and to the best of my ability you shall have it. I hardly know which to admire most, the untiring perseverance that has brought so much ancient and valuable musical matter together, or the liberality which brought it in such a handsome form before the public, both ought to be fully appreciated, but when it is known the naked state you had these rough old chaps introduced to you in order to be clothed, and when it is seen how richly you have decorated them, it is a matter of no small surprise, even to one who can make an estimate. I will venture to assert that no man without a great and versatile genius combined with a real love of the ancient music of Ireland, would have attempted the task with any hope of success, and this seems to have been easily accomplished by Edward Bunting. For my own part when I view the nature of several of the airs in this collection, I am surprised how you avoided eighths and fifths, or some unnatural progression of the harmonies, but let the Motivo run how wild it may, the controlling master-hand is shown in its accompaniment. For a specimen of learned ingenuity I would refer the Tyro in the art to the air 'Oh White Maive'. I single out this because one portion of the accompaniment is a canon in the eighth below. Thus much of my opinion, and I should not have been able to say so much, had I not had an opportunity of perusing the volume (hastily I allow) presented by you to James Sidebotham, Esq. I have not had time to peruse the literary portion of the work, nor shall I, for the volume must be returned to Mr S ——— this day; he sent it to me as a guide for me to re-engrave two pages, agreeable to your MS. so that they may correspond with the remainder of the work; they are now done, and the corrections to twenty-two other pages. Having performed a part of my duty, I will endeavour to complete the remainder in which is comprised a portion of my interest. In your last communication you ask me, to let you know what part of the year I am least occupied in answer I say just now, but I shall be always happy to render my services to your convenience. I should state that light cheerful days are the best for carrying out any work in which pains are to be taken, and as you have intimated that you have another work in contemplation for me, let me have it at your earliest convenience, and depend upon it I will use all my remaining ability to make any work of yours agreeable to your wishes. I thank you most sincerely for your liberal remuneration for all that I was able to do in the Vol. of *Ancient Music of Ireland*. It is not often that I have an opportunity of blending my humble efforts with other artists of superior ability, as in this handsome and interesting publication.

Wishing you health long to enjoy fame, and if possible fortune from an extensive circulation of the *Ancient Music of Ireland* is the fervent hope and wish of yours very sincerely,

R. THO. SKARRAT.

July 29th 1840.

CHAPTER XXVI

LAST LETTERS AND APPRECIATION

Bunting's daughter Mary seems to have paid a lengthened visit to Belfast in the autumn of 1840, after the publication of his third volume. Some extracts from letters to her exhibit a very cheery tone, in great contrast to the quotations we give from the letters written to Mary MᶜCracken during the years 1839 and 1840. To that old friend he had unburdened all the troubles and anxieties of his heart; but to his young daughter he writes good news of the favourable reviews which his book is receiving and compliments paid to him by eminent persons.

Here is the first letter to Miss MᶜCracken, written when his work was approaching completion.

15 *Dec.* 1839.

Dear Mary, I sent you a newspaper to put you in mind of your old friend, my work is now over, thank God, nearly put out of my hand and my poor wife's also, who has had a weary time of it; indeed, I may safely say for the last twelve months, the pen has never been out of her hand, copying, copying, back and forward, until both her heart and fingers were broken. As for me between the various annoyances, and other distressing things I have met, surely no one would believe how I have surmounted them, in my weakness of both mind and body without a single one to help me with their advice, except my own wise woman, and as but for her I could have done nothing, she has indeed been a good fortune to me having to struggle with every wayward appearance of ill-health, and what was, I believe, worse on her than all, the extreme irritability of my temper, not improved by the many crosses and jostlings I met with in the publication of this herculean task, and a most dreadful task it has been to me all the time; but now it begins to lighten. The entire of the letterpress is finished by Ferguson, and right well he has done it. There is a life and spirit about it now which makes it interesting, as it is itself most entertaining to read. O'Neill's book written by Tom Hughes, has furnished the most delightful stories, which Ferguson has with singular dexterity turned and manufactured into a beautiful narrative, altogether novel and simple and racy in a high degree.

45 Upper Baggott St.,

Jan. 10, 1840.

Since I wrote you I have found out another main article in Irish music, namely, the extraordinary coincidence, between the modulation as described in 1172 by Cambrensis and that now found out by your humble servant, being the identical same, as appears in our tunes this day, giving an antiquity to them of nearly seven hundred years. This new discovery followed the one found out in your house, and was consequent on it, so that everything relative to Irish music is known, and the musical people may by this new light shown to them, compose away as much as they please in the Irish style without fear of going wrong. Poor Henry Joy,[1] how he would delight in all this if alive; he comes into my thoughts with many of my old friends very often. How many we have lost within the last twenty years.

March 25, 1840.

I am better these last few days since I last wrote, and as the prospect brightens of getting my work out soon, I think my health and spirits will improve accordingly. It has indeed been a heavy concern on my mind for two years, and on my wife's also, as she says, and truly, the pen has never been out of her hand for the last two twelve months. However in giving this book to the public my mind is discharged of a weight

---

1. Henry Joy had contributed largely to the literary matter introductory to the 1809 volume.

pressing on it for nearly fifty years; but as to making anything out of it, I have given up the idea, as the cost of getting it out will amount to close on one thousand pounds. The book I hope will be published some time in May at furthest.

April 9th, *1840.*

I may make a little fame but no money I fear, and the trouble of bringing out the book to poor Mamma and me has been immense. No one would believe it, and the knowledge of it sets my brain awondering how we accomplished such a mass of downright hard work. It is certain without her active assistance it could never have been done.

May 9th, *1840.*

My labour at the Irish music is all but closed, which I am sure you are pleased to hear. My very last sheet is now printing off, and we expect to be able to publish in the course of a fortnight to the world. I begin to fear for the sale of it at last, for hitherto I never doubted, but at least we should sell as many in the course of six months as would pay the cost of publication. It now admits of doubt for many reasons; first, the taste for Irish music is on the wane, or rather weaned; and secondly, the price which we must make at one pound ten shillings each book, stands much in the way of selling a great number. There are a few ardent lovers of their country whom I think will buy it, but, unfortunately, they are indeed few. We must hope the best, notwithstanding, but the work itself will remain a monument of my unwearied perseverance and industry for nearly fifty years, and I have the satisfaction of reflecting farther, that it could not at any period of the last thirty years have come out half so well, and with so much interest to both the antiquarian and the musician as at present. My discovery of the structure of Irish music, etc., in your house stamps the work with no common interest, which discovery makes the book invaluable. As a celebrated antiquarian here said now any one may compose Irish tunes.

I have no hopes of its being of benefit to me or my family, the only remuneration, I expect, is a sort of introduction for Anthony, as the son of a man who toiled so long at the expense of both money, labour, and health. This last I add as I truly think it has in some degree shortened my stay in this world, in trying to restore (as poor Henry Joy said) a page in the history of man. What will that serve me when I shall be asleep in the grave, and very possibly be there before the fatiguing business appears. I may never see it.

In strong contrast to the sorrowful tone of these letters, in which he unburdened the weariness of his heart to his life-long friend, are the letters which were written to his daughter, Mary, already referred to. She was on a lengthened visit to Belfast during the summer when the book appeared. The letters are treasured by the descendants of that daughter, and the following extracts have been made for us. A cheerful, even jovial, spirit is evident, there is no trace of the foreboding which too truly warned of the approach of death. He boasts of the compliments paid to him, and tells of the favourable reviews.

Aug. 13th 1840.— Mrs S. C. Hall, the authoress, is praising my work up, along with the rest of the ladies.

Aug. 22nd— Long letter from Narramore, the Arch-deacon's place, wherein Miss Ball repeats her request of your visiting her, and really seems angry at our not going there, we must go some way or other, otherwise my best friend, the Archdeacon, will be displeased next. She has three tunes (Irish) for me as a bait to bring me to Narramore. Her letter, as usual, with all the letters I get nowadays, contains great praise of the Book. Miss Chapman[2] is as much elated seemingly as my other acquaintance with the success of the work. Mr Groves, too, paid me many compliments on my successful completion of the work.

---

2. A relative of Mrs Bunting.

Go over to the Doctor and ask him for the *Morning Chronicle*, in which the review of my work is, and the *Citizen* also.

The *Citizen* was a Dublin monthly, in which William Elliot Hudson, a distinguished Gaelic enthusiast and friend of Thomas Davis, the young Ireland leader, contributed articles on Irish music in the early forties.

Bunting wrote further to Mary:

Aug. 26th—— There is a critique in the *Athenæum* for 15th and 22nd of this month, both are sufficiently cold, but the last mentioned one is the musical critique which is neither true nor well done but on the whole it is rather complimentary, for tho' it censures, it praises in such a way that the reader can hardly make out whether the writer was in earnest or jest, it will advertise the work as it has a circulation of fourteen or twenty thousand which is a good thing, and will be of service to us ultimately . . . . Mr Smith is just returned from Cheltenham, he says the people there are in great love with the Books. *Petrie* is away collecting more tunes in Connaught *his pipe's out poor man* than for all that.

Aug. 29th —— Cooke, has given me an Irish tune called 'The Three Jolly Devils' he is a very queer fellow. Your mother told you of Mr Lover's grand dedication, in which he calls himself my *admirer.* Lord, the man's in love with me all at once!! he is not so wise in doing this, and acknowledging the source from which he takes the tune, as he subjects himself to an action for damages, by so doing. However, if we make what we are in hopes of doing, a remuneration by the book, we shall let him alone.

Aug. 30th —— Cooke thinks Thalberg the nicest player of the piano in Europe. Liszt has too many tricks, so much so that when he finishes his pieces the next thing you expect is that he will swallow the piano.

Aug. 30th— (At a dinner party).— Cooke sang a very pretty song, and I played to please Cooke an Irish tune or two — he is like the rest full of commendation of my efforts in restoring Irish music and of my skill. Mr Cooke was saying the Queen ought to take notice of my work in a National point of view, and make some demonstration in my favour, particularly as the Irish are so partial to her.

Buy the penny Journal, and you will see the song Lover has dedicated to me.

Sep. 1st— In the *London Sun* newspaper another grand Notice of my work, and in the penny Journal of last week another, I ought to be proud, but I am not.

Sepr. 10th— I never met with more unqualified praise than Frank Robinson bestowed on your old Daddy's labours this day, the manuscript (what he could appreciate) being so admirably set and particularly one tune had taken such hold of his imagination, that he wished it far enough, as he could not get rid of it "by hook or crook." Young Mr Irwin (Sandford) giving me a pressing invitation to see him at *Armagh is curious.* May be I may, and may be I may not comply at some future time if I live. I would be glad to shew you where *Uncle and I first drew breath.*

Sepr. 16th— Call with the Doctor, tell him to get *Chambers' Edin. Journal* for the 19th instant, a long paper "about the *young man*" who took down Irish tunes in 1792.

Sep. 24th— Think of the works being reviewed by a New York paper. I have not seen it yet as Petrie ran away with it, it has been criticised much in the English Journals of late.

A letter received by Mary from her mother about the same time gives us a glimpse of Anthony Bunting, now a widower and childless, being welcomed in his younger brother's home circle and rejoicing in his triumph.

> Sep. 16th, 1840.— Your Uncle Anthony's birthday will be this day fortnight Michaelmas Day the 29th of this month, he is engaged to dine with us on that day as he has done on every corresponding day for the last six years. He will on that day be 75 years of age.

Bunting died at his home in Upper Baggott Street as already stated in our introductory memoir. A letter from a Northern man, resident in Dublin, Mr James Orr, addressed to a Belfast friend, was published some time ago in the Ulster *Archaeological Journal*, an admirable periodical edited by Mr F. J. Bigger. The letter was dated from Dublin, 3rd June, 1845, and in the course of it the writer said:

> Amongst those friends which death has deprived us of I am sure you regretted Edward Bunting's. His death was awfully sudden. His temper was so singularly disagreeable that the very great intimacy that had existed between him and me had ceased for a length of time previous to his death, so much so that some time had elapsed before I heard he was no more. He has left three very fine children, who are peculiarly blessed in having such a mother as they have. I sometimes meet them in the street. They are all well. But was it not a most extraordinary thing that some friend capable of doing so, did not notice his death in such a way as, I am sure, his abilities and wonderful exertion in rescuing the music of his country from, I may say, annihilation, and as far as such a publication admitted, of giving so valuable a history of ancient Ireland as is contained in his two books; but not one word that I have met with gave reason to think his name was worthy of remembrance, as remembrance I am sure with all his imperfections he deserved.

This letter coming from a man with whom Bunting had been intimate and had quarrelled, has a peculiar interest, but we must not let it leave us with the impression that Bunting died without his due of honour from his countrymen, or without the affectionate regret of an intimate circle of friends.

The article by Petrie, from which we quoted so largely in the Introductory Memoir, was published in the *Dublin University Magazine*. It shows us Bunting was received and venerated within the circle of the great scholars of the era a circle which included his old friend Whitley Stokes, who survived till the year 1846, and his son, Dr William Stokes, one of the most gifted and charming of men, doubtless regarded Bunting with sympathy. George Petrie, as great an enthusiast about music as Bunting himself, was beloved by all for his sweet temper. Young Samuel Ferguson, the poet, was his chief helper in his last labours. We find his handwriting constantly among the later papers. He was a true lover of music, and we may be sure he drank in the sweet strains of 'Ceann duhb Dilish', and the 'Pastheen Finn', and many another old air from the playing of the man who had gleaned them from the harpers. His appreciation of Bunting's work, his pride in his share in it, is proved, as already mentioned, by the fact that his first gift to his betrothed was a volume of the Ancient Music.

Bunting had puzzled about many points in connection with the nature of Irish music, and here at the end light came to him when he argued and chatted with the great Gaelic scholars, John O'Donovan and Eugene O'Curry, who could quote for him the very words of the annalists and old poets of the Gael. When we read O'Curry's wonderful revelations about music and musicians in ancient Ireland, we can realise what intense pleasure Bunting must have had in taking to a man like that, though before he had accumulated his full knowledge. The scrap of paper which I referred to which has Bunting's pencilled notes on one side, and O'Curry's copy of a poem and signature on the other, suggests that there was great argument and discussion between them.

We cannot help feeling that a due need of appreciation was accorded to his work by such scholars and friends, and, finally, hear what Thomas Davis had to say about Irish music, writing, we may be sure, with Bunting's last volume before him for many of the tunes in it are named:

ATTENTION:

No enemy speaks slightingly of Irish music, and no friend need fear to boast of it. It is without a rival. It's antique war tunes, such as those of O'Byrne, O'Donnell, Alestrom, and Brien Borou, stream and crash upon the ear like the warriors of a hundred glens meeting, and you are borne with them to battle, and they and you charge, and struggle amid cries and battleaxes, and stinging arrows. Did ever a wail make a man's marrow quiver, and fill his nostrils with the breath of the grave, like to 'Ululu' of the North, or the 'Wirrasthrue of Munster'? Stately are their slow and recklessly splendid their quick marches, their 'Boyne Water' and Sıos Aꜱus Sıos Lıon, their 'Michael Hoy' and 'Gallant Tipperary'. The Irish Jigs and Planxties are not only the best dancing tunes, but the finest quick marches in the world. Some of them would cure a paralytic, and make the marble-legged prince in the *Arabian Nights* charge like a *Fag-an-Bealach* boy.

The hunter joins in every leap and yelp of the Fox Chase. The historian hears the moan of the penal days in 'Drimindhu', and sees the embarkation of the wild geese, in 'Limerick's Lamentation', and ask the lover if his breath do not come and go with 'Savourneen Deelish' and 'Lough Sheelin'.

Such was the music which Bunting devoted his life to the rescue of. Let honour and veneration, and love be accorded to him from the people of Ireland.

A Bibliography of the Publications

of

CHARLOTTE MILLIGAN FOX

CHARLOTTE MILLIGAN FOX
Musical publications

After Aughrim, [song], words by A.G. Geoghegan, music set by C. Milligan Fox. Houghton & Co, (London, 1898), Chappell & Co, (London, 1898).

My Prayer for You, [song], words by Ethna Carbery, music set by C. Milligan Fox. J.B. Cramer & Co, (London, 1898).

Bridgit Brady, [song], words by William Boyle, music set by C. Milligan Fox. J.B. Cramer & Co, (London, 1898).

The Flower of the Flock, [song], words by F.A. Fahy, etc., music set by C. Milligan Fox. Boosey & Co, (London & New York, 1899).

Erin's Lament, [song], words by E.A. Gowling, music set by C. Milligan Fox. Weekes & Co, (London, 1901).

The Ramblin' Irishman, [song], words by Edith Wheeler, collected and arranged by C. Milligan Fox. Church & Co, (Cincinnati, 1901).

Kelly's Cat, [song], words revised by A.P. Graves, music set by C. Milligan Fox. John Church & Co, (Cincinnati, 1901).

That Lass of Donegal, [song], words revised with an extra verse added by A.C. Bunten, collected and arranged by C. Milligan Fox. J.B. Cramer & Co, (London, 1901).

The Cavan Recruit - A Jacobite Ballad, [song] words by A.P. Graves, collected and arranged by C. Milligan Fox. Boosey & Co, (London & New York, 1901).

Fairy Cobblers, an Old Ulster Air, [song], words by Edith Wheeler, collected and arranged by C. Milligan Fox. Boosey & Co, (London & New York, 1902).

The Lonely Road, [song], words by F. Largesse, music set by C. Milligan Fox. Boosey & Co, (London & New York, 1902).

By the Short Cut to the Rosses, [song], words by Nora Hopper, arranged to an old Donegal air by C. Milligan Fox. Boosey & Co, (London & New York, 1902).

The Courtship, [song], words by Edith Wheeler, collected and arranged by C. Milligan Fox. Boosey & Co, (London & New York, 1903).

Ochanee, [song], words by Edith Wheeler, collected and arranged by C. Milligan Fox. Boosey & Co, (London & New York, 1903).

Spring's Ecstasy, [song], words and music by C. Milligan Fox. Boosey & Co, (London & New York, 1904).

Down There in the Meadow — Ulster Lilt, [song], words by Edith Wheeler, collected and arranged by C. Milligan Fox. J. Williams, (London, 1905).

Pulse of my Heart, [song], words by A.L. Milligan, arranged by C. Milligan Fox. J. Williams, (London, 1905).

Three Irish airs, 'Down in the Broom,' 'Kate Kerrigan,' ' With my Rureem Ra,' collected and arranged by C. Milligan Fox. O. Ditson & Co, (Boston, 1905).

Four Irish Songs, collected and arranged by C. Milligan Fox, words by Edith Wheeler and A.L. Milligan. 'The Connaught Caoine,' words in Irish by Tadhg Ó Donnchadha. Illustrated by Seaghan Mac Cathmhaoil. Messrs. Maunsell & Co. Ltd, (Dublin, 1907).

> No.1. 'The Connaught Caoine,'
> No.2. 'The Singing Bird,'
> No.3. 'An Antrim Glen Song,'
> No.4. 'Tadhg O Donnchadha.'

Songs from 'The Four Winds of Eirinn,' words by Ethna Carbery, music set by C. Milligan Fox. Illustrated by Seaghan Mac Cathmhaoil. M.H. Gill and Son, James Duffy and Co, (Dublin, 1907).

Four Joyce Songs, words by James Joyce, music set by C. Milligan Fox. Maunsel and Co. Ltd, (Dublin, 1909).

Songs of the Irish Harpers, arranged for harp or piano by C. Milligan Fox. Maunsel and Co. Ltd, (Dublin, 1910). Bayley and Ferguson, (London & Glasgow, 1910).

Mary Bannan, Ballad of '98, [song], words by A.L. Milligan, arranged by C. Milligan Fox. Vincent Music Company, (London, 1912).

Three Waterford Airs, collected and arranged for violin and piano by C. Milligan Fox. G. Schirmer, (New York & London, 1915).
>   No.1. 'Lilt: Brian the Brave,'
>   No.2. 'The Healthy Hill, Three Little Drummers,'
>   No.3. 'Bonny Lassie, Beresford's Fancy.'

Two old Irish War-Time Ballads, collected and arranged for violin and piano by C. Milligan Fox. G. Schirmer, (New York & London, 1915).
>   No. 1 'Mistress Magarth,' (words revised by
>   A.P. Graves)
>   No. 2 'Johnny I hardly Knew Ye.'

Literary Publications

[C.M.F.] 'Irish music in London,' *All Ireland Review,* vol.1, no.1, (6 January 1900), p. 5.

[with Herbert Hughes] 'Editor's preface,' *Journal of the Irish Folk Song Society,* vol.1, no.1, (Dublin, April 1904), p. 4.

'Airs: A Kerry Caoine, lament for a Druid, lament on leaving Glendowan,' *Journal of the Irish Folk Song Society,* vol.1, (Dublin, April 1904), pp. 15-16.

[With Edith Wheeler] 'Irish versions of some ballads, with examples by C. Milligan Fox,' *Journal of the Irish Folk Song Society,* vol.1, nos.2-3, (Dublin, July & October 1904), pp. 41-47.

'Portrait of Ann Carter with note by C. Milligan Fox,' *Journal of the Irish Folk Song Society,* vol.1, nos.2-3, (Dublin, July & October 1904), p. 49.

'Ballad: Moorlough Mary, air Catharine Oige,' *Journal of the Irish Folk Song Society*, vol.II, (Dublin, January 1905), p. 21.

'Ballad: Sailor's Farewell, second version,' *Journal of the Irish Folk Song Society* vol.III, (Dublin, January 1906), p. 13.

'Bailiff's Daughter of Islington (version collected in Ulster),' *Journal of the Irish Folk Song Society*, vol.III, (Dublin, January 1905-6), p. 31.

[With Edith Wheeler] 'Airs and ballads collected by C. Milligan Fox and Edith Wheeler: The Deserter; The Jolly Weaver; The Inconstant Lover; Uncle Rat,' *Journal of the Irish Folk Song Society*, vol.IV, (Dublin, 1906), pp. 19-23.

[With Edith Wheeler] 'Airs and ballads collected by C. Milligan Fox and Edith Wheeler: Lamentation on the Death of a Fox; Johnnie Taylor; Peep of Day; the Maids of the Mourne Shore; Easter Snow; The Blackbird, and a version of the ballad,' *Journal of the Irish Folk Song Society*, vol.V, (Dublin, 1907), pp. 12-15.

[With Alice Milligan] 'Gaelic airs and ballads, selected from the Bunting MSS. by Alice Milligan and C. Milligan Fox,' *Journal of the Irish Folk Song Society*, vol.VI, (Dublin, January & October 1908), pp. 15-28.

'Denis O'Sullivan,' *Journal of the Irish Folk Song Society*, vol.VI, (Dublin, January & October 1908), pp. 29-30.

[With Alice Milligan] 'Gaelic airs and ballads, selected from the Bunting MSS. by Alice Milligan and C. Milligan Fox,' *Journal of the Irish Folk Song Society*, vol.VII, (Dublin, January & June 1909), pp. 15-28.

'Songs from the Bunting MSS.,' *Journal of the Irish Folk Song Society*, vol.VIII, (Dublin, January & June 1910), pp. 19-22.

'Folk song in County Tyrone,' *Journal of the Irish Folk Song Society*, vol.VIII, (Dublin, January & June 1910), pp. 23-28.

'Airs taken down in County Tyrone,' *Journal of the Irish Folk Song Society*, vol. VIII, (Dublin, January & June 1910), pp. 29-30.

'The haunted villa — a true story,' *The Occult Review,* vol.xi, (London, April 1910), p. 158.

'Irish songs from America,' *Journal of the Irish Folk Song Society,* vol.ix, (Dublin, January & June 1911), pp. 13-15.

'Concerning the William Elliot Hudson collection of Irish folk songs,' *Journal of the Irish Folk Song Society,* vol.x, (Dublin, December 1911), pp. 5-8.

The Annals of The Irish Harpers, John Murray, (London, 1911).

'Airs from the Hudson MSS. in the Boston library, U.S.A., taken down by C.M. Fox,' *Journal of the Irish Folk Song Society,* vol.xi, (Dublin, January-June 1912), pp. 16-17.

'Folk song collecting in County Waterford,' *Journal of the Irish Folk Song Society,* vol.xii, (Dublin, October 1912), p. 11.

'Waterford airs and songs,' *Journal of the Irish Folk Song Society,* vol.xii, (Dublin, October 1912), pp. 15-26.

'Reviews: "A cycle of old Irish melodies by Arthur Whiting" and "Part II: Gems of melody by Carl G. Hardeback", ' *Journal of the Irish Folk Song Society* vol.xii, (Dublin, October 1912), pp. 35-36.

'Obituary notice: Lord Crofton,' *Journal of the Irish Folk Song Society* vol.xii, (Dublin, October 1912), p. 36.

'Ancient music MSS. at University Library, Cambridge,' *Journal of the Irish Folk Song Society,* vol.xiii, (Dublin, June 1913), pp. 17-19.

'More Waterford airs,' *Journal of the Irish Folk Song Society,* vol.xiii, (Dublin, June 1913) pp. 26-27.

'Irish folk song concert,' *Journal of the Irish Folk Song Society,* vol.xiii, (Dublin, June 1913), pp. 30-31.

'Irish folk song concert,' *Journal of the Irish Folk Song Society,* vol.xiv, (Dublin, April 1914), p. 22.

'Obituaries: Dr. P.W. Joyce; Mrs Carl Gilbert Hardebeck,' *Journal of the Irish Folk Song Society*, vol.xiv, (Dublin, April 1914), pp. 40-42.

'Irish Marches,' *Journal of the Irish Folk Song Society*, vol.xv, (Dublin, March 1915), pp. 15-18.

'Irish War Songs of Alfred Perceval Graves,' *Journal of the Irish Folk Song Society*, vol.xv, (Dublin, March 1915), pp. 19-20.

'Review of the Feis Ceoil collection,' *Journal of the Irish Folk Song Society*, vol. xv, (Dublin, March 1915), pp. 21-25.

'On versions,' *Journal of the Irish Folk Song Society*, vol.xv, (Dublin, March 1915), pp. 28-31.

'Review: Folksongs collected in Flintshire by Mrs. Herbert Lewis,' *Journal of the Irish Folk Song Society*, vol.xv, (Dublin, March 1915), pp. 32-33.

'Review: Melodies et chansons Françaises, recueillies et harmonisées par Lucien de Flagny,' *Journal of the Irish Folk Song Society*, vol.xv, (Dublin, March 1915), pp. 33-34.

'Notes and Queries: Seven Rejoices of Mary,' *Journal of the Waterford and South-East of Ireland Archæological Society* second quarter, (April to June 1915), p. 90.

APPENDIX

ON THE EDITING OF THE MEMOIRS OF ARTHUR O'NEILL

SARA C LANIER

and

ROLAND SPOTTISWOODE

Donal O'Sullivan and Charlotte Milligan Fox's
versions of
The Memoirs of Arthur O'Neill

IN THE YEARS FOLLOWING MILLIGAN FOX'S DEATH THE EDITORSHIP OF THE *Journal of the Irish Folk Song Society* remained vacant but with the end of the First World War the Irish Folk Song Society began to function again. The post of editor was offered to Donal O'Sullivan. In association with the scholar J. Martin Freeman, O'Sullivan initiated a project where the manuscript source material Bunting had collected throughout his life would be compared with the airs published in Bunting's three musical collections of 1796, 1809 and 1840. Accordingly, during the early 1920's O'Sullivan travelled frequently to Belfast in order to consult the Bunting Manuscripts. The work of the two men appeared between 1927-1939 in successive issues of the *Journal of the Irish Folk Song Society*.

With the demise of the *Journal of the Irish Folk Song Society* in 1939, only those manuscripts employed for the 1840 Bunting volume remained unedited. However, Donal O'Sullivan published an edited version of the *Memoirs* of Arthur O'Neill as an appendix to his *Carolan, the Life and Times of an Irish Harper* in 1958. O'Sullivan returned to his work on the last Bunting volume in 1965 but the work was unfinished at the time of his death. It finally appeared in 1983 in an edition edited from O'Sullivan's papers by the musicologist Mícheál Ó Súilleabháin.[1] Ó Súilleabháin's introduction to this work avoids overtly criticising O'Sullivan while describing his own difficulties in working with the severe limitations of O'Sullivans idiosyncratic approach to the material.

In the introduction to his edit of the text O'Sullivan is at some pains to dismiss Milligan Fox's earlier version of the *Memoirs*, which appeared in *Annals*, descrbing her work as containing alterations, interpolations and mistranscriptions. This critique of the work of Milligan Fox, coming as

---

[1.] O'Sullivan, Donal. *Carolan, The Life and Times of an Irish Harper*, vol.II, Routledge & Kegan Paul, (London, 1958), p. 144.

it did so many years after the publication of *Annals*, and from as canonic a source as O'Sullivan, has never been questioned. However, a closer look at the original manuscript texts serves to raise questions concerning O'Sullivan's interpretation.

Arthur O'Neill's blindness ensured that he himself could not write. Accordingly, he required the assistance of an amanuensis to transcribe the words from his dictation. This work was carried out at Bunting's request in 1803 by a close friend of the McCracken family, the Belfast solicitor Thomas Hughes. The manuscript O'Sullivan employed was an initial draft that was taken down from O'Neill's dictation during a first working session. This first rough draft, Bunting MS.46, was re-drafted by Hughes at a later date, when it was extensively corrected by O'Neill, who dictated a series of revisions to Hughes. This second, revised version is now Bunting MS.14. The running script of the revised text contains a number of significant stylistic alterations which suggest that MS.14 was carefully amended to read more smoothly during an initial corrective session, possibly with the intention of developing the first transcript into a definitive text for contemporary publication. The author and his scribe then evidently returned to the text on a number of occasions and made further careful revisions. This work must have been undertaken over a series of sessions as the corrections, crossings out and superscript emendations that have been added although all in the same hand, display a number of slight differences that suggest different periods of composition.

Charlotte Milligan Fox acquired this second, carefully revised text, Bunting MS.14, with the manuscripts gifted to her by Bunting's grandson Dr MacRory. The uncorrected first draft of the text, MS.46, remained in the possession of MacRory's sister Lady Deane until after Charlotte's death in 1916. It was finally deposited among the Bunting Papers only in 1917, when Lady Deane sold her Bunting manuscripts to Queens University after Milligan Fox's collection of Bunting papers had finally come into the university's keeping.

Despite some minor changes to bring elements of the manuscript into conformity with the practices of her own time with regard to taste and to eradicate a few insignificant slights on persons whose descendants might find the comments offensive, Milligan Fox closely duplicates the final version Hughes had prepared with O'Neill and reproduces the text's chapter arrangement with much of its original spelling and expressiveness. All of the O'Neill/Hughes additions and alterations present in Ms.14 are given her careful critical attention in preparing her published text.

In preparing his edition of the *Memoirs* of Arthur O'Neill Donal O'Sullivan selected material from the two manuscript texts held at Queen's University Belfast: Bunting MS.46 and MS.14. The text published in his *Carolan* drew mostly upon Bunting MS.46. O'Sullivan erroneously assumed that Milligan Fox had had both copies in her possession while preparing her version for publication. His comments on Milligan Fox's edit quite inaccurately stating that she primarily used what he describes disparagingly as "the fair copy," Lady Deane's uncorrected text, Ms.46, in preference to what he calls "the original," the corrected second draft, Ms.14, to which she sticks closely.[2] O'Sullivan accuses Milligan Fox of dealing with the material in a manner which can not be justified.

O'Sullivan's own edit of the *Memoirs* employs both texts quite arbitrarily, selecting material from both manuscripts with no regular system of editing evident beyond his desire to combine some of the early draft raciness of Bunting MS.46 with the clear advantages of style offered by the revised version, Bunting MS.14. O'Sullivan has also divided O'Neill's narrative into seven chapters, an arrangement that is entirely his own and that has no precedent in either manuscript version. In addition he has extensively revised the punctuation of the material he selected from the two manuscripts, altering the original phonetic spelling of Irish names and terms by Hughes to conform with the modernised Irish spelling of the 1950s, therein erasing the valuable historical etymology of both of the original texts.

---

2. O'Sullivan, Donal. op. cit. p. 144.

Milligan Fox's edited text is a carefully reproduced version of Bunting MS.14. with a few insignificant portions cut. She critically employed all of the revisions O'Neill prepared with his scribe, Thomas Hughes. In so doing she offers us a text that more faithfully reflects the intentions of O'Neill. In the version of the *Memoirs* Donal O'Sullivan has reproduced in *Carolan*, he has capriciously selected material from both manuscripts to construct a composite, modernised text that shows scant respect for O'Neill's creative process and more accurately reflects O'Sullivan's personal sensibilities and concerns.

This display of mean spiritedness by O'Sullivan can be explained, with the clarity of hindsight, by both his personal prejudices and his circumstances. O'Sullivan was inimical to Irish traditional music and his hatred of the genre has been described by Breandan Breathnach in the biographical entry for O'Sullivan in *The Companion to Irish Tradtional Music*[3]. This dislike was behind his decision as editor of *The Irish Folk Song Society Journal* to discontinue the publication of articles on folk music. He preferred to use the journal as a platform to publish his academic work on the Bunting material.

It would seem that in his erroneous judgement in regard to the scholarship of Milligan Fox, O'Sullivan was indulging a common arrogance of attitude of the professional academic, that of using the criticism of work, often of equal if not greater merit, undertaken by the amateur, who by being outside the profession has no recognised right to reply, in order to further his own career and reputation. It is time that the generous soul of Charlotte Milligan Fox and her brilliant scholarship was redeemed from continuing to suffer such a calumny.

---

3. See, Vallely, Fintan. *The Companion to Irish Traditional Music*, Cork University Press, (Cork, 2011), p. 536, (also see p. 292 in the 1999 edition).

INDEX

INDEX